CHINA

ON THE

EDGE

CHINA

XINJIANG

GA

QINGHAI

TIBET

YUN

HEILONGJIANG

JILIN

GXIA

INNER MONGOLIA

LIAONING

•Beijing

HEBEI

River

SHANXI

SHANDONG

SHAANXI

HENAN

JIANGSU

• Shanghai

River

HUBEI

ANHUI

ZHEJIANG

JIANGXI

HUNAN

ZHOU

FUJIAN

Pearl River

GUANGDONG

TAIWAN

UANGXI

•Guangzhou

HAINAN

CHINA

ON THE

EDGE

**THE CRISIS OF
ECOLOGY AND
DEVELOPMENT**

HE BOCHUAN

CHINA BOOKS AND PERIODICALS, INC.

Cover design by Laurie Anderson
Text design by Robbin Henderson and Linda Revel

Library of Congress Catalog Card Number: 91-70073
ISBN 0-8351-2447-9 (casebound)
ISBN 0-8351-2448-7 (paperback)

Printed in the United States of America by CHINA
BOOKS
& Periodicals, Inc.

▊ CONTENTS

Foreword by Lester Ross, author of Environmental
Policy in China   IX

Author's Preface to the English-Language Edition   XIII

A Note on Weights, Measures, and Currency   XVII

Publisher's Aknowledgements   XVII

1. Population Shock: China's Number One Problem   1
2. The Ecological Crisis: A Grim Legacy   21
3. The Economic Earthquake   43
4. Energy and Transportation: Two Weak Links   65
5. Problems in Industry and Agriculture   89
6. Wrangling at the Window to the Outside World   113
7. Questions of Pace and Regional Development   139
8. Educational Dilemma   157
9. Nature's Ungrateful Children   175

Notes   195
About the Author   209
Map   II

■ FOREWORD

China on the Edge was authored in the late 1980s for a domestic audience in the People's Republic of China (PRC). It examines present-day environmental, economic and social conditions and paints a chilling prognosis for the PRC's future unless various long-term trends are altered. Written in a highly dramatic style for such a somber theme, although some of the flair is regrettably lost in translation, the book has evoked a strong response from its readers in Taiwan and Hong Kong as well as the PRC.

The book is not intended to provide a hard-science investigation of discrete problems, nor is it a rigorous social science study of public policy or the relationship between the Chinese people and their environment. Rather, it is a broad survey of the PRC's often disquieting environmental, economic, and other conditions. Drawing upon some of the limited statistical data that exists as well as the author's understanding of Chinese history, *China on the Edge* describes a country whose economic potential and the well-being of whose people are gravely jeopardized by population pressure, inefficiency, illiteracy, pollution, deforestation, loss of natural habitat, and other perils.

Readers will be particularly dismayed by the litany of policy failures recounted in the book. Some are relatively well-known, especially the conscious rejection of population control in the 1950s attributable to the late Communist Party Chairman Mao Zedong. Economists and demographers who advocated population control at the time, most notably Ma Yinchu, suffered grievous sanctions for their impudence in speaking truth to power. More than a decade was wasted before the PRC finally began to address the need for population control, during which time population pressure with its attendant short- and long-term consequences grew even more acute. The belated recognition of the severity of the problem, coming amidst the demise of rational discourse during the Cultural Revolution, inclined the leadership of the Communist Party to adopt desperate, even inhumane measures to curtail population growth when the dimensions of the problem were finally grasped. Moreover, as stressed in *China on the Edge*, precipitous efforts to belatedly control population growth have distorted the age profile of the population, presenting the PRC with a major elderly care problem early in the next century.

Other policy failures are less widely known. For example, the PRC in the 1960s embarked on a massive effort to expand strategic industry in the interior of the country in a rather quixotic effort to limit vulnerability to foreign attack. This so-called "Third Front" strategy proved to be enormously expensive and prevented the PRC from undertaking much-needed infrastructural and other improvements in the coastal areas, where the payback would have been much faster.

One shortcoming of the book, however, is a tendency in places to project past trends into the future without sufficient attention to the potential for improvements to be gained by changing policies. For example, as noted in the book, there is very severe air and water pollution in many parts of the PRC, and a number of pollution-related problems like the treatment and disposal of solid and hazardous wastes are only just beginning to be addressed.

It would be a serious mistake, however, to dismiss the accomplishments that already have been achieved in pollution reduction through the upgrading of industrial facilities, the introduction of modern technology and district heating, among other measures. Although capital will continue to be a critical constraint on the PRC's ability to finance pollution control, spending on environmental protection is rising, not just in absolute *renminbi* but also as a proportion of national income. Officials at every level of authority have become much more aware of the dangers of a one-sided pursuit of economic growth, and are more sympathetic to environmental protection than their counterparts of a decade ago. Furthermore, the PRC and its relevant officials are becoming ever more deeply engaged in dialogue with the global scientific community and organizations such as the World Bank with environmentally-influenced mandates, which increases the likelihood that PRC policy will become more sympathetic to environmental concerns.

Similarly, as discussed in the book, the PRC faces serious water shortages, particularly in urban areas. Part of the problem is due to the relationship between population size, economic activity, and the resource base. In addition, however, water rate schedules bear little relation to scarcity prices, particularly in the agricultural sector, which is the largest user. Rate reforms, more efficient irrigation techniques, and a reduction in farming in urban areas would lower demand and also reduce the problems of waterlogging and salinization.

Readers will be provoked by other questions involving *China on the Edge*. For example, the book was published in the PRC in 1988. At that time, Chinese politics were in a reform phase, during which there was relatively broad freedom of expression. Such freedom was reduced in the aftermath of the tragic Tiananmen Incident of 4 June 1989, when Party General Secretary Zhao Ziyang was purged. How permanent is the effect of the crackdown on freedom of expression, economic reform, environmental protection, and other policy sectors? Several think tanks have been suppressed, and support for price reform and other economic rationalizations that would enhance efficiency and indirectly improve the environment has diminished. Moreover, there is even less freedom than there was before to oppose controversial, big-ticket, high-profile projects such as the Three Gorges Dam.

On the other hand, however, the opponents of economic reform have not succeeded in presenting a coherent and workable alternative, although they have drastically slowed the pace of reform. Looking at other policy areas, the overall momentum in favor of environmental protection among regulators and scientists appears to be unaffected, although reliable attitudinal data is lacking. Notably, new statutes and regulations continue to be promulgated, including some innovative provisions pertaining to implementation and liability, although much more remains to be done. New pilot projects have been started in search of more efficient and comprehensive solutions to pollution problems. Additional nature reserves have been created, timber production quotas have been reduced, and forest management measures have been strengthened.

From my own perspective, the author paints an unduly bleak, even Malthusian picture of the PRC's future prospects, while slighting present and potential policy changes as well as more recent data which indicate that some, although not all, problems are or are capable of being ameliorated. *China on the Edge* nevertheless performs an admirable service in highlighting the economic, environmental, and social problems facing the PRC.

—LESTER ROSS

■ PREFACE TO THE ENGLISH-LANGUAGE EDITION

Many "reflections" were going on in China during the past decade—reflections on China's own true cultural traditions, etc. This book was seen by some commentators here in China as part of a new wave of reflections on the concrete actions of the government.

Reflection is another word for "critique." To devote a whole book to the critique of the government, in China, is almost unimaginable. Hence, hardly any surprise that this volume encountered some complications.

This book has been widely circulated among the middle and upper echelons of the Chinese government and academia. Over 430,000 copies were printed in Chinese since its first publication in 1988. However, since the June 4th incident, printing was abruptly halted by decree from above.

Far too many are the sweet lullabies Chinese propaganda machines have sung for themselves over the last 40 years. And far too many are the biased and distorted pictures of China presented in the Western media. Between the two extremes, to take an even-handed and clear-headed approach to the vast diversity of dilemmas and problems facing China today is the goal this book had set for itself—though I must admit that the goal is probably far loftier than what has actually been accomplished.

For its own survival, humankind has accumulated its knowledge, pushed forward its technology, enormously expanded its production, recklessly gobbled up scarce resources, devised arcane social experiments, and created fanciful patterns of relationships between society's members. Every interest group seeks forcefully to adjust its environment to itself, and would never bother to attempt the reverse. Today, everywhere in the world, ordinary social behaviors are threatening to descend into a gigantic sequence of organized madness. More and more people are coming to realize that in its self-congratulatory flaunting of its supposed accomplishments, humanity has in reality harmed itself, wounded itself, in a way that borders on the absurd.

Richard Nixon commented somewhere that the 20th century was the bloodiest and most spectacular of all. Now we are witnessing a serious threat to the very survival of humanity because of global depletion of resources and decay of the environment. The whole human race is crowded on this increasingly small spaceship, yet every political and military machine in every nation continues on its mad spin, intent on continuing to create more glory smeared in blood. When this introduction was being written, the last trickle of sand had just flown through the hourglass timing the Persian Gulf crisis. Another brutal gamble to exchange blood for oil was about to begin.

As all of us are inevitably crowded into one ship, China's position becomes all the more significant. If the machinery of China becomes jammed and her support system becomes clogged, the rest of the world will also suffer the consequences. If people only understood how, over the last few decades, the Chinese had almost completely chopped away their tropical rain forests—one of the most precious jewels of nature's endowment on earth—it would be clear that large scale, conscious or unconscious destruction of nature is not only the shame of the Chinese, but of all humanity.

Currently China faces severe soil erosion, increased frequency of natural disasters, forest depletion, and pollution of water resources. Worse still, it has no effective or feasible measures to reverse the trend in the foreseeable future. If the Chinese take another wrong step in certain other areas, it would be difficult to prevent the outbreak of large-scale and uncontrollable irrational behavior.

No one could deny the vital importance which the Sino-American relationship holds for the future of this earth. A friend of mine who works on Capitol Hill in Washington and who is an authority on China once commented that, while there is much concern in the United States on the issues of human rights in China, there is little interest in the problems of the Chinese environment. But if problems in the social sphere are caused by human behavior, so are the problems in the natural sphere. Why should they be treated differently?

The title of the book might have posed a bit of a difficulty. The word I used in Chinese for "mountain ridge," *shan ao,* is one for which a direct translation probably cannot be found in English. The Chinese dictionary defines *shan ao* as "flat areas within a mountain." Normally, there are three places in a mountain where flat areas can be found: in the valley, on the top, and along some turning points on the path leading up. The last kind of flat area is usually flanked by dangerously slippery slopes, or sometimes cliffs. And these present the most treacherous phase in mountain climbing: if the right turn is made, the path may open to the top; but if a wrong step is taken, one may plunge into oblivion. With this comparison, I wish to underscore the point that in China today, an ill-conceived choice on an important issue may result in the permanent loss of the opportunity ever to correct the mistake. China has gone past the point of no return.

—HE BOCHUAN
Guangzhou, January 1991

A Note on Weights, Measures, and Currency

In general, this text follows the author's use of the metric system for measures of volume, distance, and weight. Consequently, when the term "ton" is used, it refers to the metric ton (1,000 kilograms —2,205 pounds). But where the author uses the traditional Chinese land unit *mu* (.1647 acres), it has been converted into the British system's acres. Also, because the metric system's land measure of hectares (10,000 square meters—2.47 acres) is still unfamiliar to many, hectares have been converted to acres.

Monetary units follow the author's use of Chinese yuan (about $.18 at the time of this publication), and the U.S. dollar when he states a sum in dollars.

Publisher's Acknowledgements

China Books is grateful to the following team for translating this book from the original Chinese, *Shan ao shang de zhongguo:* Jenny Holdaway, Guo Jian-sheng, Susan Brick, Hu Si-gang, and Charles Wong.

We would also like to thank Jim Nickum for offering us a perceptive evaluation of the original text. We are also grateful to Pam Burdman, Madelyn Ross, and Rachel Saidman for their contributions to this project.

1

POPULATION SHOCK: CHINA'S NUMBER ONE PROBLEM

The greatest single threat to the Chinese nation is population pressure. Overpopulation lies at the heart of China's environmental and development crisis, making its other problems pale by comparison.

China's growing population is mercilessly gobbling up the advances made by development. By the year 2000, China will have to increase grain production by approximately 9 million tons each year, just to keep everybody fed. By that time, the swelling population will have caused per capita natural resources to drop by a further one-seventh, and the space for development will have been squeezed to practically nil, especially in the Southeast, where 92% of the arable land and 95% of the agricultural population are concentrated.

The population problem has three major aspects: sheer numbers, structural distribution, and overall educational level. The difficulties arising from these have cast us into a profound dilemma, but before plunging into a detailed explanation, it is instructive to begin by examining the history of our own perception of it.

The dire warnings of Thomas Malthus, first sounded in the 18th century, are now common knowledge throughout the world. Food shortages, dwindling per capita resources, the lack of capital, and the destruction of the ecological balance have been largely the result of overpopulation. Population pressure puts a strain on natural resources, which is manifested in excessive cultivation, fishing, herding, etc.

The destruction of the environment in turn creates economic pressures: falling production and efficiency, unemployment, inflation, and unequal distribution of wealth and resources which subsequently produce social pressures in the form of hunger, a poor level of social welfare, neglect of education, and moral decline. Eventually these break out in mounting political tensions, and may lead to wars or other violent conflicts.

Unfortunately, the prophecies of Malthus were perhaps too incisive and radical for his time. For the next century-and-a-half after his thesis, the vast majority of politicians, economists, and social philosophers were unwilling to confront the issues he raised, and tried to counter him by arguing that each additional mouth came with two working hands and a smart brain, and that fair distribution and education in social justice and equality would effectively neutralize the threat posed by overpopulation.

This period of history has some important lessons for the Chinese because our politicians and academics decisively rejected Malthus's theory. The blind optimism that resulted from their "thorough and conclusive refutation" of Malthus has been the source of our deepest disasters. Classical contributors to Marxian theory tended to underestimate natural and environmental constraints, and had inordinately high expectations of social revolution and human initiative. They often drew conclusions before a multitude of variables had become apparent and consequently they often raced far "ahead of the times," leaving the practitioners who followed to bump into cold hard walls of reality.

Interestingly enough, one of the earliest thinkers to warn about the population problem was the Chinese philosopher Han Fei. More than 2,000 years ago he commented, "Nowadays people don't consider five children to be too many. But if each of those five children goes on to have five more, the grandfather will be blessed with 25 grandchildren before he dies. The result will be more people with less goods to use, and more labor with less food to share." No one would have thought this simple admonition of more than 20 centuries ago would turn out to explain the crux of many seemingly insoluble problems facing the world today. China bears a large share of responsibility for these, and given that the nation is already running on overload, it is clear that the race between efforts at development and the mounting pressure of population can only become more severe in the future.

It is also appropriate to mention two distinguished individuals who sounded a warning in the modern period, Ma Yenchu and Zhong Huilan. After conducting field research in Zhejiang Province in 1954 and 1955, Ma concluded that there was a dangerous trend towards rapid population growth, which already exceeded 2% annually. The 72-year-old scholar presented his results to the Supreme Council of National Affairs in February 1957, under the title "A New Thesis on Population," and at the time he actually received praise from Mao Zedong himself. On 5 July of the same year, *People's Daily* published his entire thesis.

Two days later, however, Mao made his famous speech "Counter the Attacks from Bourgeois Rightists" at a cadre meeting in Shanghai, and from then on, quotes from the Great Helmsman like "it is not a bad thing to have more people"; "there is no basis for the pessimistic view that there is currently an overgrowth of population in our country," and "of all things in this world, man is the most precious," were used as weapons against "A New Thesis on Population." Ma was reviled as a "Chinese Malthus" and disgraced.

In 1957, the other "Chinese Malthus," Zhong Huilan, former director of the Chinese Medical Association, warned on the basis of detailed calculations that unless policy adjustments were made immediately, China's population would reach one billion within 20 years. Zhong later met with the same fate as Ma Yenchu, but a greater misfortune still was that his prediction came true.

The Chinese spared no effort in refuting the ideas of these two Malthuses, and the price we have paid as a nation has consequently been much higher than that of any other country. During the 14 years from 1962 through 1975, about 350 million babies were born in China. (Historically, it took a whole 4,000 years, from the time of the Yellow Emperor (circa 2300 B.C.), when China's population was estimated at 13 million, to the reign of the Manchu Emperor Jiaqin in the 18th century, for the total to reach that size). If all the children born during those 14 years later reproduce at the rate of two babies per couple, this group alone will have added another 350 million babies in next 30 years.

Eventually, of course, population growth will run into natural constraints. Song Jian and others have concluded that "if within a hundred years or so, the overall quality of our diet is to match the present level of France or the United States, the optimal population would be under 680 million."[1] A different but simple method of calculation, which allows five acres of arable land per person, puts the optimal number at around 300 million. Another, which divides the total grain output by 500 kilograms per person per year, gives 600 million. Taking the various methods of calculation into consideration, one could conclude that an optimal population level would be around 500 million. The sad thing is that we had already broken all these limits as early as 1963 (when the total population was estimated at more than 691.7 million), and in that year, the annual natural population growth rate was 3.333% (a net increase—after deaths are subtracted from births—of 33 people per thousand.) During the following decade, the natural growth rate remained between 2.089% and 2.838%, and only after 1974 did the rate gradually drop below 2.0%.

In the December 1987 issue of *Wide-Angle Len*s magazine, I presented this case for an optimal population level of 500 million, making the analogy that if an excellent meal for one were shared by two, it might still be tolerable; but if it were divided among three, all would end up starving. The point was, that the absolute maximum level of population China could tolerate would be 1.5 billion.

This standard was confirmed in a study sponsored by the Chinese Academy of Science on China's land resources, their productive potential, and the size of the population they could support.[2] The study concluded that the maximum potential output of China's land resources was about 7.26 billion tons of dry goods per year, which theoretically could be considered capable of supporting a maximum population of between 1.5 and 1.6 billion. This finding is worth noting because that figure may very well be reached by 2020.

By 1979, China's population growth rate had dropped to 1.161%, due in large part to the government's population control efforts. However, after the official goal of "keeping the population below 1.2 billion within this century" was set, the growth rate actually climbed again. In 1980, it was 1.187%; in 1981, 1.455%; and 1982, 1.449%. Although it dropped to a low of 1.081% in 1984, it began climbing again in 1985, reaching 1.408% by 1986, remaining above 1.40% since, and hitting 1.433 in 1989. The official census which was begun in July 1990 counted 1.133 billion.[3] By March of 1991, official government statistics added another 10 million to the census total, bringing the population of China to 1.143 billion, with the natural growth rate still up at 1.439% *(see figure 1.1)*. Even if the rate falls back down to 1.1% in the future, the 1.2 billion mark will be passed by 1998.

Another estimate by Tian Xueyuan predicts that it will be impossible to reduce net population growth to near zero until between 2020 and 2030 *(see figure 1.2)*. Due to the serious mistakes made in population policy in the 1950s and 1960s the population leapt from 700 million to a billion within just the decade and a half from 1964 to 1981. Even assuming strict enforcement of the official "one child policy" (one child per couple), it would take as long as 90 years to bring it back down to 700 million. Besides, this policy has serious side effects and could not realistically be sustained over a long period of time.

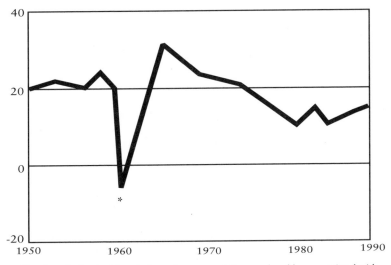

FIGURE **1.1**
CHANGES IN THE GROWTH RATE OF THE CHINESE POPULATION, 1950–90

* (The sharp decline in this period was due to crop failures and problems associated with the Great Leap Forward, 1958–59.)

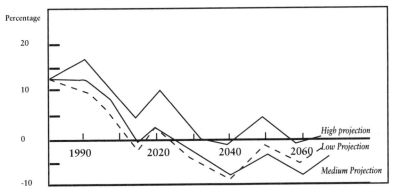

FIGURE **1.2**
PROJECTED CHANGES IN NET GROWTH RATE OF THE CHINESE POPULATION, 1970–2070

▌ From the Days of the Yellow Emperor to the Shock Wave of the Next Century

In addition to the failure to curb population growth in recent times, there are profound historical reasons for the enormous population crisis that China faces today.

During the long feudal period, which was marked by intermittent social upheavals and general economic stagnation, China's population growth actually remained relatively stable. The seeds of the later explosion were first sown in the early 18th century. Around the 23d year of the reign of Emperor Kangxi (1684), the population passed the 100 million mark for the first time. In 1712, Kangxi adopted the policy of "fixed taxes that would favor more births," and in 1723, Emperor Yongzhen extended the same policy by merging the poll and land taxes, effectively revising the poll tax, which had prevailed since the days of the Qin and Han dynasties, into one that was essentially land based. With the tax levied on land instead of individuals, there was no longer a disincentive to reproduce.

From that time on, the population grew at a formidable pace of over 2.5% annually. By the 27th year of the reign of Emperor Qianlong (1762), the 200 million mark was passed, and by the 55th year of his reign (1790), the population reached 300 million. By the eve of the Opium War (1834), China already had a population of well over 400 million.

At that point, the second edition of the famous *Principles of Population* by Malthus was already 30 years old. One might have thought that criticism of that worthy mathematician might have been tempered by the example of China, where the erosion of the environmental and ecological balance, the decline of productive forces, and the intensification of class conflict seemed to provide a perfect footnote for his thesis. Marx and Engels themselves did in fact take note of the Chinese population problem, pointing out that the excess population "has long since aggravated social conditions which have become shackles on the majority of this nation's people." Extensive research on materials containing estimates of historical population levels has yielded some very valuable results *(see figure 1.3)*. After breaking the 100 million mark, China's exponential population growth between 1684 and 1834 created conflicts and pressures that eventually led to a general collapse. Luo Ergang once suggested that the Taiping Rebellion (1851–1864) was largely the result of population pressure. Despite criticisms that it "ignores class contradictions," there is considerable validity in this thesis. The Taiping rebel chief Hong Xiuquan made his appeal from a remote corner of the Southwest, but his cause received an enthusiastic response throughout China. The general sense of restlessness this reflects was undoubtedly related to the expansion of the population.[4]

In addition, from a strictly statistical point of view, we are forced to consider the fact that the tragedy of the Taiping rebellion did partially alleviate the pressure of overpopulation. During the decade-and-a half period of the rebellion, the population was reduced by more than 100 million, or one-fourth of the total.

It is a great shame that despite all this upheaval, the basic structure of the small-scale agricultural economy that spurred population growth was never disturbed. Instead, along with the adjustments in political and economic relationships, and increases in production, the rate of population growth quickly regained its former momentum. And from 1949 on, China entered a period of what might be called "hyper-exponential" population growth, dragging the nation into the most serious crisis it has ever faced.

According to the comprehensive population records for the period 1949 to 1989 China's population grew by an average of 100 million every 7 years. In 1981, 39 babies were born every minute (by 1990 this had risen to 43). What is more, another 200 million births are anticipated within the next 20 years, four-fifths of the population of the USA, or almost two Japans.

FIGURE 1.3
HISTORICAL CHINESE POPULATION LEVELS

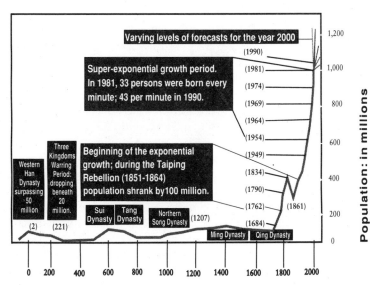

In 1979, Song Jian and his co-researchers made detailed forecasts for the growth trend of China's population over the 100 years between 1980 and 2080.[5] A look at the figures indicates that over the last few years the average number of children per couple has been 2.5. If this trend persists, by the year 2000 we will reach the daunting figure of 1.3 billion *(see table 1.1)*.

A fresh peak in births looms because despite population control, the birthrate in China has been rising again at an alarming pace in recent years. To be sure, the birth rate has been brought down since the 1960s, when it was in the 35 to 40 per thousand range, but it has in fact

TABLE 1.1

FORECAST FOR THE TOTAL CHINESE POPULATION

Average no. of births per couple	Average annual natural growth (%)	Total population by 2000 (billions)	Total population by 2080 (billions)
1.0	0.27	1.0549	0.2880
1.5	0.73	1.1506	0.6775
1.7	0.91	1.1888	0.9220
2.0	1.16	1.2463	1.4324
2.3	1.40	1.3032	2.1337
2.5	1.55	1.3421	2.7542
3.0	1.92	1.4380	4.9833

been rising since the mid–1970s. In 1979 it was down to 17.82, but it was above 20 for all but 3 of the next 10 years. In 1986, the birthrate rose to 2.08% from 1.78% in 1985, 50% higher than planned. The 1990 census revealed that in the year before the census was taken there were 23,540,000 births, a birth rate of 20.98 per thousand.

In some provinces, the proportion of women having their third child jumped by as much as 60%, and was continuing to rise. Estimates by some population experts, indicate that only about 10% of women of childbearing age in China are actually having only one child. A new peak in births is on the horizon, yet grain output actually declined in the years between the harvests 1984 and 1989.

Unless there is an overall improvement in the level of education and the quality of life, it is quite unrealistic to expect a sudden change in the traditional Chinese belief that "more babies bring greater fortune." As it is, the population problem can be expected to worsen in the short run, because of the sheer number of women now of childbearing age.

Table 1.1 presents another, more recent forecast. Using the figures already cited, and some other estimates made by foreign experts,[6] we may deduce the growth curve shown in figure 1.3.

■ Other Threats from Overpopulation

The structure and distribution of China's population have several important features which form the basis both for policies aimed at containing the population, and also for measures designed to counter the adverse effects of population pressure. The existing structure presents five major threats: a shortage of employment for the young; a disparity between the sexes; the future burden of an aging population; the unbalanced geographical distribution of the population, and low-quality education.

The first threat we will encounter is the pressure to find employment for the disproportionately large number of young people in the population. This is one of the most important characteristics of the population structure *(see table 1.2 and figure 1.4).*

Well over a third of the population is under 14. Over two-thirds are under 30. Over 600 million people were born after 1949. According to the 1982 census, the mean age of the population was 21 years, and the average was 27.1 years. This last number, for example, was 6.8 years less than the corresponding figure for Japan in 1980. The ratio of the elderly to minors in China was 14.61%, whereas in 1980, the

FIGURE 1.4
CHANGES IN RATIO OF ELDERLY PEOPLE IN CHINA, 1978–2030

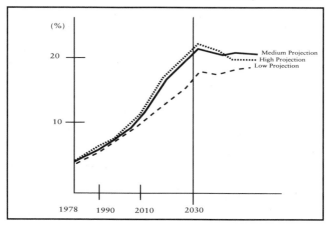

TABLE 1.2
CHANGES IN THE AGE STRUCTURAL DISTRIBUTION OF THE CHINESE POPULATION (%)

Year	0–14 years old	15–64 years old	Over 64 years old
1953	36.3	59.3	4.4
1957	38.8	56.5	4.7
1964	40.4	56.1	3.5
1975	36.8	58.4	4.8
1978	35.8	59.4	4.8
1982	33.6	61.5	4.9
1989	27.5	66.5	6.0

average figure for developed countries was 47.83% and for less developed countries, 7.3%.[7] What China has is a typical "young" population, and this offers hope and danger in equal measure.

The vast and growing working population has already become something of a burden, and the situation can only worsen as today's children reach working age. If we apply the standard which designates working years as the ages 15–64, by 1985 China's potential working population was already over 680 million, or 61.5% of the total. Applying China's domestic standard, which includes only those 16–59, gives a lower figure of 600.85 million. By 1990, it had reached 700 million (or 673 million by another estimate). The average ratio worldwide of the working population to the total population was 59%.

In the 11 years from 1953 to 1964, China's population grew by more than 22%, while the working age population only increased by 13.9%. However, during the 18 years between 1964 and 1982, the total population increased by 44.5%, but the working age population grew by 61.3% This growth trend cannot possibly be reversed before the year 2000. Xiong Yu has calculated that the total projected increase in the working population between 1981 and 2000 would be 440 million (a yearly average growth of 22 million, and even this may be on the low side). Of the total increase, cities and townships are likely to account for 110 million *(see table 1.3 for details).*

The enormous pressure of employment is also related to a rather disadvantageous pattern in the distribution of the urban population. According to data from the 1990 census, the total population of cities and towns was 297.2 million, or 26.23% of the total population. However, a substantial number of these people actually belonged to the suburban agricultural population, so the urban population in the strict sense of the word is somewhat less. The total non-agricultural population of areas under city administration in 1989 was about 146.13 million, or 13% of the total population (considerably lower than the world average of 40%). The total non-agricultural population of cities of 500,000 or more was only about 80 million.

Many questions also surround the issue of urbanization in China. The Chinese Urban Planning Department has planned that by the year 2000, China will have 27 super-large cities, 32 large cities, 72 medium sized cities with populations of over 0.2 million, 283 small cities with populations of under 0.2 million, and 3,178 townships. With the further development of the existing 53,000 large agricultural villages, a total of 140 million people, or roughly two-thirds of the anticipated increase in the population over the next 15 years, could be brought into newly developed townships and large villages.[8]

Significant obstacles will have to be surmounted even to achieve this goal. The trouble is that the current strategy focuses only on absorbing new increases in the urban population, while the crux of the problem really lies in absorbing excess labor from rural areas. Allowing for future increases, this is expected to amount to 330 million people. Obviously, plans for urbanization alone will not be sufficient to resolve this problem.

This is the first of several considerations that were overlooked when the urbanization program was first proposed by the respected

TABLE 1.3
FORECAST ON THE LABOR RESOURCES OF CHINA (1981–2000)

MEASUREMENTS	Y E A R S			
	1981–1985	1986–1990	1991–1995	1996–2000
Total population reaching working age (millions)	133.3	130.47	97.28	85.00
Share of urban residents in total population (%)	23	25	27	30
Total urban population reaching working age (millions)	30.00	32.60	26.26	25.50
Total rural population reaching working age (millions)	103.3	97.87	71.01	59.50

sociologist Fei Xiaotong. If the newly developed townships are to absorb the 140 million of the population increase, the other 350 million, including surplus labor from the rural areas and their families will somehow have to be accommodated into the cities. Even if it could be done, it would require 350 cities with the capacity to house a million people each to absorb them.

This is aggravated by the dearth of capital. On the conservative assumption that 2,000 yuan in housing construction and 10,000 yuan in capital stock would be required to accommodate each additional fulltime laborer into the city, and assuming also that only 150 million of the 350 million are to be employed, the total capital investment required would still be 2 to 3 trillion yuan—a substantial amount even for the wealthiest of nations.

Another difficulty, which will be discussed further in the chapters on ecology, is that based on present patterns of development in the new townships, the price we would pay in terms of the destruction of arable land involved in building new cities would be 11 times higher than if we simply allowed this population to be absorbed into the existing large cities.

We must also consider the fact that the labor force is overwhelmingly uneducated. After the contract labor laws and the bankruptcy laws are implemented on a large scale, we may encounter enormous problems of structural, preferential, and frictional unemployment. It is quite apparent that the possibility of successfully absorbing excess agricultural labor into new townships by 2000 is still largely theoretical. In view of this, there is little place for blind optimism.

The second major threat has to do with the discrepancy between the sexes or, more specifically, with the dangerous preponderance of males over females in the population. This is a situation which could potentially aggravate an already rising social dislocation.

Historically, the sex ratio of the world population (taking the female population as the percentage denominator) has hovered around 103 to 107 men to every hundred women, but in China it has floated between 110 and 115 men to women in some areas. No research has yet shown whether this difference is the result of biological or geographical factors, or whether it is due to a sexist preference for males. According to the *Future of World Population* published by the United Nations, the sex ratio worldwide has been approaching unity since 1950, and is not expected to rise to 101.2 until 2000. In China, however, the sex ratio for all new births has been 108.47 males to 100 females, falling far short of the equalizing trend that has prevailed elsewhere in the world.

A report published in the first 1984 issue of *Youth Research* indicated that among youths of marriageable age in a county in Shaanxi Province, males outnumbered females by 5,706 and the young women were continuing to leave through marriage or taking jobs outside the county. Many families with marriageable daughters took advantage of this opportunity to demand exorbitant betrothal gifts from the bridegrooms' families, who often went totally broke as a result. The situation was clearly becoming a threat to social stability in the area.

In the 1982 census, total female population of China was 488.7 million meaning that men outnumbered women by almost 30.4 million, or 5.72% of the total male population. Since, as in most other countries, females far outnumber males among the elderly, an adjustment of the statistics indicates that as many as 9.33% of males of marriageable age will not be able to find a spouse: that amounts to approximately 48.5 million bachelors—and the 1982 census failed to include people currently serving in the military. Later, on the advice of international population experts, the National Council announced in June 1985 that there were 4.24 million active service persons in 1982. Among them, men outnumbered women by 3.16 million. If this adjustment is taken into account, males then outnumbered females by more than 33 million.

According to the 1990 census, the ratio of male to female stood at 106.6, with 584,950,000 males and 548,730,000 females, a difference of more than 36 million, and .3% higher than figures for 1982.

Stricter enforcement of the "one child policy" would probably only serve to aggravate the discrepancy in the sex ratio because of the strong pressure to produce a male heir. According to a survey carried out in 13 counties and cities in the Jinzhou region of Hubei Province in 1982, the discrepancy increases as the age of the babies decreases. The age and the sex ratio (male:female) were as follows: 4 years, 104.1:100; 3 years, 104.6:100; 2 years, 105.1:100; and 1 year, 106.2:100.[9]

Surveys carried out in 1986 among unmarried people between the ages of 30 and 59, who numbered 9.48 million, showed that 95% were male. This trend has been aggravated by the lingering tradition for women to marry early. In 1982, of the 4.24 million young people who were considered to have married early by legal standards, women outnumbered men by 1.5 times. Correspondingly, there was also a relatively high rate of early childbearing. For example, research by Professor Tian Xinyuan indicates that 65% of Chinese women became pregnant within the first three months of marriage, and 85% within a year.

In China, traditional family and social pressures still favor early marriage and childbearing, and reinforce the preference for male babies over female ones. Unless there is a fundamental shakeup of deep-rooted traditional beliefs, and perhaps a transition to a more practical norm of early marriage and late childbearing, the task of population control will continue to be a truly daunting one.

Another related problem is the question of female infanticide. In June 1985, at the Twentieth International Conference on Population in Florence, the American scholar Judith Banister delivered a paper entitled "The Impact and Verification of Some Results from the 1982 Chinese Census." In it she calculated missing data on birth and death rates in China over the preceding years. The figures she derived showed discrepancies during the highest years of more than 20% and 40%, respectively. She commented, "Assuming that the real sex ratio for births in 1981 was 106:100 (male:female), there must have been at least 230,000 female births that were never reported . . . and if the cases of female infanticide reported in the Chinese media were statistically significant, which was not reflected at all in the 1982 census, then there is a strong indication that some families did not report to census personnel the births and unnatural deaths of these victims."[10]

Regardless of its cause, if we cannot prevent this cruel slaughter of female babies, China will surely become the target of severe denunciation from the international community. It would be much more reasonable to encourage a more open and flexible practice of free sexual relations but late childbearing rather than in effect tolerating the sexist and inhuman practice of drowning of female babies in certain regions. It is a pity that in the realm of marriage and family, old Chinese traditions are most stubbornly preserved and have so far proved unshakeable.

The natural process of procreation cannot be manipulated like a mechanical gadget. The historical burden of a large population is tied up with everything else, and must be solved with time and patience. The backwardness of technology that still prevails in rural areas makes it extremely difficult to insist on limiting families to one child. Without the kind of technology required to reduce the need for physical labor, the peasants still feel a right to demand a bigger labor force to support their families. Consequently, even today, one often sees couplets in front of northern Chinese country homes that read: "Horses and carts before the door do not mean lasting wealth; A home with sons and grandsons may have greater Fortune." This ancient Chinese worldview corresponds to the nation's current level of economic development. An "optimal strategy" for births can be artificially defined through numerical curves and models, but we must not forget that the people having the babies are real human beings who exist within the confines of traditional customs and practical constraints, and are swayed by limitations of their own knowledge, psychology, and other character-istics. The pessimists were not wrong, and their predictions have been proven more reliable than other, rosier visions. The Chinese govern-ment recently made some modifications to its "one child policy," and this should be lauded as a wise decision. We must also realize that only a general rise in income, consumption, and the level of education can provide strong incentives for family planning. Forcible measures will only bring a trail of disaster in their wake.

The third major threat is the rapid aging of the population as a whole that will occur in the not-so-distant future. China has had some success in limiting the growth of the total population by lowering the birthrate. This is a commendable achievement, but one inevitable side effect is a rapid increase in the proportion of senior citizens in the population as a whole. The faster the bottom of the pyramid shrinks, the thicker the lump already appearing in the middle will grow. Thus, as a result of conscious policy decisions, we are gradually transforming a disproportionately young population into a disproportionately old one.

According to international norms, if more than 10% of the population is over 60 years old, or more than 7% is over 65, the population as a whole can be considered elderly. France was the first country to see its population transformed from a young one into an old one. There, the process took 150 years, which gave the country time to adjust. In Japan it took 50 years for the proportion of citizens over 65 years old to rise from 5.3% in 1920 to 7.1% in 1970.

The percentage of senior citizens 65 and over in China will rise from 6.0 in 1990 to 7.1% in 2000. Within the space of only 10 years, China will join the ranks of "elderly" nations: an unprecedentedly fast rate of transformation. This will lower the overall quality of the labor force, and will also place an inordinately heavy burden on the younger generation and society in general.

If we use instead the official retirement age in China, which is 60 for men and 55 for women, census figures for 1953, 1964 and 1982 suggest that the proportion of senior citizens in the population was 8.4%, 7.8% and 9.26%, respectively, and by 1990 it reached 9.83%. The total number for 1982 was approximately 93 million out of a total population of 1.004 billion. For the city of Beijing alone, the total population is projected to increase 2.66 times by 2000 from its 1956 level. But over the same period, the population of senior citizens (over 60 years old) is expected to increase by 8.7 times, to reach 14.65% of the total population (this does not include mechanical increases, which were 8.95% in 1985). This would amount to well over 2 million elderly people in Beijing. In the Xuanwu District of Beijing, surveys carried out in five different residential areas showed that senior citizens over 60 years old comprised 9.2% of all residents.[11]

By the end of 1985, there were more than 1.59 million people over 60 in Shanghai, over 10% of the city's population. By United Nations standards this would be the first city to reach old age in its overall population. The ill omen extends outward from Shanghai, with adjacent cities like Nanjing, Suzhou, and Wuxi reaching the same level around the same time, and the whole province of Jiangsu reaching it in 1988.

According to a different forecast, put forward during an international conference on population held in Vienna in September 1982, by 2000 there will be about 130 million people over 60 in China (in 1986 there were about 80 million), by 2025, 300 million (50 million more than the current total U.S. population), and by 2050, over 400 million. Even if we extend the definition of "old" to 65, the figure will jump from 50 million at the time of the 1982 survey, to 100 million by 2000 (7.9% of the total population), and in 2040 it will peak at 260 million or 17.4% of the total population (the corresponding world average in 1985 was 6% and is expected to rise to 9.5% by 2025).

If the present trend persists, by 2025 one out of every four or five persons in China will be a senior citizen. The aging of the population began late in China but it is proceeding apace, and as the crisis starts to set in, every Chinese will begin to feel the shock.

Supporting this large number of elderly citizens is going to be expensive. For example, due to the cadre retirement system, the amount paid out for pensions from the Beijing municipal budget had increased six-fold since 1978, amounting to $1/10$ of the total wage income in the city (and this figure does not include vast increases in medical payments).

Currently, 13% of all state employees are drawing retirement benefits. In the future, even if reduced birthrates lower the budget for raising children, we may see the benefits drained away immediately to support our senior citizens, shattering our hopes of attaining a higher standard of living.

Poor as China may be in economic terms, the country has always been rich in arcane arts designed to promote longevity, and vast improvements in health care and diet since 1949 have increased the lifespan. By 1985 average life expectancy for women had risen to 71 years, and for men to 67 years, giving an average of 68.92 years. By contrast, average life expectancy was only 35 in 1949.

16   China on the edge

▪ A Conservative and Stable Distribution Structure

The distribution of the Chinese population is another major difficulty. As noted, the geographical distribution of China's population is heavily concentrated in the Southeast.

In his 1935 paper entitled "The Distribution of the Chinese Population," Hu Huanyong proposed dividing the country in half by drawing a straight line from what is now Aihui in the Northeast to Tengchun in the Southwest. He discovered that the northwestern part covered 64% of the landmass but had only 4% of the population, and the corresponding figures for the southeast were 36% and 96%, respectively. A reappraisal of the census figures collected in 1982 revealed minimal changes: the total population of the Northwest had risen to 5.6%, and that of the Southeast had dropped to 94.4%.[12]

Indeed, even without drawing the lines, just adding up the total population of Inner Mongolia, Xinjiang, Tibet, and Qinghai, which cover roughly half the landmass of China, reveals that these regions contain a mere 3.8% of the population. As for population density, the number of people per square kilometer in the whole of the Northwest is only 17, which is less than 10% of the national average. In Tibet, there are less than 2 people per square kilometer. In Qinghai, there are only 6.2 per square kilometer, whereas the figure for Shanghai is over 2,300, and for the province of Jiangsu, 670.

Geographical differences are also evident in the sex ratio. Figures 1.5 and 1.6 were compiled by Gu Zushan using the data on the sex ratio presented in table 1.4, and were presented in his paper "The Geographical Distribution of Discrepancies in the Sex Ratio." He drew a line, based on discrepancies equal to or larger than 107/100 (male/female), that separates China into an eastern region (excluding Shanghai) and a western region.

There are 19 provinces and autonomous cities in the eastern region, which accounts for roughly 83% of the population and 36% of the land; and 10 provinces or autonomous cities (including Shanghai) in the western region, which has 17% of the population, and 64% of the land.

The eastern regions show a higher level both of population density, and of discrepancies in the sex ratio (albeit with a natural growth rate that is lower than the West). Generally speaking, lower-altitude and more densely populated areas of China (with the exception of Shanghai) also tend to have a higher discrepancy between the sexes. The differences may be the result of environmental and histori-

TABLE 1.4
SEX RATIOS IN DIFFERENT PROVINCES, CITIES AND AUTONOMOUS REGIONS

Anhui	112.5	Guangxi	110.7	Guangdong	110.5
Henan	110.3	Shandong	109.9	Hunan	109.5
Shanxi	109.3	Xhannxi	109.2	Zhejiang	108.8
Fujian	108.6	Hebei	108.2	Sichuan	107.9
Jiangsu	107.9	Jiangxi	107.9	Jilin	107.8
Tianjin	107.7	Liaoning	107.1	Beijing	107.0
Hubei	107.0	Heilongjiang	106.9	Guizhou	106.8
Nei Mongol	106.8	Gansu	106.3	Qinghai	106.2
Ninxia	106.2	Yunnan	106.2	Xinjiang	106.1
Shanghai	105.4	Tibet	101.3		

cal factors and may be impossible to alleviate. Nonetheless, the pressure that results from the discrepancy will continue to mount, and cannot be ignored. The strain on the larger cities is particularly heavy and they will increasingly face shortages of land and housing, the depletion of water and energy resources, a shortage of many services, rising unemployment, and all the attendant social problems.

Researchers studying the pattern of shifts in the center of gravity of the population in China have also shown that for almost 14 centuries up until 1393, the center of the Chinese population was shifting towards the southeast at the rate of roughly 0.43 kilometer per year. For the 535 years between 1393 and 1928, it moved back up northwest at roughly the same speed. From 1933 to 1953, the center started to shift northward at a rate 7 or 10 times faster than previous shifts and then it swung west, albeit at a much slower pace. (The shift between 1978 and 1982 appears somewhat exaggerated because the 1982 census figures included the populations of Hong Kong, Macao, and Taiwan.) After 1953, the center consistently remained east of its position in that year. The shifts that occured in later years inclined further southeast, worsening the imbalance in distribution.

It is hard to predict when the center will shift west of its 1953 position. Li Xijun has argued that moving the population physically will do little to redress the imbalance in the long run. A real shift will only occur if there is a change in the relative natural population growth rate. [13] It is not impossible to envision a strategic westward shift of the center beyond the 1953 position, but this will probably not occur before the year 2000.

Since 1953, the population center has been shifting within a triangle of less than 159 square kilometers. This trend will not alleviate the pressure of high population density in southeast China. But as we shall see in the next chapter, it is doubtful whether the fragile environment of the West and Northwest can bear the strain of substantially increased migration there anyway.

The fifth major problem is the high percentage of illiterates in the population. According to the 1982 census, there were roughly 238 million illiterates in China. The 1990 census did indicate some progress in this area, with the number of illiterates down to 180 million, a drop from almost 23% to about 16%. Although progress has been made in higher education, with the number of college graduates doubling in the past decade, only about 14 in every thousand Chinese today have a college education, and 80 out of a thousand a high school education, a total of less than 10% of the population, far lower than the more advanced nations.

FIGURE 1.5

DISTRIBUTION OF POPULATION VOLUME AND SEX RATIO BETWEEN THE EASTERN AND WESTERN PARTS OF CHINA

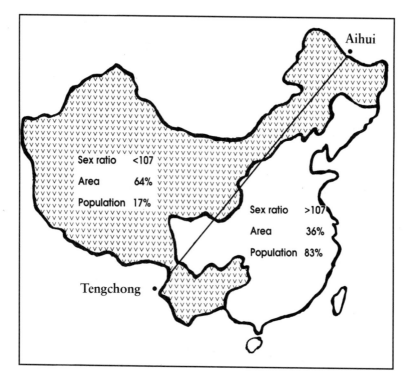

FIGURE 1.6 DISTRIBUTION OF CHINESE POPULATION NATURAL GROWTH

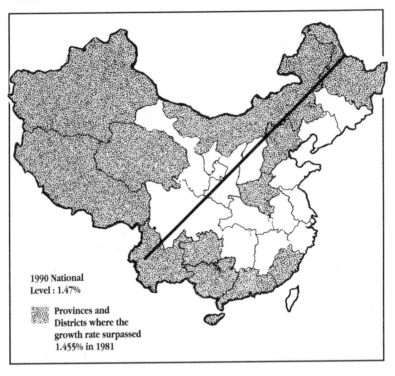

1990 National
Level : 1.47%

Provinces and
Districts where the
growth rate surpassed
1.455% in 1981

Among a working population of about 553 million, only slightly more than 5% are professional specialists, and only 13 million, or 2.5% of the workforce, have received technical school training or more. If we include all those who finished secondary school, the total is about 200 million, still less than a fifth of the total population. China's low level of productivity, bad management, and poor utilization of new technologies can be traced to this generally low level of education.

To conclude, a closer look at the population crisis reveals that, in addition to presenting the enormous challenge of merely feeding and housing ourselves, this crisis has given rise to various other unforeseen social and economic difficulties. Controlling population growth clearly remains China's single most formidable task.

2

■

THE ECOLOGICAL CRISIS:
A GRIM LEGACY

■ A Seventh of the Land Has Become Desert

1972 may have marked an important transition in mankind's perception of nature. That year, a report entitled "There Is Only One Earth"
was delivered at a conference on the environment in Stockholm. The
report, which synthesized the opinions of 152 experts from 58
countries, was the first attempt to present all the ramifications of
environmental protection from a political, economic, and social point
of view. It signalled an awakening to the global dilemmas of ecological
decline and scarce resources.

Since then, people the world over have been forced to confront
two threats that hang ominously over the future of the human race: the
possible exhaustion of energy resources, and the rapid deterioration of
the environment. Unfortunately, in 1972 a good part of China had
barely emerged from a nightmare of massive political upheaval, and
the problem of environmental decay was completely ignored.

Indeed, there was a general silence about environmental problems in China until the mid-1980s. On 12 December 1984, Du
Runshen, who was then the Director of the State Council Agricultural
Commission, concluded a speech delivered at an agricultural working
conference by saying, "What I am most worried about is the protection
of the environment. The situation is becoming serious and nobody is
discussing it."

The relentless progress of desertification is one of the most serious environmental problems China faces. Even as government officials and academics were earnestly debating grandiose schemes to open up the expanse of virgin land in the Northwest, the "yellow dragon" of desertification was devouring it.

This is nothing new: the desert began to spread centuries ago. The ancient city of Tongwan, which was the capital of the Mongol chief Helian Bobo, has vanished from sight. The famous Silk Road that spiraled across the southern slopes of the Heavenly Mountains and the northern foot of the Kunlun Mountains has faded into sand dunes, and the grand prairie of Erdos that was known for its wild lushness a thousand years ago is now nowhere to be seen. Whatever trace remains is being rapidly licked away by the voracious tongue of the great "yellow dragon."

The disappearance of the Silk Road is already part of Chinese history, but the stark process of desertification continues today. One of the recent victims is a 300-kilometer-long green corridor at the lower reaches of the Talimu River in Xinjiang Province, which has played an important role in checking the southward expansion of the Taklamakan Desert. Many poplar trees and red willows are dying, the roads are strewn with rocks and sand, layers of dust cover the rooftops, and the underground water table has receded to a mere eight or nine meters.

This is primarily the result of excessive logging and herding, and the failure to conserve water resources over the last few decades. Lake Luobupo was once the largest water source in the Central Asian region, but it lies dangerously close to the Taklamakan, China's largest desert (in the local language the name means "you can go in but you won't come out"). By the early 1980s the lake had been reduced to a vast wasteland strewn with the corpses of dead birds.

In 1987, at the annual conference of the Scientific Association of Xinjiang, representatives from the Bortahla Mongolian Autonomous District made an urgent appeal to "save Lake Aibei." The lake, which lies northwest of Jinghe County at the southeastern corner of the Ahla Mountain Pass, on the border with Russia, is the center of water resources in the Jungre Basin of northwestern Xinjiang; 77,400 acres of arable land surround the lake, and it also provides the main local source of salt. Hundreds of thousands of people from 13 different minority nationalities have made their livelihood on and around the lake over the centuries.

During the early 1950s, Lake Aibei covered about 1,620 square kilometers: now it is down to about 500 square kilometers, and still shrinking. Severe sand storms, called *karaburan* in the local dialect, and hazy sand-filled fogs have become more frequent, and a 30-meter-wide protective bank of trees has been engulfed by the sands. (A protective belt of trees planted in dry regions is part of the Chinese authorities' strategy to combat desertification. The width of the plantings ranges from 30 to 70 meters, depending on regional weather conditions. This particular layer in the Aibei region is about 80 kilometers long.) Farmland is being swallowed up by the desert, and the nearby vegetation has withered or died due to the receding water line. A new saltworks that took 11 years to construct, at a cost of 6 million yuan, is unable to begin production due to the falling water level.

There is abundant historical evidence to support the thesis that most desertification has been due to manmade factors. Oscar Wegel, the German Sinologist, is convinced that the disappearance of Lake Luobupo also falls into that category. For many years, the Chinese government actively encouraged pioneering "marches" into the great Northwest. Wastelands were plowed up, farms were developed, and logging and herding were carried out on a massive scale. This merciless assault on nature has brought retaliation from an army of sand dunes.

Some estimates conclude that up to 160,000 square kilometers of China's deserts are of human origin. If effective controls are not instituted promptly, another 70,000 square kilometers of land will go the same way by 2000. By and large, original vegetation has disappeared, and one-fifth of the cultivated land is becoming salinated. Nor do these figures include an additional 9,700 square kilometers of land in the semi-arid regions that have been reduced to a dust-bowl.[1]

Other studies have claimed that in the Erdos Region of Inner Mongolia alone, the area desertified due to human factors over the last 30 years exceeds total natural desert expansion over 2,000 years. Official statistics have shown that between 1949 and 1980, 65,000 square kilometers of land in 11 provinces and 207 counties were lost to the desert. Currently, deserts and semi-arid regions cover 1,496,000 square kilometers, or one-seventh of China's total land area. Of this, 71% of the inhabitants, 72% of the declining farmland, and 68% of the withering grassland are concentrated in the desertified parts.

In addition, 158,000 square kilometers of uncultivated wilderness are in the process of becoming desertified. Approximately 9.7 million acres of farmland, 12.2 million acres of grassland, and nearly 2,000 kilometers of railroad are currently threatened. Grasslands are deteriorating at a particularly alarming rate, and by the mid-1970s, about 15% of the total grassland area was affected. By the mid-1980s, this had increased to 30%, or more than 132 million acres. At the beginning of the 1950s, about 1.6 million acres of the famous Erdos

Grassland were semi-desert. By the beginning of the 1980s, this had leapt to 10 million acres, or almost 50% of the total.[2]

■ The Threatened Forests

Intensive cultivation, soil loss, and lack of investment in infrastructure are thought to be among the major causes of this rapid deterioration. Although the human causes of this massive desertification are still not entirely clear, the destruction of forests has certainly been a contributing factor. The disastrous effects of deforestation on air, soil, vegetation, and water supplies have been well-documented all over the world.

Like desertification, the deterioration of forests in China has been taking place over a long period of time. The Yellow Earth Plateau, situated in the center of northern China, was once known for its dense forests and rich grassland. Nowadays travelers to the area see only a shadow of its former grandeur in an endless stretch of barren hills. Archaeologists and environmentalists estimate that in 900 B.C., approximately 53% of the area was covered with forests. This has decreased steadily over the years to 40% between 200 B.C. and A.D. 600, 15% in the 1600s, and to 1% in this century. The annual state budget allocated to soil preservation projects in the area is now as low as 100 million yuan, or 1/200 of equivalent expenditures in Japan. In view of this, there is little hope for improvement in the near future.[3]

Zhejiang Province in southeastern China provides another example of this problem. In historical records, the province is described as a fertile rice-growing region with abundant water supplies and high mountains. The province has a warm, humid climate and a mountainous terrain, which in ancient times was covered with lush primal forest. As late as the middle of the 10th century, herds of elephants still lived among the hills in the south. The crops were once varied, and included a fair amount of dry grains. Only much later on did rice replace other grains as the main crop.

Despite significant southward migration during the Jin dynasty (circa A.D. 300), the geographical characteristics of the mountainous regions were not seriously altered, but changes started to occur following another wave of migration to the province in the Song dynasty (A.D. 960–1279). It was at this time that the shortage of grain became a problem, and at some later point, two new crops—corn and sweet potatoes—were imported from across the Pacific. These alleviated the pressure of the growing population and brought a revolution in land utilization, but no one anticipated that the new crops would also contribute to severe soil erosion and the destruction of native vegetation.

Chen Qiaoze, a specialist on the history of land cultivation and deforestation in Zhejiang, has found that from the reigns of Emperors Kangxi and Qianlong (A.D. 1661–1795), around the time corn and sweet potatoes were introduced, a large part of the population began to settle in the mountainous regions of the province. This massive migration disrupted the natural growth rate of the population, causing rapid increases which necessitated cultivation on an ever larger scale. The mountains were stripped of their native vegetation, leaving the soil exposed to erosion, and a vicious cycle of population growth and the deterioration of the ecological balance began. Even today, the province is still suffering the negative consequences of that period.[4]

Similar experiences of waves of cultivation in the mountains leading to the destruction of forests were recorded in many other provinces. However, the events of the last few decades make it clear that this important historical lesson has yet to sink in. Massive destruction was wrought during the "pioneer" campaign initiated by the Chinese government in the late 1950s and 1960s which encouraged and sometimes forced young people from the densely populated cities to migrate and resettle on farms throughout the Northwest. These prolonged "pioneer" movements, using primitive techniques like burning large areas of vegetation to clear ground for plowing, dwarfed the damage done in any other period in history.

Recent research on the Changbai Mountain Area in Heilongjiang, shows a significant discrepancy between deforestation and efforts at reforestation. The forest has been shrinking at the rate of 5 million cubic meters of wood, or 86,450 acres, per year. In the Yichun District, annual lumber production has been 5 million cubic meters, but the local residents have been burning as much as 3 million cubic meters per year.

Eight of the 40 bureaus under the administration of the Heilongjiang Forest Industry Bureau had run out of any forest to administer, and another 22 had just enough to last about another 10 years. Nevertheless, by 1985, the annual lumber production exceeded the state plan by 39%, or almost 5 million cubic meters. If measures are not taken immediately to reverse this trend, the whole province will be stripped of its natural protection and its forest-related industries will face collapse by the year 2000, with all the ensuing ecological repercussions.

In Sichuan Province, another major forest area in China, deforestation has been equally severe. According to some estimates, the ratio of trees felled to trees planted was as high as 10 to one. Over the last three decades, a total of 60 million cubic meters was felled. The local inhabitants were said to be "replacing the forest of trees with a forest of arms and axes."

If the unrestrained activities of local and provincial enterprises and greedy individuals continue at this rate, the western Sichuan Forest will not last more than 13 years. At the upper reaches of the Ming River, forest cover fell from around 30% in the 1950s to 18% in the 1980s. The corresponding figure for the entire province fell from 20% to 13%. The entire Hengduan Mountain Region boasts the second largest forested area in China after the Northeast, but it too is plagued by excessive logging.

In the Xishuang Banna Autonomous Region, a famous tourist destination, forest cover has been reduced from 60% in the early 1950s to about 30%.[5] And in neighboring Guizhou Province, which was once similarly endowed with abundant forest, cover has been reduced to 14.5%. This has had a demonstrable impact on the local climate. In much of southwest China, the typical weather pattern has changed from one of mild winds and adequate rain to one of sporadic storms and drought. The once deep and gently flowing rivers have dwindled to paltry streams, occasionally swelled to roaring torrents by flash floods. Soil erosion on the hills has turned the rivers a muddy brown, and there are also more frequent land and rock slides.

In the 2,300-kilometer-long valley of the Jingsha River, which winds through 20 different counties in Yunnan Province, there is a saying that "not a tree can be seen for 10,000 miles." According to local statistics, the average household burns 3.38 cubic meters of wood a year. In addition, two kilograms of wood are consumed for every half kilogram of sugar manufactured, and three kilos for every half kilogram of tobacco. In 1985 alone, Yunnan Province burned 2 million cubic meters of wood, just in the production of tobacco.

At the time of this writing, the massive scale of excessive logging had not been halted. Recent policy has transferred the administration of forest-related enterprises from the central government to local authorities, and the wages of the swollen local workforce are being paid through even more deforestation. For example, the Luhuo Forestry Bureau at the upper reaches of the Yangtze River employs a workforce of 2,500 people, and it takes an annual harvest of at least 120,000 cubic meters of logs for the enterprise to remain self-sufficient. Other enterprises and individuals in the area require another 30,000 cubic meters to pay their expenses, bringing the total to 150,000 cubic meters, and the annual growth rate of the county's forests is only 40,000–50,000 cubic meters.

If timber consumption continues at this rate, within 20 years there will be nothing left of the county's 178,000 acres of forest. In addition, 900,000 tons of logs are burned for heating and other purposes every year in the Ganzi District in which Luhuo County is located. Fir and dragon spruce, which are the main types of wood in the county, have typical cutting cycles of between 80 and 120 years, making it difficult for reforestation to keep pace with consumption.

Hidden away in a remote corner of Hubei Province is one of the few areas in which China's original vegetation has allegedly been preserved. Shennongjia (the name means "home of the magic peasant") has an air of mystery about it, and unconfirmed legends claim that prehistoric people still reside there. In July 1990, I toured the area with a few associates and was shocked to find that only a few acres of original vegetation remain. Over 80,000 loggers were burning and chopping furiously, day and night, and 90% of the trees were gone in all the areas accessible on foot. Only young trees as slender as porcelain seemed to have been spared, and these pathetic, isolated clusters are all that remain of the magic forest.

The situation in the less renowned forest areas is even more horrifying. Every year, Fujian Province grows 18 million cubic meters of trees, but 25 million cubic meters are felled for industrial and commercial use, and another 10 million cubic meters are burned by local residents for domestic purposes. Little remains of the forests in Fujian and resultant soil erosion has caused a rapid increase in the silt carried by the province's rivers. Between 1967 and 1977, the volume of silt discharged at the lower reaches of the Min River increased 2.6 times over its 1951 to 1966 level. By 1976, soil loss from erosion was estimated at 89.8 million tons. That is the equivalent of stripping 105,410 acres of land of its top soil.[6]

The government's reforestation efforts are losing ground to the assault. Between 1949 and 1988, 231 million acres of new forests were planted throughout China, but only 69 million acres, or 30% of these remain.[7] Since 1970, the forest areas of the Qin and Guan Mountains have been reduced by 15.9%; and the forest lines have receded by an average of 5 to 10 kilometers. In the Baoji Region of Shanxi Province, only 51,000 of the 395,000 acres of new trees planted since 1954 have survived; a preservation rate of only 12.8%. At this rate, it would take 250 years to completely reforest the area's barren hills.

False reporting, ineptitude, and bad management are the main causes for the huge discrepancy between the impressive claims and the meager results of China's reforestation campaign.

The theft and blatant looting of forest resources has never been effectively checked. After an antimony mine opened in Shaoyang

County, Henan in 1987, hordes of peasants from the nearby counties of Shaoyang, Xining, and Dongan descended upon the area. Arriving in droves of more than 3,000 a day, they proceeded to start digging and blasting holes in the ground, causing severe damage to the surrounding forest. The local Hebo Forestry Enterprise reported to the higher authorities that forests near the mining area were in danger of complete destruction, but all the local government could do was plead with the offenders through loudspeakers. As many peasants came from different counties, the proclamations fell on deaf ears.

During that year, civil courts in China prosecuted more than 75,000 cases of forest-looting involving the destruction of 247,000 acres of forest. In the first half of 1988, another 20,000 such cases were prosecuted. Since then it is said that many reports on such cases have been suppressed, and of all the cases that went before the courts, less than 10% actually resulted in some kind of indictment, a dismal indication of the level of ignorance regarding forestry, and the impotence of government enforcement measures.

As part of the fresh outburst of propaganda following 4 June 1989, the 10 March 1991 issue of the *Guangming Daily* reported that over the last decade, more than 10 billion trees had been planted in nationwide volunteer tree-planting campaigns, a total of 2 billion days of voluntary labor. The reports claimed that over 27 million acres of protective forest had been planted along the Northern Plains, and 1.7 million acres along the Yangtze River valley. Figures furnished by a bureaucracy eager to demonstrate its efficiency and zeal are rather suspect, but in any event it is amusing to see how Chinese media reports emphasize output rather than input when discussing production figures, and vice versa when it comes to volunteer labor.

It is instructive to compare China's experience with forest preservation to that of the United States. The initiative China could learn most from was the Civilian Conservation Corps, instituted during the Roosevelt administration, partly to cope with drought conditions caused by overcultivation and partly to create employment during the Great Depression. Between 1933 and 1941, more than 2.5 million unemployed young people were recruited to plant trees, build roads and trails, and work on a host of other projects in an effort to reclaim and develop the country's natural resources. The program made an important contribution both to the environmental quality and economic potential of the United States in later years. China should seriously consider the possibility of a similar program.

The latest official statistics put forest coverage in China at around 13%, but some experts put it much lower at 8% (it was 13%

in 1949).[8] Satellite photos suggest an even lower figure. But even accepting the more optimistic version, coverage is still only just over half the global average of 22%. The total forested area is estimated to be 301 million acres, or less than 0.3 acres per capita. Stocks of raw wood are around 9.9 billion cubic meters, which leaves less than 10 cubic meters per capita. Those figures are much lower than the global per capita average of 2.5 acres of forest and 83 cubic meters in stocks of raw wood.

TABLE 2.1
COMPARISON: FOREST COVERAGE RATE OF CHINA
AND SOME OTHER COUNTRIES (%)

World Average	China	Finland	Japan	USSR	USA	France	India
22	12	69	66	34	33	26	26

During the last three decades, a quarter of the forests in China have vanished. At the current level, annual national consumption of raw wood is 300 million cubic meters, yet annual growth of timber remains at 230 million cubic meters. Between 1949 and 1981, 164.7 million acres of forests were destroyed in China. Forestry experts estimate that if a country's forest cover slips below 20%, it ceases to be self-sufficient in raw wood resources. According to official reports, timber consumption for construction and industrial use did decrease by 6.3% in 1990, dropping to 54 million cubic meters from the previous year's total. But it is obviously easier to regulate the amount of wood processed as timber than to control massive cutting for firewood. Short of something as drastic and effective as the Conservation Corps, the forest problem will surely prove to be a major obstacle to China's development.

■ Soil Erosion: Bleeding from the Main Artery

In China, planning is often far removed from reality, and this is nowhere so apparent as in the policies to counter soil erosion. According to recent statistics, due to the destruction of original vegetation, soil loss now affects an area of 1.5 million square kilometers. That translates into a soil loss of 5 billion tons per year, and the trend continues to worsen.

In August 1975, a major flood in Henan demolished the Banqiao and Shimantan Reservoirs, with disastrous results for the regions on the lower reaches. In 1983 an overflow of the Yellow River affected 12 million people, and in 1984, massive floods erupted in Sichuan, Shanxi, and Heilongjiang. In June and July of 1989, torrential rain in Jiangxi damaged or demolished 1,927 bridges and nearly 9,000 reservoir facilities, affecting a population of 3.5 million. [By mid-July 1991, according to official reports, summer floods had killed 2,000 people in China, causing 40 billion yuan ($7.5 billion) worth of damage while destroying 618,000 acres of farmland and causing a 30% decrease in grain production in the affected regions.—EDITOR.]

In some areas, the bed of the Yellow River is already 3–10 meters higher than the fields on either side. The river is contained only by embankments and has literally been "suspended" by soil deposits on the bottom. If a major flood occurs, causing a flow of more than 22,300 cubic meters per second, the embankments could collapse, endangering the lives of tens of millions of people, and wrecking numerous development projects on the Yellow River plains.

The Yellow River's annual silt discharge is currently as high as 1.6 billion tons (37.7 kilograms per cubic meter of water: the equivalent figure for the Nile River is 1 kilogram).

Currently, the river-bed of the lower reaches of the Yellow River is still rising 5–10 centimeters per year. Projections by the Yellow River Committee show that over the next 50 years or so, the riverbed will have risen 4–6 meters in some sections. It would take an investment of 700–800 billion yuan to raise the banks correspondingly, and that is not considering the damage that would occur if the banks ever gave way.[9]

Lake Tai, in southern Jiangsu, provides another example of this problem. The lake basin covers only 0.3% of the nation's total area, and has 1.3% of its arable land, but it yields more than 10% of the gross national product, and one-fifth of national income. It also sustains hundreds of towns and a population of 34 million. In 1983, floods drenched more than 823,500 acres of farmlands, and completely or partially destroyed crops over an area of 361,000 acres. The total economic loss was estimated to be in excess of 800 million yuan. Some experts believe that if flooding were to recur on a similar scale, 40% of the farmland and countless towns would be submerged, causing losses of over 10 billion yuan.

The recent opening of free markets in lumber and logs has brought a new intensity to what is called "living off the mountains." Reports from the Chengde Region north of Beijing, show that as early as 1981 total soil loss was equivalent to 7,590 acres of farmland, and the loss of fertilizers was one-and-a-half times the total volume of chemical fertilizers used in the whole region in 1980. At this rate, the Miaogong Reservoir constructed in 1961 will be rendered completely useless within 30 years.[10] Of the once famous sea of luxuriant pines, only a scattering of withered bushes remains, and what was once the elegant summer resort of the emperors is in danger of becoming a "desert retreat."

Further to the south, the volume of silt discharged into Dongting Lake, the second largest fresh-water lake in central China, has been increasing steadily due to a similar phenomenon in a whole section of Yangtze branches. The bottom of the lake has been rising yearly, and there has been a corresponding drop in volume of water.

A few years back, there were debates over whether the Yangtze might end up like the Yellow River. The answer should be clear by now. Jingsha River, as the upper third of the Yangtze is called, saw an increase in silt discharge of 0.4 kilograms per cubic meter between 1982 and 1985. The implications of this become clear when it is compared with the increase of a mere 0.2 kilogram per cubic meter over the 35 year period between 1941 and 1976, and a similar increase during the six years between 1976 and 1981.

Furthermore, the Yangtze River discharges 500 million tons of silt annually into the East China Sea, roughly one-third that discharged by the Yellow River, and equivalent to the total discharge of the Nile, the Amazon, and the Mississippi Rivers combined.[11]

The decline of the Yellow River basin area, the cradle of Chinese civilization, was partly due to soil erosion. Frequent warfare and massive southward migration may also have played a part, causing a shift of the population to the Yangtze River basin. If the Yangtze ends up like the Yellow River, a similar decline may threaten this region as well. Some people may wish to speculate that the future center of Chinese civilization may shift down to the Pearl River basin, the main river in Guandong Province, but unfortunately things do not bode well for the Pearl either, as its eastern section is already looking rather "yellow."

From the large reservoir where the Mei and Nin Rivers (upper branches of the Pearl) join, one sees only barren hills and the gaping craters of collapsed mountains. Mud and soil clog the river, and the reservoir is badly silted. Many tributaries of the Pearl have been reduced to a trickle of yellow mud, and the water near the Maple Bank Reservoir (at the upper reaches of the Eastern Pearl) is a ghastly amber red. The area used to boast ancient trees with such a girth it took several pairs of arms to span them, but none remain today. Even smaller trees are few and far between.[12]

In Liaoning, soil loss affects 14.2 million acres, or 40% of the province's land area. In nine counties in the east of the province, arable land has shrunk by one-third since 1950, primarily due to soil loss. The most severe case is the Zhaoyang Region, where erosion has affected 78% of the total land area. The climate has also been affected. Over the last century, there were 46 years of fair weather and 14 years of droughts and floods, but during the 23 years from 1958 to 1981, the ratio was 5:18. Four of the six years from 1980 to 1985 saw droughts.[13]

Fujian Province has only 3 million acres of arable land. This is 0.13 acres per capita, or half the national average, but there is no evidence that this vital resource has been treasured. From 1979 to 1981, rural housing construction and state industrial projects swallowed up 29,000 acres, including 15,000 acres of arable land. The population of the province is growing at the rate of 430,000 per year, which will increase the heavy burden on the land. Since 1958, massive human and capital resources have been invested to turn landfills into farmland, but this has destroyed the fishing industry, leading to a two-thirds reduction in the province's fish harvest. Fish have completely vanished from some coastal regions.[14]

▌ Visions of an Apocalypse

We will discuss the dangers facing agriculture in another chapter, but it is worth raising one of them here. By 1977, China had lost arable land equivalent to the combined land areas of Guangdong, Guangxi, and Sichuan (970,000 square kilometers), including the commercial crop base of the Tai Lake Basin, which is in danger of shrinking into insignificance. The transfer of the labor force into small village industries over the years has cost another 13.2 million acres of farmland.

The Chinese population is 21.5%, or about one-fifth of the total world population, but China has only one-thirteenth of the world's total arable land, and this is shrinking as the population grows. In 1981, the population of China increased by 14.5 million, while arable land was reduced by 2.5 million acres. Between 1979 and 1984, the country lost a total of 19 million acres of arable land, a yearly average of 3.8 million acres. In 1985 alone, when the economy was growing rapidly, 11 million acres were lost. Since then, over 4.1 million acres have been lost every year. Industrial construction alone has claimed 1.5

million acres yearly, while and residential construction in the countryside took another 82,500 acres.[15]

China's arable land continues to shrink. Per capita acreage has
already fallen below 0.165 acres in nine provinces. Furthermore,

TABLE 2.2
CHANGES IN THE CULTIVABLE LAND IN MODERN CHINESE HISTORY

Year	Total Cultivable Land (millions of acres)	Per capita Cultivable land (acres)
1915	237.50	0.55
1918	216.42	0.48
1935	219.38	0.47
1946	232.22	0.50
1955	270.50	0.44
1960	259.07	0.39
1965	255.94	0.35
1970	249.85	0.30
1975	246.39	0.27
1980	245.40	0.25
1990	236.37	0.21

estimates based on samples from 236 cities suggest that urbanization
drives will require an extra 74 square meters per person on average.
The large new coal mine discovered in Shanxi will claim another
1,320,000 to 1,980,000 acres by 2000. Further increases in the rural
population will mean allocating an extra 200 to 266 square meters per
person, and rural irrigation projects will claim an additional 2.5
million acres by the year 2000.[16]

In fact, it is hard to be sure how much arable land we really have.
Figure 2.1 presents some historical data, but because different governments used different units of calculation, it is impossible to draw a
clear curve. Nonetheless the data from 1915 on is quite clear, and the
curve for this period slopes steadily downward at an alarming angle,
especially after 1949.

Current statistics are grossly unreliable and we also lack precise
figures on grasslands, water resources, and available land for industry.

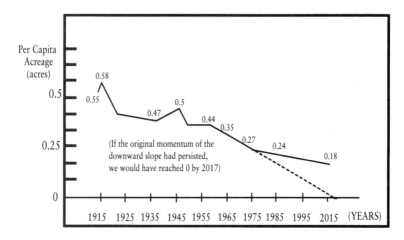

In many regions, the reported figures have been deliberately understated to conceal real resources. Reports on the unit productivity of agricultural resources are often inaccurate, and certain administrative organs knowingly collude with regional authorities under their jurisdiction to pass up the false figures.

Table 2.2 shows that China has a total of less than 240 million acres of arable land. However, an important study by He Binli demonstrated that much of the data on which this conclusion was based was unreliable. According to some samples, it is common for a region to have 20% more arable land than reported by local authorities. Separate analyses based on satellite photos reveal that China might actually have between 363 million and 380 million acres of arable land. Recent surveys, based on more reliable methods, have also arrived at an estimate of between 330 million and 345 million acres.

Even after adjusting for these differences, China still ranks eighth from last among the 76 nations that have a total land area of more than 100,000 square kilometers. Assuming that China may have a third or even half as much more arable land than the official figures show, the nation would still have only between one-eighth and one-tenth of the world's total arable land.[17] This would seem to be a matter for rejoicing, but if this estimate is correct, it also means that agricultural productivity is much lower than the reported figures. And although this extra land may provide some breathing space in the face of the still enormous pressure of land erosion, it offers little consolation.

China also has about 33 million acres of undeveloped land, some of which might be converted into farmland. But even if half of this could be brought under cultivation, it would still only be an increase of less than 0.02 acres per capita. In addition, further damage to the environment might be caused by conversion efforts.

All in all, serious worries remain. We must also consider that the existing arable land is very unevenly distributed, and of inferior quality; that three quarters of the land is more than 500 meters above sea level; that multiple cropping has vastly reduced the productivity of the land; and that over 16.5 million acres of farmland have become salinated.

The serious deterioration of soil in China also demonstrates that a vast majority of government and agricultural officials have not yet realized that land is a precious and scarce resource. It can take many years to restore the ecological balance of a large geographical area, 60 to 70 years for a full layer of vegetation to grow, and 50 to 60 years to restore the productivity of land through forestation.

■ Water, Water, Give Me Water!

Water resources have always been extremely precious in China and the water crisis may be even worse than the shortage of grain.

China's water shortage mirrors a worldwide problem. According to United Nations statistics, the earth has a total of 1.36 billion cubic kilometers of water, of which 97.5% is ocean or other salt water, and only 2.5% is fresh water. Furthermore, 70% of the fresh water is concentrated in glaciers around the two poles, and only about 0.34% of it serves directly to sustain human communities. The remainder is suspended in the atmosphere as vapor.

According to the same report, the use of water for agricultural purposes worldwide increased by a factor of eight during the first three quarters of this century, and for industrial purposes, it increased by a factor of about 21.[18] At the present time, 63 different countries or regions face a water shortage.

China has traditionally been a water-poor country, with per capita fresh water stocks of 2,700 cubic meters, or a quarter of the world average. A glance at figure 2.2 makes it abundantly clear that at least half the country will be severely affected by a severe water crisis. As early as 14 November 1980, a Xinhua News Agency report acknowledged that the area of lakes throughout the country had been reduced by over 3.3 million acres, or over 35 billion cubic meters of water.

That is but a quarter of the world per capita amount and puts China 84th among the nations in the world. The distribution is also very uneven. In cubic feet per acre, the Yangtze and Pearl River basins boast 2.5 and 3.5 times the national average, respectively, while the Yellow, Huai, Hai, and Liao river basins have only 17%, 15%, 10%, and 13% of the national average, respectively. On a cubic feet/per capita basis, the Yangtze and Zhu river basins have roughly the equivalent and 2.7 times the national level, respectively, while the other four river basins come to only 26%, 15%, 11.5%, and 21%.

These four river basins account for 63.7% of the nation's arable land and 46% of the population, but their annual water flow is only 17% of the national total. The southeast, southwest and Huanan regions have only 36.3% of the arable land, and 54% of the population, but the annual water flow is 83% of the national total. In the arid northern regions weather cycles and the seasonal needs of the crops coincide poorly, with drought often striking when the crops are most in need of water, and heavy rains falling when they most need sun.

Some estimates put the total volume of water used in China at 477 billion cubic meters a year.[19] Of this, 88%, or 419 billion cubic meters is used for agriculture. At the same time, northern China has a total of 2.2 million machine-drilled wells, supplying 28 million acres of farmland, or one-third of all irrigation in the north. This demonstrates that agricultural irrigation consumes not only a lot of water, but also a great deal of energy to pump the water out of the ground and to the fields. The recycling of agricultural water has been almost completely ignored, while only 20% or 30% of water used in industry is recycled, resulting in an estimated waste of 31.2 billion cubic meters of unrecycled water.

Annual per capita water use in China is currently 490 cubic meters; only one-fifth of the U.S. level and half that of the USSR. Some authorities estimate that by the year 2000, total demand for water in China will reach 700 billion cubic meters, with 80% of this used for agriculture. However, the supply can only provide 600–630 billion cubic meters. The areas that will suffer the severest shortage will be the North China Plain and parts of the Northeast Plain.[20] It is not certain whether our economic planners have already taken this projection into consideration.

Large new industrial projects, like the northwest chemical complex, the energy complex in Shanxi Province, and the comprehensive development planned for the Central Plains, will put increasingly high demands on the Yellow River. Though supplied primarily by atmospheric circulation, the river flows through the driest parts of North China. Statistics from years of observation at the Huayuankou station show an annual water flow of only 48 billion cubic meters, or one-sixth that of the Pearl River. Quite a few tributaries of the Yangtze carry more water than this.

Over a long period, 96% of the water from the Yellow River was used for agricultural irrigation, and only 4% by rural inhabitants or for industry. Surveys indicate that about half the villages in China with a chronic grain shortage are located in the Yellow River basin, where both per acre yields and per capita consumption of grain are the lowest of the seven major river basins in China.

Even according to the most optimistic scenarios for improving storage and increasing capacity by technological means, the maximum amount of extra water that could be drawn from the Yellow River is 10 billion cubic meters. This is still far short of projected demand for the surrounding provinces. There is also the danger that an excess draw of water might reduce the capacity to discharge silt, further raising the river bottom and increasing the risk of floods— a serious consideration on a river which has overflowed its banks once every three years for the last 2,000 years.

The overall level of development around the seven major rivers in China is low. The Huai, the Hai and the Liao rivers have been best utilized. These three river basins, which cover about 1/12 of the nation's total area, produce a quarter of the gross national product.

There has been a lot of talk about the extra wealth that could be created if all the seven major river basins (4.37 million square kilometers) in China could be developed to the level of Hai or Liao River. But little or no attention is paid to the fact that the price of development will be the depletion of water resources. The Yellow, Huai, Hai and Liao river basins have a total population of 330 million, 106 million acres of farmland, the vast majority of the nation's energy and industrial installations, and 40% of the gross national product. However, if a drought of medium severity (25% water reduction) were to hit the region, projections show that the whole area would be short 30 billion cubic feet of water.

▌ Water Shortages Affect Both Cities and Countryside

Bositeng Lake in the center of Xinjiang Province, was once, like Lake Luobupo, one of the largest fresh water lakes in Northwest China, and has met a similar fate. By 1980, gradual depletion had caused the lake's water to become slightly salty. Dongting Lake, which used to stretch over 400 square kilometers, has had 60% of its total area filled over the last 30 years, and is now in danger of complete extinction. Boyang Lake is still the largest fresh water lake in China, but has shrunk to half its original size over the last 20 years, and currently receives more than 21 million tons of silt every year from the Gan River, causing the lake bottom to rise about 20–30 millimeters a year.

Baiyang Lake on the North China Plain was once known as the "Jewel of the North," but in the spring and summer of 1984, it dried up completely for the second time.[21] The once sparkling lake is now a wasteland of yellow mud and grass. In 1949, Hunan Province had 1,066 lakes and was known as the "Province of a Thousand Lakes": by 1981, only 309 remained, and the total area of surface water had shrunk by three quarters.

The onslaught of soil erosion and diminishing land productivity have undermined the effectiveness of irrigation projects and other investments in agricultural infrastructure. Between 1982 and 1986, the area with effective irrigation was further reduced by 8.4 million acres, causing an estimated loss of 10 billion kilograms in grain output for 1985 alone.[22]

On 1 April 1986, an article in the *People's Daily* on the ecological crisis in Hebei province, disclosed that Beijing and Tianjin would face a serious water supply crisis in the near future. At that time, a quarter of the farmland in Hebei was experiencing drought, a sixth of it was deteriorating into semi-desert, and a tenth of all farmland in the area already had a saline level of over 0.2%. Soil erosion affected 50% of the land, causing a loss of 1.55 million tons of fertilizers annually, or 42% of the province's annual fertilizer production; the clogging of reservoirs by silt had caused the equivalent loss of one medium-sized reservoir every year; and silt in the rivers had rendered a third of the flood prevention structures ineffective.

Currently, the annual demand for water in the whole province is 27.3 billion cubic meters, but the annual supply has been less than 20 billion cubic meters. Excessive draw on underground water has exacerbated the drying up of the rivers and lakes. Since 1983 alone, 30 lakes in Hebei have dried up completely, and there has also been a significant drop in the volume of water flowing from Hebei into the ocean each year.

There was a proposal to draw Yellow River water into Beijing to counter the approaching crisis, but it would have required an investment of at least 1.1 billion yuan. In the Huai and Luan River basin areas, the per capita volume of available water was just 430 cubic meters; a twentieth of the world average, and even lower than Saudi Arabia. On a cubic meter per acre basis, the volume of water resources around the Huai, Hai, and Luan River basins is only 40% of the national level. Yet a whole set of water-guzzling economic ventures have been set up there, including the inappropriate attempt to develop large paddy fields in the region.[23]

The plundering of underground water supplies has resulted in the depletion of over 90% of these resources in the Beijing-Tianjin-Tangshan region. It is estimated that more than a third of the original water reserves beneath the Liao River Plain, over half those beneath the Yellow River Plain, and more than 90% of reserves under the Hai River Plain have been extracted. This has had serious consequences. The level of the land has sunk, the quality of the water has deteriorated, its salt content has increased, and hundreds of thousands of wells have dried up. When a serious drought strikes, over 100 million people will be affected.

Underground water reserves in other areas are also being depleted. There have been many complaints about the water shortage in Shandong Province, where there is a shortfall of 18 billion cubic meters per year for agriculture. However, due to the indiscriminate use of underground water, an area of about 7,000 square kilometers shows evidence of being overdrawn. In the coastal region particularly, sea water has permeated underground water reserves, raising the salt content by 3–15% and making the water completely undrinkable. Local agriculture has also been severely affected.[24]

Discovery of water shortages can present obstacles to optimistic development projections. For example, when Qinghai Province was preparing to step up its development effort, some advocates claimed that underground water reserves beneath the Chaidamu Basin amounted to 340 billion cubic feet, or the equivalent of three Qinghai Lakes. A more professional report reduced that projection to 4.44 billion cubic meters, and cautioned that only $1/77$ of that could be used in ordinary circumstances.[25]

Many cities and townships in China are pursuing development on a massive scale. By the end of the 1970s, total water use in China had reached 470 billion cubic meters, 5.7 times the 1949 level. Over the same period daily water use in urban areas increased 9 times; and industrial use 23 times. The strange thing is that urban water use has never been earmarked as a separate concern for long term planning and coordination.

Guo Tao, a member of the Water Power Research Institute attached to the National Council, has studied water resources in areas around dozens of cities and towns in the country.[26] His research reveals increasing shortages due to population growth and the extraction of underground water at a rate exceeding that of natural refill. Some areas have had to spend large sums to "borrow" water from other regions. He found a lack of overall coordination and frequent competition between different industries and sectors for precious water supplies.

Guo's study also found that silt clogging lakes and rivers, damage to embankments, and the lack of effective repairs are intensifying the risk of flooding nearby cities, and cities with good water transportation networks have been forced to abandon them because of increased silting. The sewage system has been thrown into chaos, in some cases causing dangerous spills into lakes and rivers, and polluting the water supply. There is also a lack of detailed legislation to define water use rights, and the decentralization of economic decision-making in this area has resulted in a state of near anarchy.

■ Lack of Central Control

In large urban areas, numerous authorities have jurisdiction over different aspects of water use, like supply, sewage, flood control, water transport, suburban irrigation, environmental control, and water quality control. These functions are in the hands of entirely different officials, who may be in disagreement or even at loggerheads with each other.

With each bureaucratic institution maintaining independent authority over water use in its area, it is hardly surprising that chaos results. The logical arrangement would be for the natural supply of water to dictate constraints for water use by agriculture, industry, and the population. But in fact, because lack of coordination leaves each sector to find its own means of supply, there is no incentive to manage water in an orderly, efficient, and economical fashion.

There should be many ways to recycle used water, but the recycling rate for agricultural irrigation systems in China is only 0.4%–0.5%, and for industrial water it is 2%. On one hand there are severe shortages, and on the other, enormous waste.

The cities are particularly hard hit. Historically, there were reputed to be eight rivers around the city of Xian. Today the subterranean water line is falling and wells have been drying up. Tianjin, once known as "the meeting point of all the rivers," is now the center of droughts. In 1979, 154 Chinese cities were suffering water shortages; by 1984, 188 were affected, and 88% of the 289 major cities have

FIGURE 2.2 DISTRIBUTION OF CHINESE WATER RESOURCES

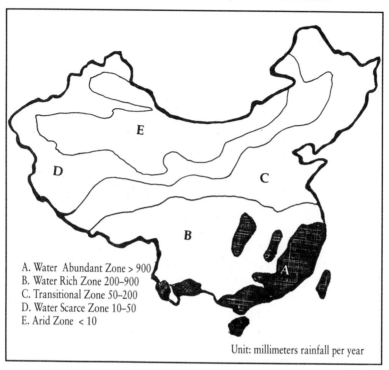

A. Water Abundant Zone > 900
B. Water Rich Zone 200–900
C. Transitional Zone 50–200
D. Water Scarce Zone 10–50
E. Arid Zone < 10

Unit: millimeters rainfall per year

periodic problems with water supplies, while 40 of them have reached a crisis point, with a total daily shortfall of 12 million tons. Since the summer of 1986, some industrial plants in the north have had to ration the supply. Some foreign experts in Beijing have pointed out that if very strict legislation is not introduced within five years, China's modernization plans will be severely impeded by water shortages.

In the greater Tianjin area, the ground has been sinking at the rate of eight meters per year, the most severely affected spot being the Northern Railway Station, which sank two meters between 1959 and 1982. The situation is not much better in the cities of Cangzhou and Handan. In various regions north of the Yellow River, 30 spots have been located where subterranean water has been descending in a pocket-shaped zone. In Cangzhou, as of October 1979, the deepest point was 68 meters underground, and the level had been falling at the rate of six meters per year.

Beijing has probably seen the greatest increase in water consumption among cities. The total extraction of underground water increased 31 times between 1949 and the mid–1960s. It doubled again in the 1970s, and again in the 1980s. By 1979, the total consumption had reached 4.6 billion cubic meters, stretching the upper limit of the pool of supply. At some times, "running water" ran only at night, and not even then for the upper stories of some buildings. Beijing's per capita water supply is 470 cubic meters, less than one-tenth that of Tokyo. [27]

The quality of the water is deteriorating rapidly. With ground subsiding due to excessive extraction, sea water is permeating the underground reserves, and increased salination could permanently prevent fresher water from resurfacing. Some researchers are already seriously contemplating whether the capital should be relocated away from Beijing.

Grandiose plans such as transferring water from the south to the north offer some hope, but they would be extremely expensive. According to projections, an astronomical investment of 24 billion yuan (the cost of the Baoshan Steel Works) could draw 875 billion cubic feet of water from the Yangtze into the Hai River. Unfortunately the flow of the Yangtze itself has been steadily declining over the last 20 years (100 billion cubic meters), and right now 58 gigantic sand dunes are already exposed above the water level from Wuhu on.

Even more ominous is the fact that the sea water has already penetrated to the borders of Changshou, and residents between Changshou and Shanghai must bear with drinking slightly salty water for three or four months in the year. The Baoshan Steel Works has to rely on fresh water from Dianshan Lake, 70 kilometers away, to operate its heavy machinery. In addition, if water were ever to be transferred from the Yangtze it would obviously have severe effects on weather conditions in the Yangtze and Yellow River basin regions, and on the local fishing industry.

3

THE ECONOMIC EARTHQUAKE

▌ The Economics of the "Wartime Guarantee System"

The economic difficulties faced by a number of socialist countries are an indisputable fact. In recent years the most influential critique of their economies has been the analysis presented by the Hungarian economist Janos Kornai in his 1980 book *Economics of Shortage*.[1] These economic difficulties are a major factor in environmental problems because they create the inefficiency, waste, lack of innovation, and ineffective use of capital which compound environmental damage and obstruct solutions to it.

China's own mistakes in economic theory are primarily the result of regarding the economy as a wartime system. From the 1950s to the 1970s, our basic development strategy was to strengthen centralized management, strive for self-sufficiency, and prepare for a possible invasion. The key concepts underlying economic policy were guaranteed supply, production, allocation, adjustment, subsidies, and so on. These terms all have a wartime flavor, and China's brand of economics could be called "wartime guarantee economics" *(zhanshi baozhang jingjixue)*, or "wartime supply economics" *(zhanshi gongji jingjixue)*.

The concept of "guarantees" in economics was coined by Mao Zedong. As early as August 1933, in an article entitled "Attention Must Be Paid to Economic Work," Mao asserted that "material conditions must be improved in order to guarantee supplies for the Red Army." In 1942 [during the long war against Japan] he raised the slogan "Develop the economy and guarantee supplies" which became the overall strategy for the nation's fiscal and economic work for more than 10 years to follow. One can still see this slogan on the walls of big cities like Zhengzhou today.

Mao's concept of "guarantees," like the theory of "distribution" Lenin proposed after the October Revolution, was the product of military pressure, a weak infrastructure, and poverty. What differs between them is that Lenin later realized the policy had to be changed, while we Chinese continued to cling to Mao Zedong's directive until the reforms of the past decade.

Even today there are people in the Ministry of Commerce who consider "guaranteed supply" the basic starting point for fiscal and economic work. Even though it implies a system of controlled supply and allocation, they still believe that the policy of "guaranteeing the basic essentials of life must not be infringed in any way," and that this principle is a clear indication of the superiority of China's socialist system. It is hard to see how these ideas can be reconciled with the new policies of developing a commodity economy, emphasizing the law of value, and promoting competition.

Essentially, the "wartime guarantee economy" is still a barter economy. This is reflected in all the campaigns to "Provide enough food and clothes for ourselves," "Be self-reliant," and "Prepare against war and natural disasters." Even the campaigns to "Take grain as the key link" and "Make steel the leading industry" were the inevitable product of this kind of economy.

The result was often the irrational use of resources. In order to realize regional self-sufficiency in coal, between 1966 and 1977, 4.1 billion yuan was invested in the coal industry in nine provinces and cities south of the Yangtze River, a region which has only 2% of the nation's coal reserves. By 1978, annual output was still only 87 million tons. Meanwhile, total investment in the coal industry in Shanxi, which has one-third of the national coal reserves, was only 3.1 billion yuan for the whole 30-year period prior to 1981, yet in 1978 annual output exceeded 100 million tons, and investment per ton of coal produced was one-half to one-eighth that in the former region.[2]

The self-sufficiency drive meant inefficient small-scale production in many areas. In 1978, for example, the whole country produced only 150,000 automobiles, and these were scattered across 26 provinces, cities, and regions. At least 110 factories had an annual production capacity of under 1,000 cars, 17 factories produced fewer than 100 vehicles, and some made just a handful of cars at a cost of 20–30 thousand yuan each, double or triple the cost of a larger operation like the Number One Automobile Factory. By contrast, the average output of foreign truck factories is anywhere from 10–50 thousand cars per batch.

Agriculture was similarly affected. In the Hunan-Hubei region it takes an acre of sugar cane to produce one ton of sugar (whereas it requires only 0.25 acre in Guangdong), and in Henan province it takes more than 1.6 acres of sugar beets (the yield per unit is only one-seventh that of Heilongjiang), yet both the low-yield areas operate sugar factories to supply their own needs. It seems as if every region must make a prison within its borders and be totally self-reliant before there can be any "guarantee" worth talking about.

Another practice that grew inevitably out of "guarantee economics" was the policy of subsidy economics implemented in many economically backward regions, particularly in national minority areas. In Inner Mongolia, for example, the ratio between the region's fiscal revenue and financial subsidies from the central government in 1984 was 1 to 2.45.[3] Most construction projects in the region relied on state investment and subsidies, and economic construction was sustained mainly by state subsidies.

The original intent behind such policies was to promote the economic development of backward regions and quickly eliminate the inequalities that existed between the different nationalities. Unfortunately, as time passed, people became inured to the subsidies, and with no active measures being taken to offset this trend, the state seems destined to bear this burden for a long time to come. Meanwhile, the regions concerned remain dependent on state assistance.

As well as being contrary to the avowed spirit of self-reliance, this policy has also suppressed the local drive for development and delayed self-initiated growth. These areas have been kept alive on transfusions from the center for so long that they have lost the capacity to sustain themselves, and this has served only to increase the gap between them and the advanced regions. These areas must change from subsidy economics to a self-supporting economy before any real development occurs.

A wartime mentality has also colored the style and terminology of economic policy. Hence the talk of the industrial front, the agricultural front, the university front, and the United Front, and slogans like "Closely follow the Party Central Committee!", "We must carve out a bloody trail for ourselves!", and "Charge across! Hack a way through!" These are the slogans and methods used in times of war, in a period of destruction. That is why ex-soldiers who had their "university education" in the army were more successful under this system than graduates from Beijing University. The application of the same crude tactics to the long-term and complex task of economic reconstruction was the root of the chaos, backwardness, and decline that ensued.

Kornai has systematically analyzed some shortage phenomena that are representative of the problems inherent in socialist economies, and has pointed out that "shortages are not the result of the backwardness of the economy, but are caused by certain systemic factors." The system he is talking about, seen from the point of view of the wartime guarantee economy, is the "guaranteed distribution system" or the "guaranteed supply system."

Kornai distinguishes between two kinds of modern economic systems: the demand-constrained type (the free-competition capitalist commodity economy), and the resource-constrained type (the traditional socialist economy). The latter he calls the "shortage economy" or the "suction economy."

▌ Waiting for Political Reform

Kornai's economics of shortage or "suction" economics is essentially the same as our wartime guarantee economics or "common pot" (daguofan) economics. One could almost say that the Hungarian's model has "Chinese characteristics." The shortages that Kornai speaks of are equivalent to the "grabbing for supplies" that inevitably takes place under the "common pot" system.

It is interesting to consider whether it is possible for a resource-constrained economy to eliminate the phenomenon of shortages by means of normal reforms. In fact, the best way to answer the question is to look at the nature of the economic reforms that are currently in progress. According to a report in the World Economic Herald on 18 June 1984, the main contents of the current reforms to the economic system fall into the following seven categories:

1. Reform of the unitary system of "ownership by the whole people," [state ownership] and the establishment of an ownership structure led by the state sector, but with a reasonable disposition of various other economic forms and management methods.

2. Reform of the planning and management system in which too many quotas are set by directive, planning is too unified, and the market is excluded. Introduction of a system where economic planning plays the leading role, supplemented by market adjustment, and where important projects are closely controlled and small projects given a looser rein.

3. Reform of the policy-making system in which there is no clear demarcation of responsiblity and power between the central and local governments; in which the division of labor between the Party, the government, and enterprises is irrational; and in which too much

power is concentrated in administrative departments. Introduction of a multi-level policy-making system in which important powers are concentrated and lesser powers dispersed, and in which there is a reasonable division of work between the Party, government, and enterprises.

4. Reforming the way in which the economy is divided into horizontal and vertical segments *(tiaokuai)* and urban and rural areas, in which the various departments, regions and sectors are cut off from each other, and economic management is carried out in accordance with administrative districts. Introduction of a management system based on economic sectors in which cities play a major role, and horizontal and vertical segments are combined.

5. Changing the present system of using administrative methods to control the economy. Introduction of a management system that unites responsibility, power, and profit, and combines economic and administrative methods.

6. Increasing the authority of enterprises to make their own decisions, and setting up a distribution system in which responsibilities, authority, and profit are clearly defined and in which the economic powers and interests of the center and the regions, the state and enterprises, collectivities, and individuals complement each other.

7. Reforming the system of unified control of revenues and expenditures, prices, deposits and loans, the allocation of labor, the rigid eight-level wage system, and so on.

It is clear that, in terms of its theoretical framework, the reform of the economic system currently in progress has four main elements: a dominant state-run sector; management by planning; the concentration of important powers; and the unification of vertical and horizontal administrative districts. If these four are maintained, the original socialist planned economy will be retained. The other reforms mostly relate to minor adjustments aimed at dealing with certain excesses that need to be modified.

According to Kornai's theory, if the four principles above are upheld, it should still prove impossible to avoid shortages because the basic structure will not have changed. But if these changes do not eliminate shortages, then the phenomenon cannot be the inevitable product of the structural factors Kornai described. The economic reforms currently taking place in China thus provide a perfect opportunity to test Kornai's theory.

Ever since the "Decision of the Central Committee of the Chinese Communist Party Concerning the Reform of the Economic System" was promulgated in autumn 1984, the nation's economists have been troubled by a series of theoretical problems.

A whole string of questions and contradictions has arisen. For example, has China ever really had a system of "ownership by the whole people," or was it essentially either ownership based on centralized power, or ownership by no one at all? Again, how can a planned economy and a commodity economy be combined? What is the essential characteristic of socialism: a planned economy, a commodity economy, common ownership, or associated labor? Is a planned commodity economy the same thing as a "planned market economy"?

On the subject of labor, why is it that people only talk about a "labor market" and not a market for labor power? It seems unlikely that one can be betrayed and not the other. They say that "our labor power is not a commodity," but what about workers who are sent to work overseas, and those who work for private employers and foreign and joint venture enterprises? And if there is a labor market under socialism, what happens to the old status of the laboring people as the "masters of society"?

At the moment, they say that "our nation's land and resources are not commodities," but if this is true, then how can we use land and resources as capital to invest in joint equity ventures? Is it really possible to separate the ownership of enterprises from management? And if they are separated, to whom should the new increase in the capital goods of state-owned enterprises belong? In a situation where new increases in capital goods account for an ever higher proportion of total fixed assets, will this change the nature of the system of ownership? After enterprises become independent economic entities, will the state lose control of the macroeconomy?

The role of the state in the economy raises a host of other questions. Should the state control production capacity or the scale of capital construction? Can the state control the scale of investment throughout society? Is it possible to use high consumption and low savings to stimulate the economy and control the inflation of demand at the same time? In setting the goal for price reforms, how do we choose between planned prices, floating prices and free prices? Is the foundation of prices the equilibrium price, the production price, or the market price?

Should wages and bonuses be routinely allocated, paid according to work performance, or neither, and should the relationship between wages and prices be direct (index linked wages) or indirect (fixed periodic adjustments)? Is it possible for government and enterprises to separate their functions before there is a smoothly functioning commodity market? Will developing a commodity economy not result in people just seeking financial gain and so be contradictory to the aims of socialism? What is the difference between a "planned commodity economy" and a capitalist market economy where some planned adjustment of the market is carried out by the state?

What is the relationship between competition and communist morality? What happens when enterprises go bankrupt and people are unemployed? Is the fact that some people are getting rich first purely the result of implementing compensation according to work? Is the widening of income differentials permitted so that inequalities can be eliminated in the end? Will the development of the private sector not result in the emergence of a privatized society?

At the moment, many people are confused about the implications of the growth of the private sector *(geti jingji)*. From 1978 to 1984, the number of people working in the private sector multiplied by 87 times, but only seven times as much tax was collected. At least 50% to 80% of the tax is being lost through tax evasion. The surprising results of a survey carried out by Zhu Qingfang in 1986 showed that private employers, (some of whom already employ a thousand people) exploit their workers and treat them cruelly, and that the incomes of workers and employers differ by a ratio of between 1 to 5 and 1 to 211.

The increase in hired labor has also forced some people to leave their jobs or quit school. One enterprise in Wenzhou hired more than 700 child workers between the ages of 10 and 16, most of whom were girls. In addition, bribery, string-pulling, and speculation are standard practice among private employers, with fortunes being made by such illicit means.[4] Some delegates at the 1988 National People's Congress were of the opinion that there must be at least 10 individuals in the country worth over 10 million yuan.

The evils of our economic system are concentrated in five areas:

1. Highly centralized control over supply, production and sales, and over personnel, capital, and materials has deprived enterprises of independence and decision-making power, and turned them into appendages of the administrative structure without any initiative of their own.

2. Enterprises do not have independent economic interests, so they lack incentive.

3. Using administrative measures to manage economic activities has led to the growth of a bloated state bureaucracy.

4. Leaders of enterprises are only responsible to the next level of the state bureaucracy and not to the staff and workers of the enterprise.

5. The laboring masses are prevented from combining directly with the means of production.

In addition to these problems, there is a shortage of competent managers, and the majority of existing managers and policy makers are habituated to military methods of organization and command. We also lack talented theoreticians: many of China's economists have burrowed their way into *Das Kapital* never to emerge again. They use rigid and simplistic methods of analysis, and terms like "equilibrium price," "decreasing marginal return," "comparative cost," and "opportunity cost" have very low status in their economic vocabulary.

No matter how the theorists rack their brains, it will be impossible to find a comprehensive and consistent solution to all the problems we face in reforming the economic system, especially if these reforms continue to leave the political system completely untouched. It was only in the early 1980s when officials mentioned formally for the first time that China's current economic reforms would involve reform of the political system.

At present, the aspects of the political system most frequently criticized are the dual-leadership system (by Party and government), the lifelong tenure and selection systems for cadres, the high concentration of power, the lack of a comprehensive legal system, insularity, arbitrary policy-making, the suppression and waste of talented people, the unfair and irrational distribution system, and the stifling of innovation and creativity. In these areas we will have to wait for further stages of reform, especially when it comes to steps towards any real change with regard to political democracy and freedom.

The decentralization of power has been a constant feature of political reform throughout the world. The United States has a land area of 9.36 million square kilometers, slightly less than China's 9.6 million square kilometers, and its population is less than 25% of China's, but it is divided into 50 states. France (550,000 square kilometers, even smaller than Sichuan province, with a population of 56 million, less than that Hebei province), carried out decentralization in 1983, making the nation's 22 administrative regions independent units for development, each of which could formulate and implement its own development policy.

In a system accustomed to concentrated power, decentralization is one of the big stumbling blocks of reform, especially where leaders think that power is everything. Many people have observed that China's reforms tend to involve a bout of impulsive theorizing followed by ad hoc implementation, and that there is never a scientific and feasible overall plan. This is equally true of the current round of reforms. However, until reform of the political system achieves concrete results, and particularly in political democratization, liberalization, and legalization, and systems for enforcing them, it will be impossible to devise an overall plan for China's current reforms.

■ The Persistent Imbalance in the Economy

Anyone who does research on China will soon discover that theory and practice, what people say and what they do, can be two entirely different matters in China. Nor is this simply an individual trait: sometimes the state behaves the same way. The problem also pervades the economic sphere, where there is a big discrepancy between propaganda and fact.

Over the last 30 years, China has already experienced several cycles of rash surges of economic development followed by adjustment. For many years, we have been harping on about the need to cut back capital construction projects, but in many places the result is like kneading bread: the more you squash it down, the more it expands. The state calls for concentrating capital to guarantee infrastructures like energy, transportation and other key construction projects, but in fact people everywhere are producing refrigerators, television sets, radios, and washing machines, and small-scale tobacco factories, fertilizer plants, and breweries are springing up all over the place.

Meanwhile construction in energy and transportation is making even less progress than it was before the slogan came out. Regions compete for power supplies and withhold raw materials; they employ policies that protect backward industries and prevent competition. Small projects squeeze out large ones and outdated industries hinder the development of more advanced ones. Low quality products pile up in storage, while demand for brand-name goods exceeds supply. The state promotes policies that emphasize capital construction rather than production, and high accumulation at the cost of efficiency. It is prepared to waste people's energy to fulfill meaningless quotas and pays no attention to the actual results.

This has led to notorious and chronic situations like that reported for 1981 by the State Statistical Bureau, when 70 product lines worth a total of 14.5 billion yuan were backlogged in storage. Although there were excess inventories of one billion meters of terylene cloth, for example, the following year various regions were still competing to exceed production quotas. They produced just for the sake of producing, regardless of demand for the product: output was the only consideration.

In publications and at exhibitions the propaganda boasts of

breakthroughs, development, progress and prosperity, but the actual figures reveal losses. Losses in grain production, in forestry, in foreign trade, in industry. Losses which number in hundreds of millions.

According to a report in *Jingji cankao* (Economic Reference), at the end of August 1985, 5,176 large-scale enterprises throughout the country were showing a loss, 518 more than at the end of 1984. Total losses were 1.58 billion yuan, and 30% to 40% of this was considered to be due to bad management. Two-thirds of the loss-making enterprises were small-scale regional or county-level ones. When Wuxi City carried out a reorganization of its 86 television assembly plants, more than 70 were found substandard and closed down. The losses for state-owned industrial enterprises continued to mount in the 1980s, causing grave concern among officials. In 1990, according to government statistics, profits dropped by 58% from the previous year. According to the State Statistical Bureau, over 35% of these firms were losing money in 1991, while they had an inventory of over 133 billion worth of unsold products. Economists are quite understandably calling for massive reforms in this sector of the economy.

From January to August of 1986, accumulated losses in industry were 68.8% higher than the same period the previous year, and had already passed the acceptable level of losses planned by the state for the whole year. By October, 7,000 basic level supply and marketing cooperatives throughout the country were sustaining losses, and more than one-fifth of all such cooperatives incurred losses totalling 0.458 billion yuan.

In 1987, *Caijing yanjiu ziliao* (Finance and Economic Research Materials) reported that the budgeted proportion of capital used by state-run industries and enterprises to produce finished products in 1986 increased 6.1 billion yuan over the previous year (an increase of 21.8%), but at the end of the year 5.8 billion yuan of faulty products were piled up in stock. This accounted for 11% of all inventories and it cost 0.6 billion yuan just to dispose of them.

In the same year, the gross output value of state industries grew by 6.2%, but costs for comparable products increased by 6.6%. The most significant causes of this were bad management, inefficiency, and waste. For example, the utilization rate for steel was only just over 60% and some enterprises had a defective product rate of up to 80–90%. But even though production costs were much higher than the sale price, they kept on producing. In 1987, 70 billion, or 30% of the state fiscal revenue of 220 billion yuan went to subsidize losses. In 1988, total losses of state-run enterprises increased by 27% over the previous year. Losses have averaged 40 billion annually in recent years, even with heavy state subsidies (52 billion budgeted for 1989 alone).

In 1987 Lu Jian made a detailed statistical analysis of the cyclical fluctuations in China's economy and concluded that from 1953 to 1985, this economy has undergone seven cycles: 1953–1956, 1956–1958, 1958–1965, 1965–1969, 1969–1975, 1975–1978, 1978–1985. The average length of the swings is between four and six years (between 1795 and 1973, the United States experienced seventeen cyclical economic fluctuations, with an average duration of 8.35 years). The average amplitude of the Chinese cycle was 23.1% and the highest (the third), at 66.2%, approached that of the Great Depression in the United States in the 1930s (70%). There were also four periods of negative growth, and two of stagnation.

On average, the economy grew at a rate of 3.9% a year, but for every 1% increase in investment, it only grew by 0.3%. The fusion of politics and economics, and high concentration of power exacerbated the starvation of the planned economy, and continuous increases in investment to ensure that quotas could be met induced the cyclical fluctuations associated with rapid growth. It is not surprising that an outside observer like Thomas Finger, Head of the China Section of the Intelligence and Research Department of U.S. State Department said in 1986 that he would be amazed if any of China's policies could be sustained for more than five years.

There are of course theories that hold that the cycle of growth and contraction in the national economy is a normal occurrence. However, the phenomena and conditions it refers to do not apply in China's case. It is more important to note that if this persistent imbalance continues, there may be a sudden economic collapse. In the early 1960s, immediately before it went into recession, the overall economy was still growing. Within the space of a year, the growth rate for heavy industry plummeted by 40%, and for light industry by 30%, with almost half of the production capacity suddenly lost.

On that occasion, the government took the drastic measure of sending people back to the countryside, thereby solving the problem of feeding 20 million urban dwellers. Such a solution cannot be applied today, so careful research into potential crises is more important than ever.

Apart from the persistent imbalance in the economy, we must also pay attention to crises that may emerge out of the current economic reforms. Specifically, there are 10 major questions:

1. Uncontrolled inflation of aggregate demand may result in the reforms, which rest on the expansion of the market forces, being unable to proceed, or may induce fierce inflation, which would undermine the reforms.

2. Excessively rapid economic development may force the state to step up planning of production and distribution in order to ensure the completion of key projects, unintentionally working against the thrust of the reforms.

3. Shortages of some goods and commodities may keep enterprises in the trap of pursuing only quantity of output, instead of quality and efficiency.

4. Capital may be lacking for the supplementary projects needed to support the reforms.

5. It is important to grasp this opportunity and make sure that reform is implemented quickly and thoroughly, so that we do not end up pursuing contradictory goals. At the same time, however, certain adjustments have to be made before we can adapt to thorough reform. This presents the question of whether adjustments and reforms should take place concurrently or separately. The wrong choice could cost us dearly.

6. Planning, regulation, supervision, and organization form a chain within the economic system, but the current policies of separating enterprises from government, simplifying government, and decentralizing power are intended to be done simultaneously. But where cadres are incapable of adapting to the new model, it may result in loss of control over the macroeconomy and a vacuum of management at the microeconomic level. If there are no suitable policies and regulations to deal with this, the reforms could get snarled up at the lower levels.

7. Some outfits may change their form by merging, downgrading, or devolving power, but remain essentially the same as before. It is possible that this "label changing" game, where "committees" turn into "companies", will continue during the reform period. If the same old team is still in charge, reform will be merely superficial.

8. Reform of the price system and the encouragement of competition will produce a complex response among certain political elements and institutions. Enterprises that cannot withstand the pressure will go out of business, and this will revive the controversial problem of how to integrate reform with our political system. We will face thorny questions concerning the real nature of the labor market, such as how to deal with enterprise debts and capital, structural unemployment, professional employment agencies, and temporary and seasonal workers.

9. The relationship between policy and public opinion is also problematic. In the 40 years since the founding of the PRC, basic policy has undergone six or seven major changes of direction and, as Finger remarked, no policy has been pursued consistently for more than five

years. Very few countries have seen so many dramatic policy changes over such a short period.

Everyone in China now understands the need for stable policies, but although this is a relief in itself, it is unfortunately not reflected in practice. Reform naturally has its ups and downs, and these small but unavoidable uncertainties are disturbing, especially when many people were nervous to begin with. Changes in popular feeling affect policy, and the lack of stable policies makes the public more uneasy. As a result, enterprises, collectives, and individuals all take preventive measures based on their assessment of whether policy is likely to change. This undermines the effectiveness of policy and reverberates throughout the economy.

10. The most vexing problems in our current economic reforms are that the allocation of work is not fair, there is no equality of opportunity, and income differentials are unreasonable.

Consider some examples of the last point. In Guangzhou, a bus driver earns only 100–200 yuan a month, but it is not unusual for a private taxi driver to make over 1,000 yuan. In some areas, a private taxi driver can earn more than 8,000 yuan a month, while a school teacher's monthly salary is only 24 yuan. It is right to encourage the development of the private sector, but that does not mean it is healthy for it to thrive at the expense of collective and state-run sectors. We want to increase income differentials but at the same time we restrict the mobility of labor, which is tantamount to deciding arbitrarily who is allowed to prosper and who is denied the chance.

People tend to think this situation is more serious in the south than in the north, but the amazing situation I encountered in Shanxi in 1985 illustrates the severity of the differentials. Wutai Mountain and Heng Mountain are only 60 kilometers apart, at opposite ends of a valley. In Wutai, many peasant households make more than 100 yuan a day. While there, I interviewed the Liangs, a family of three that already had 120,000 yuan in savings, and an income of almost 100 yuan a day.

A few hours later, arriving at the foot of Hengshan mountain, and on the way to the top, I saw people carrying huge logs up the mountain on their backs. Each log weighed about a hundred kilograms, and it is almost an hour's climb from the foot of the mountain to the peak, but the wood-carrier said that he was paid only 2.4 yuan for carrying a log to the top.

In economics, the Gini Coefficient is used to measure the extent of inequality in income distribution. If the Gini coefficient is high, it indicates a high level of inequality, and if it is low, it implies that egalitarianism is strong. Current United Nations figures for capitalist countries indicate that the highest Gini Coefficient is 0.6 (e.g. Brazil), and the lowest is 0.2. Taiwan's Gini Coefficient was 0.5 in 1954, and 0.28 in 1981. Using this method to assess wage differentials in Shanghai before and after the wage adjustment of 1979, Tang Guoxing and others at Fudan University found that the Gini Coefficient was 0.142 before adjustment and 0.139 afterwards, which shows that the wage adjustment among cadres strengthened the tendency toward absolute egalitarianism in this group of state-employed workers. In 1982, a calculation made by Yang Xiaokai for Hubei gave a Gini Coefficient of 0.1332.[5]

According to figures from the State Statistical Bureau for 1984, compared with 1983, wage increases (including bonuses and benefits) were highest in the financial industry, with an increase of 23.5%. Commerce was 22%, construction 20.6%, and industry 18.9%, while cadres saw the lowest increase at 4.2%, and teachers and hygiene workers were about the same. Even without making the calculations, we can see that this draws the Lorenz curve representing the Gini Coefficient straight out along the low income side, bringing it closer to the straight line of absolute equality.

A survey of the net income of 1,646 specialized households in Shijiazhuang in 1984, indicated that those engaged in cultivation earned only 228 yuan, whereas those in transportation earned 2,683 yuan, or more than 12 times as much. In the state sector wages are moving closer to the standard of absolute equality, while in the private sector the gap in income distribution is reaching almost unimaginably unfair proportions. It is hard to see what rationale there can be behind this.

■ Enticing Targets — Appalling Results

For the last few years, economists have concentrated their attention on five major issues: compensation according to work, the theory of productive forces, the purpose of production, the commodity economy, and development strategy. The last question is still the topic of heated debate, especially the goal of "quadrupling" output by the year 2000.

In China today many important decisions are known by foreigners before ordinary Chinese find out about them. Important news is like high quality goods: it gains credibility by being produced for export and then sold locally. So it was that the target of quadrupling China's per capita GNP by the year 2000, and reaching a "comfortable standard" of living was proposed by Deng Xiaoping when he received the Prime Minister of Japan in December 1979.

Based on 1979's per capita GNP of US$253, a fourfold increase would give a per capita GNP of US$1,000, and a GNP of US$1 trillion. Not long afterwards, an article entitled "Everyone will definitely reach US$1,000 by the year 2000" came out, but later it was noted that if the estimated population increase were taken into account, per capita GNP would in fact only be US$800. Later, the 12th Party Plenum formally proposed that "on the premise of continually improving efficiency, we should strive to quadruple the gross value of the nation's agricultural and industrial output" by the end of this century, and raise people's material and cultural life to "a comfortable standard."

Some commentators assert that this target was based on careful calculations, and to the traditional Chinese way of thinking, perhaps this is already cautious enough, but the very way in which the target was proposed, and the fact that population increase was originally not even brought into the calculation suggests that the projections were anything but careful.

In particular, confusion later developed over the use of the terms "quadrupling" and a "comfortable standard." This was because in propaganda reports three different targets: the gross value of industrial and agricultural output, national income, and GNP[6] were all being used at the same time. In 1980, the Secretariat of the Central Committee pointed out in response to questions about this that a "comfortable standard" of living referred to GNP (a per capita GNP of US$800 and a GNP of US$1,000 billion) and that only when talking of "quadrupling output" was it permissible to use any one of the three indicators.

On 12 October 1983, *People's Daily* carried the following explanation from Zhao Ziyang: "When we speak of quadrupling output, it means we want to increase the wealth that is actually created, but the quadrupling people are talking of now is calculated according to the gross value of industrial and agricultural output. There are a lot of disadvantages to calculating in terms of gross output."

In fact, the average per capita national income in 1979 was US$223. Increasing this fourfold would give US$900 billion, and a per capita national income of only US$720 (based on a population of 1.25 billion). According to the Political Report of the 12th Party Plenum, quadrupling the gross value of industrial and agricultural output by the end of the century would give 2,800 billion yuan, equivalent to US$1,879 billion (converted at the 1980 exchange rate) or US$1,503 per capita. So it is clear that there is a substantial difference between the target figures for national income and the gross value of industrial and agricultural output.

A "comfortable standard" of living is a vague concept which is hard to quantify and, as Zhao Ziyang pointed out, there are a lot of disadvantages to using the GNP as an indicator of national prosperity. But is it doubtful whether it is any more appropriate for propaganda to use both a per capita national income of $720 and a per capita gross value of industrial and agricultural output of US$1,503 as targets for the year 2000 without distinguishing between the two.

Working on the target of quadrupling the gross value of industrial and agricultural output (GVIAO), we would only have to have maintained an annual average growth of 7.2% from 1980 to 2000 in order to reach our goal. From 1952 to 1980 the average annual increase in GVIAO was 8.2% and according to statistics, since the 1950s, 18 countries (including the Soviet Union, Romania, Bulgaria, Yugoslavia, East Germany, West Germany, and Japan) have reached the target of quadrupling per capita GNP within 20 years.

If it were merely a question of quadrupling output, few would doubt that the Chinese people would have much difficulty. After all, the quota increase set for steel production during the Great Leap Forward was much higher. The real problem is that of the actual benefits, of making efficient use of production inputs and ensuring that production satisfies the real needs of society. This is even more important when using quotas for GVIAO, which includes large amounts of transferred value which may be counted more than once.

First, the inefficiency of China's economy is truly remarkable (as we will see in later chapters on energy, transportation, agriculture, and industry). For example, one large electric power station in China employs 8,900 people to produce only 1.2 million kilowatts per year, while the Japanese Hitachi power station employs only 5,500 to generate 10 times this amount. In 1978 average per capita gross labor productivity in China was 9,000 yuan, while the equivalent figure for the United States was US$69,000, more than 20 times as much. The following table *(table 3.1)* is a composite of various materials relating to this topic.

If efficiency were not a concern, and it were just a question of racing to quadruple output, we would have no trouble reaching the target. But the inevitable consequence would be another convulsive round of huge economic swings. If we continue using the present technology, products, and industries, while frantically pouring in more inputs, as we did in the past, we will also succeed in reaching our goal, but the technology gap between China and advanced industrial countries will grow to unimaginable proportions, while the actual benefits will be minimal.

In fact we have always suffered from a very low capital utilization rate and inefficiency. As late as 1987, the State Planning Commission admitted that 70% of the liquid capital was tied up in inventories, losses were huge, subsidies were increasing and the cost of capital construction projects was higher than ever. In 1989, the overall efficiency of the state-run enterprises that account for 70% of all industrial production continued to decline sharply, and production costs for the first quarter alone were up 15.8% over the same period of the previous year, while profits were down 14%. The deficit for Shanghai's state-run enterprises for the same period increased 3.9 times.

TABLE 3.1 CHANGES IN THE EFFICIENCY OF CHINA'S ECONOMY AND COMPARISON WITH OTHER NATIONS

Industrial output per yuan of fixed capital (in 1983, China had 650 billion in fixed capital)	1970		1980		1990	
	1.78		1.2		(n/a)	

Energy consumption per US$100 million of national income (in 10 kilotons of coal)	PRC	USA	JAPAN	GERMANY	UK	FRANCE
	32.5	12.1	5.5	6.5	10.6	5.7

Amount of liquid capital used for every hundred yuan of output (yuan)	REST OF COUNTRY	SHANGHAI
	29.7 (1982)	19.7
	19.5 (1957)	

Increase in labor input (%) yearly average (1952–1980)	TOTAL	AGRICULTURE	INDUSTRY
	2.4	2	5.5

Rate of increase in labor productivity (yearly average 1952–1980)	*by total output*		
	TOTAL	AGRICULTURE	INDUSTRY
	5.6	1.4	5.3
	by net output—added values		
	TOTAL	AGRICULTURE	INDUSTRY
	3.5	0.3	4.3

■ 20 Flaws in the Target for the Year 2000

As soon as one considers efficiency, quadrupling output becomes not just an extremely complex matter but also a very difficult goal to achieve. Listed below are a series of conditions which, if not satisfied, could mean that we are unable to reach the target of increasing output fourfold by the year 2000 while ensuring efficiency. It is easy to see from these indicators that there are many weaknesses in the target set for the year 2000.

1. Political stability. There must be no major political movements, or the time spent on them must not exceed 1/12 of the labor hours. No major wars must break out.

2. The population must be contained to below 1.25 billion (see chapter 1 for a discussion of the population question).

3. There must be no major or prolonged natural disasters. We can see by the billion yuan losses caused by the Grade 7 typhoon that struck Guangdong province in July 1986 and the floods of the summer of 1991 that natural disasters are a threat that cannot be discounted. Furthermore, grain production must grow by a guaranteed yearly average of 8 million tons, and reach at least 480 million tons per year by the year 2000. It was 321 million tons in 1980. Between 1980 to 1990, production increased from 321 to 435 million tons, an average of 10 million tons a year. However, we must be cautious when assessing these gains. Although the grain output in 1989 hit 408 million tons, surpassing the previous peak year of 1984, the per capita grain consumption in 1990 was actually less than in 1984, because grain production was not keeping pace with the population increases.

4. There must be no serious policy mistakes like the errors made in the distribution of construction projects in the early 1960s, when they were assigned to mountainous, remote or subterranean sites. In one province alone, 81 fairly large construction projects had to be scrapped due to policy mistakes, 41 because the factory site was unsuitable, four because the product was obsolete by the time they were completed, 27 because they failed to reach production capacity over a long period, and nine because of lack of coordination in the design. In recent years there have been similar problems with many of our technology import projects.

5. The average increase in GVIAO must be no lower than 7.2% starting from 1981. Broken down into sectors and time periods, the target for industry is 5.7% for the first 10 years and 9.5% for the second 10 years, and the corresponding figures for agriculture are 5% and 5.5%. But according to the analysis of American economist

Dwight H. Perkins in his book *Agricultural Development in China from 1368 to 1968* the average yearly increase in agricultural output has never been more than 2%.[7] American economists Robert F. Dernberger et al. in their book *China's Future: Foreign Policy and Economic Development in the Post-Mao Era,* published in 1977, predict that up to 1992, it will remain at that level.[8] It will certainly not be easy to reach and sustain a 5% average yearly increase in agricultural output. One fundamental problem is that the potential of small-scale production has already been exhausted and it has not yet been possible to make a smooth transition to large-scale production

6. We cannot continue to rely on widespread extensive development. Labor inputs in industry and agriculture grew at an average yearly rate of 2.4% between 1952 and 1980 (2% for agriculture and 5.5% for industry) but it is estimated that annual yearly increase from 1981 to 2000 must be only 0.82% (0.63% for agriculture and 0.18% for industry) if intensive growth is to be achieved.

7. The obstacles presented by high accumulation, over-rapid development, and inefficiency must be overcome. Labor productivity in industry must rise at an average yearly rate of 5.8% (between 1952 and 1980 it was 5.3%, and between 1980 and 1982 it was only 2%). Of this, labor productivity in agriculture must rise at a rate of 4.6%, and industry at 6.2% to reach average per capita levels of 27,345 yuan for industry and 1,750 yuan for agriculture. This calculation assumes that the percentages of the total population and total labor force working in industry and agriculture will remain at 1980 levels of 36.45% and 85.5% respectively, so if the population in 2000 is taken as 1.2 billion, there will be more than 437 million people working in industry and agriculture, and if the population is taken as 1.25 billion, there will be a further increase of over 18 million people.

8. The education system must be able to provide about 20 million technical school graduate personnel (starting from 1983). To accomplish this, expenditure on education will have to increase to 6% or 7% of the national income. We must attend to the fact that one-fourth of the population is illiterate or half illiterate, and a third have almost no education.

9. A corresponding increase in the quality of life must be ensured and inflation must be prevented (it would be a disaster if prices were also to quadruple by the year 2000). Income distribution must be made fairer, and something must be done about the fact that one-fifth of the population has a per-monthly income of less than 20 yuan.

10. Activities that cause serious pollution or wide-scale damage to the environment must be prevented. Pollution and the destruction of the environment are not only too high a price to pay for reaching the

target, but could in themselves be factors in preventing us from reaching it.

11. Natural resources should be used sparingly and rationally. In the long run it is not worthwhile to use huge quantities of resources that far exceed necessary inputs in order to achieve some goal.

12. The uncontrolled growth of the cities must be prevented, or the cost of resolving urban problems will cancel out the benefits of achieving the target.

13. National security, and social order and stability must be ensured.

14. We must avoid accumulated debts, (or having a zero financial balance), either of which might result in a premature outbreak of vicious inflation.

15. The shortage of capital must be resolved. It takes at least a billion yuan to build a hydroelectric plant with a 1-million-watt generator, and more than 2 billion yuan to lay a thousand kilometers of railroad track. An open face coal mine with a capacity of 20 million tons a year costs over 3 billion yuan, and it is predicted that by the year 2000, investment in highways alone will require a capital of 100 billion yuan. Based on the previous 1 to 1 ratio of average outputs to investment, quadrupling output by the year 2000 will require capital inputs of 2,800 billion yuan. Even if the output-input ratio can maintain the 1981 level of 1:0.6, it will still take huge capital inputs of 1,700 billion yuan to reach targeted growth.

There are several ways of solving the capital problem. For example, if the economy could be made really efficient, about 50 billion could be saved by increasing the capital turnover rate. Making good use of part of depreciation funds and part of the increase in urban and rural personal savings could provide a total of 12.5 billion yuan in investment capital (annual fixed asset depreciation funds total 20 billion yuan a year, and if one third of this were used for investment, it would yield over 6 billion yuan.

16. An additional 200 billion yuan is needed for equipment and plants that urgently need replacement, and a further 20 billion to repair school buildings and warehouses.

17. Twice as much energy will be required to support a quadrupling in output. This would be an unprecedented feat, and no country has managed it so far. The prospect amazes many Japanese, because the savings on energy needed to do this would be higher than Japan's current energy savings. Japan's current energy utilization rate is already 57%, while China's is only about 30%. Further, energy consumption from 1966 to 1974 indicates that for every 1% increase in gross national income and output value, we must increase the energy

supply by 1.41%. On this basis, energy supplies would have to increase by 568% to support a fourfold increase in output. At present, China's energy consumption is third highest in the world, about the same as Japan, although it has a GNP only about a quarter that of Japan.

18.   The Engel coefficient (the proportion of income spent on food) must be around 0.4 to 0.5. It remains about 0.5 in the big cities and is about 0.7 to 0.8 in many areas. In developed countries it is usually 0.2 to 0.3.

19.   The personnel, labor and work allocation systems must be changed from their present forms, in which they hinder and even prevent the development of productive forces, into forms which will encourage a positive attitude and innovation in the work force.

From the point of view of China's existing system, energy presents the most difficult challenge, and security is the easiest factor to ensure, but we cannot afford to be complacent even about that. Of the 19 indicators we have listed, the eight major items of politics, population, energy, transportation, personnel, capital, science and technology, management, efficiency and the rational use of resources are the most important.

Even if all these conditions can be satisfied and we can reach the target of US$800 per capita income by the year 2000, it will still only be 1/20 of the current U.S. average per capita income of US$17,000. At an average growth rate of 6% a year, it would still take more than half a century to reach the current U.S. level. By the year 2000, the U.S. average per capita income will probably reach US$20,000, so China will clearly lag even further behind the developed nations than it is today.

At the moment, the biggest problem facing the reforms is the transition from the old system to the new, and maintaining coordination and balance in the process. We want to develop new industries, but at the same time we must guarantee supplies of some traditional products. We want to promote the vitality of the market, but we must not throw the overall plan into chaos. We must transfer out surplus labor power, but we also want to ensure the relative stability of the production system and avoid unemployment. We want to eliminate excessive control, but we have to guard against inflation. This will all be much easier said than done.

Finally, we may also encounter the following situation. In the 1950s we tried desperately to overtake the United States and Britain by increasing steel production, and only now do we realize the need to use a compound indicator that reflects the whole of the national economy. In addition to GNP, it is important to consider other indicators, like the quality of life and education. It may be that by the year 2000 we will still find ourselves with a "unitary index," while many other countries have shifted their development targets from increasing the quantity of output to a more pluralist concept of value. So we may discover that we should have been pursuing a target different from GNP all along.

4

ENERGY AND TRANSPORTATION: TWO WEAK LINKS

Development in any country involves numerous interrelated factors, and to be successful, a reasonable balance must be achieved among them. Otherwise, one weak link can thwart advances in other areas. China's infrastructure is seriously unbalanced, with the major weak points being energy and transportation. In the effort to quadruple output by the year 2000, these two factors will present constraints even more serious than the pressure of a growing population, the shortage of capital and technological resources, dated management, and environmental damage and pollution.

China started to make energy a priority in the early 1960s. But due to poor technology and over-ambitious plans for heavy industry, development resulted in an even more severe shortage of energy. When policy changed and investment in heavy industry was cut back, investment in energy was also severely affected. In addition, the lack of other suitable export products led the country to export energy resources, which is the last thing a developing nation like China should be exporting. In the 1980s China was exporting approximately 10 million tons of crude oil each year, at an annual loss of US$800 million due to falling oil prices. In 1988 and 1989, this increased to about 25 million tons per year, only serving to make the energy problem even more acute.

In the attempt to quadruple output by the year 2000, the most difficult task will be to increase the GNP fourfold with only doubled energy production. This energy policy is unprecedented: no country in history has ever quadrupled its GNP within 20 years with only a doubling of its energy supply.

After the production target was set, the first outline for an energy policy in China, entitled "An Outline Proposal for the Development of China's Energy Resources" was proposed by energy experts in November 1982. Based on a total annual energy production of 640 million tons, and an annual consumption of 600 million tons of converted standard coal in 1980, the most optimistic estimate of the energy supply by the year 2000 was equivalent to 1.1 to 1.2 billion tons of converted standard coal.[1] But it was thought that this supply could support a GNP of 2,800 billion yuan.

China's decision-makers and media often forget the conditions the experts laid down. In this case most of the experts who participated in the energy policy-making process said that if all economically cost-effective indexes could be significantly increased, if energy saving measures could double energy efficiency, if energy flexibility indices could decrease from 1.42 to 0.5, it would not be impossible to reach our target with only a twofold increase in energy supplies. Unfortunately their conclusion that it was not impossible was a logical conclusion to a theoretical discussion rather than a reflection of reality. Table 4.1 (1980 indexes are used for comparison) gives an idea of what was really involved.

The data indicate that China faces a severe energy shortage, that consumption efficiency and per capita consumption are low, and that consumption in production is high. In addition, uneven energy distribution, a severe capital shortage, poorly developed energy technology, the lack of trained personnel, and outdated management, all make the implementation of the energy policy extremely difficult.

In the early 1980s, China's energy flexibility index[2] was P = 1.42, compared to 0.8 for the average industrialized countries. To reach the goal set in the energy policy, it needs to be 0.5, one-third better than that of the industrialized countries. Calculated against the current energy consumption level of 100,000 tons of standard coal for every 100 million yuan of products, 2.8 billion tons standard coal will be needed by the year 2000. Even taking into consideration possible improvements in technology and energy-saving measures, a minimum of 2 billion tons will be required. There is a 40% gap between the 2–2.8-billion-ton demand and the output of 1.1 to 1.2 billion tons. This is obviously a key problem.

Since the goal of quadrupling economic output was proposed, a puzzling phenomenon has occurred: energy needs have increased dramatically but energy production has not increased correspondingly. In 1981, total energy production was only 630 million tons, with a low

TABLE 4.1
COMPARISON OF ENERGY AMONG CHINA, USA, THE USSR AND JAPAN

COUNTRY	CHINA	USA	USSR	JAPAN
coal production	62013	76295	71640	1804
oil production	10595	48500	60300	
natural gas	143	5464	4350	
hydraulic power	1605	6000	3150	2380
energy production (100 million)	6.4	21	19.4	0.4
power generation (100 billion)	3.0	22.9	12.8	4.8
energy consumption per $1.00 GNP (kilogram of standard coal)	2.50	0.92	1.22	0.35
energy efficiency (%)	30	51		57

590 million ton consumption in standard coal. In 1989, total energy consumption was 1.016 billion tons, with a 969 million-ton consumption of coal. In addition, a greater percentage of coal, a serious source of pollution, is being used than previously. Between 1980 and 1990, the percentage of coal as a part of the total energy usage rose from 69.4 to 74.1, with natural gas dropping from 3% to 2% of the total, while hydropower's share rose less than 1%, from 3.8 to 4.6.

A few examples illustrate how long this problem has existed. A report from Jiangsu Province indicates that in 1983, there was a 600,000 kilowatt shortage of electric power (20% of total operating capacity), while the electricity supply was 3 billion kilowatt-hours

(15% of total electricity consumption), causing production losses of 10 billion yuan.

Liaoning Province reported a 130% increase in industrial production between 1970 to 1983, but electricity production increased only 89.5%, and there was actually a 4.9% decrease in coal production. Up to 1985, 20% of the industrial capacity of the province was not utilized. The East China Power Network, the biggest in China, supplied 1.145 billion more kilowatt-hours of electricity than the quota allowed for in 1982, and since then, the power consumption quota has been growing daily.

At the same time, many power-intensive industries, like iron and steel, construction, chemicals, paper, and fertilizers were still expanding rapidly. The first phase of the Baoshan Steel Works and the second phase of the Jinshan Petrochemical Works were in operation for a long period without any new high-capacity generators being installed. The old system was left intact, hard pressed by shortages of capital and fuel, and obsolete management. Shanghai plans to reduce its energy consumption from 2.57 tons per 10,000 yuan of industrial output in 1980 to 1.40 tons by the year 2000. But energy consumption in 1985 was 37 tons for fertilizer production, 25 tons for cement, lime, and bricks and tiles, 11 tons for glass, and 6 tons for paper; a far cry from the goal.

With the major industries in this position, it is not difficult to imagine the rest. According to available statistics, the whole country is currently short 10 million tons of crude oil and 10 million kilowatts of electricity. As a result, 30% of the nation's production capacity lies idle. Many factories operate four or sometimes even only three days a week.

Meanwhile, massive amounts of electricity are consumed by facilities like luxury hotels, which have no productive function. A medium-sized modern hotel consumes 10 million kilowatt-hours of electricity a year. And refrigerators consume over 6 billion kilowatt-hours per year. When energy is short, profits from sales of non-productive, energy-intensive goods and services are made only at the expense of losses in industry. From the late 1970s, the whole country suffered annual losses of about 100 billion yuan in industrial output due to electricity shortages.[3] This is over 6% of the annual GNP, and no one even seems to be aware of its significance. By contrast, the developed nations were convulsed when the 1973 oil crisis brought losses of 3.1% in the United States, 11.9% in Japan, 4.8% in West Germany, 4.8% in Britain, and 2% in France. It will take at least three to five years before any fundamental improvement will be seen in China.

Two major causes of the prolonged energy shortage in China are the inefficiency and waste caused by outdated equipment and technology, which are aggravated by a third problem: the unreasonably low price of electricity. In many cities the price of electricity is lower than the cost of producing it; 10 fen (2 U.S. cents per kilowatt-hour for industry, 5 fen (1 U.S. cent) for big industrial consumers, and 6 fen (1.1 U.S. cents) for agricultural use.[4] There is little incentive for efficiency under such circumstances.

China's energy consumption per unit of GNP is the highest in the world. Our energy consumption for every dollar increase in GNP is eight times higher than Japan, and about four times higher than the world average . China's total energy consumption has been equal to Japan's for quite some time, but our GNP is only one-sixth that of Japan.

In 1979, energy consumption per 100 million yuan of GNP was 174,000 tons standard coal, 89.5% higher than the 91,800 tons consumed during the first Five Year Plan (1953–57), and 27.9% higher than the 136,000 tons consumed in 1965. In 1980, energy consumption per 100 million yuan of GNP was 21.5% higher than in 1965. Even with below-cost energy prices and heavy government subsidies, energy costs still make up 20% to 70% of total production costs. The country is developing in the direction of high energy investment and consumption.

The fourth key problem is getting the energy where it is needed. China is forced to transport millions of tons of coal and billions of kilowatts of electricity to locations hundreds of kilometers away from their sources. Coal has to be shipped from the North and West to the south, and electricity from the West to the East. This requires heavy investment and high technology, and also places an unbearable burden on the woefully inadequate transportation network. About 90% of the known coal deposits in China are in the remote provinces of Shanxi, Shaanxi, Gansu, Ningxia, and Inner Mongolia. Only 2% of these are in central, eastern, or southern China. Similarly, about 70% of water power resources are in the remote provinces of Yunnan, Guizhou, Sichuan, and Tibet. In 1984, however, 71.2% of the country's industrial production was concentrated in the 15 coastal provinces, which have less than 10% of the country's total energy resources.

The slow pace of energy exploration and the development of new resources is the fifth problem. China does not have adequate proven energy reserves. Much of the crude oil from the Daqing Oil Fields was extracted at a high cost in electricity (2,000 yuan per kilowatt-hour). Electric pumps force down water to displace the oil, but the volume of oil extracted is only 10%–20% of the water pumped down. To maintain annual production of 100 million tons of crude oil, a new capability of 8–10 million tons each year is needed. However, no other oil field comparable in size to Daqing has been found on land. There is a promising field in southern Xinjiang, but it is a week's drive from Urumqi.

Offshore exploration has not been satisfactory either. Exploration of the once highly promising oil fields in the South China Sea is proceeding at a much slower pace than anticipated, and foreign investment is decreasing. Some sources estimate that to the year 2000, energy investment in China will only reach between 20.5–28 billion yuan. To reach the original plan of a daily output of 3.5 million barrels from fields in the South China Sea in 2000, an investment equal to US$35 billion will be needed. Even if half of this comes from foreign investment, it still leaves a heavy debt.

▌ Low Per Capita Energy Supply

As with arable land, China's energy resources are not scarce at all in absolute terms, but when measured against the population, they appear pitiful. In terms of per capita recoverable energy reserves, China is an energy-poor country.

China has coal reserves of 1,440 billion tons, ranking third in the world, and accounting for 13% of total reserves worldwide. But per capita recoverable reserves are only 101 tons, or 40% of the world average. China has the world's largest hydroelectric resources, with a capacity of 680 million kilowatts. But the recoverable capacity is only 378 million kilo-watts, 1,965 kilowatt-hours per person, or 81% of the world average. Likewise, China's per capita natural gas and crude oil reserves are only 50% of the world average, one-seventh that of the Soviet Union, and one-tenth that of the United States.[5]

China's energy shortage is most acutely reflected in the rural areas. At a time of recovery and development of the agricultural economy, the seriousness of this problem should not be underestimated.

In the vast expanse of rural China, there are less than 200 coal-fired electric power plants, and these are low capacity, poorly managed, and inefficient. Over 40% of the nation's production teams still do not have electricity, and households among these teams burn 500 million tons of crop stalks, over 100 million tons of firewood, 9 million tons of dung, and 5 million tons of coal each year for fuel. Half the rural households in the country are short of firewood for 3–6 months a year. Due to the low thermal efficiency of household stoves (18%), 500 million tons of the 600 million tons of stalks and firewood consumed are wasted. This is the equivalent of 300 million tons of standard coal, more than two times total consumption for thermal power production nationwide in 1981.

This energy consumption is destroying the nation's forests. According to an estimate for Guizhou Province in 1980, annual forest production is only 9 million cubic meters, or only three-fifths the annual rural firewood consumption in the province. Dunhuang County, in Gansu Province, used to have 75,300 acres of forests and woods, but since 1949 they have shrunk at the rate of 1,650 acres each year due to household consumption, and have now almost vanished.

In 1980, 180 million cubic meters of firewood were consumed nationwide. In 1984, industrial wood consumption was 55 million cubic meters, but households consumed 3.54 times as much again over the same period. It is estimated that China's 180 million rural households consume 1.7 billion tons of stalks for household energy (each household needs 4,500 kilocalories of energy, which is equivalent to 13 to 13.5 kilograms of stalks).[6] If this problem cannot be solved, vegetation will be further damaged, and water and soil conservation will be impossible.

In 1986, China's urban per capita electricity consumption was 34 kilowatt-hours, only 1.1% of that of the United States. Per capita coal consumption was 0.88 tons of standard coal, less than a third of the world average. Analyses of energy in 84 developing countries worldwide indicate that it requires annual per capita energy consumption of the equivalent of 1.6 tons of standard coal to achieve an annual GNP of US $1000 dollars per person. But even by the year 2000, China's per capita annual energy consumption could only reach 1 ton.

∎ Policy Shifts Haven't Helped

A hasty decision was taken to convert coal-burning boilers to oil burning ones and there was a lot of publicity about the advantage of burning oil. Soon after the conversion, though, it was decided to convert back to coal again, and the disadvantages of burning oil were publicized. Several billion yuan was lost in the process.[7] Although China's energy policy calls for coal as the primary source of energy in the future—and it must be, because the technology for other sources is not yet developed—coal is a problematic source of energy.

China's coal reserves were documented in Geographic Records (*Shan hai jing*) as early as in the Warring States period, and archaeological discoveries indicate that our ancestors used coal as early as six or seven thousand years ago during the Neolithic Age. Historically, then, China was quite "developed" in this sense but, unfortunately, it is astonishingly backward now.

In the past, individual peasant-operated coal mines were sharply criticized because they damaged coal reserves, but following an approving comment from the top leadership, the media immediately started publicizing the advantages of liberal policies that allow peasants to open small coal mines. For example, on 22 July 1985, the *People's Daily* carried a report article headlined "It benefits both the country and the individual for peasants to open coal mines." By mid-1985, the number of small, village-run coal mines had grown from 17,800 in 1978 to 61,000 nationwide, a 340% increase, but coal production increased by only 220%. In 1984, coal production from peasant-run coal mines made up 27.5% of total national coal production (almost double the 14.5% in 1978). Some provincial officials even expound the idea that "coal mines should be given to the peasants to run."

No one can say how much is being lost due to this irresponsible attitude. Take, for example, the high quality Taixi coal produced in Ruqigou in the Ningxia Autonomous Region which is highly competitive on the international market.[8] Because of the policy of allowing state, collective, and individially run coal mines, and because there are no regulations for minimum coal extraction, more than 200 small coal mines have been opened in an area of 11 kilometers.

In 1985, the state-run mines in the area produced 630,000 tons of coal, consuming 800,000 tons of coal reserves (the recovery rate was 79%). By contrast, the small coal mines produced 800,000 tons of coal, but their reserve consumption was as high as 4.04 million tons, and the recovery rate was lower than 20%. At present, that mining area is losing 2.23 million tons of high quality coal each year. If half of it is exported, the loss is more than US$100 million. Total reserves in the area are about 230 million tons. Since 1966, 70 million tons have been mined, but actual production was only 15 million tons, giving a recovery rate of 21%. If this situation persists, the remaining 140 million tons of coal will be exhausted in less than 20 years.

Savings made by small scale production are not always worthwhile. Locally operated mines have smaller reserves, and lack exploration facilities and investment for capital construction. There are few technical personnel, and management is poor. Such mines have a bad safety record; there are many serious accidents, and the death rate per million tons of coal produced is much higher than in state-run mines. Production, supply, and marketing are also completely uncoordinated. But the most acute problems are the low return on investment and the severe waste of resources. Even China's well-developed coal mines have a recovery rate of only 40% to 50%, while the rate for county-run mines is 20% to 30%, and for locally run mines only 20%. Although the Resources Code is now in effect, its guidelines are too simple and are hard to implement. Meanwhile, waste and the abuse of resources worsen by the day.

The low price of coal is also a factor in the underpricing of energy. Although subsidies to the coal mining industry are common worldwide, the problem is particularly acute in China. At present, a truckload of sand costs more than a truckload of coal in Beijing, and the price of coal in China is only one-fifth to one-sixth that in other countries. In relation to other products, its value is only one-third to one-fourth that of other countries. For example, according to the statistics provided by China Coal Economics Institute in 1985, in the United States, Great Britain, Japan, and West Germany, a ton of coal could be exchanged for 0.102 to 0.222 tons of steel, while it China it can be exchanged for only 0.025 tons.

Coal production costs keep rising because mines are being dug deeper and tunnels are being extended, making extraction more costly. According to reports from the China Coal Economics Institute, the average depth of new mines nationwide grew by 10 meters each year. In 1964, the average length of tunnels was 9,194 kilometers, but it was up to 25,324 kilometers by 1983. The fast turnover of mining personnel, the low standard of construction of new mines, the length of time required to reach full productive capacity, rising compensation for landslides, damage to arable land, to surface construction, and to water resources all add to the rising costs.

According to a recent survey of 44 mining areas, between 0.1 and 1.45 acres of arable land is damaged for every 10,000 tons of coal produced. Forty production teams in the area under the jurisdiction of the Huainan Coal Mining Board have already run out of farmland, and 73 teams under the Xuzhou Board have less than 0.1 acre of farmland per person.[9] In addition, increased employee benefits and bonuses, retroactive salary increases, the nationwide increase of material prices, and rising supplementary expenses (for the workers' union, education, travel, conferences, interest, subsidies, and so on) have all added to the cost of energy.

The pay and living conditions of coal mine employees reflect an even more profound problem in China's energy production. As the heart of the coal industry, Shanxi Province has made a great contribution to China's economy. Coal mining began in this area as early as 1,500 years ago, and now five railroads cross the province. According to the National Bureau of Statistics, every 10 million tons of coal exported from Shanxi yields an increase of 17 billion yuan in the gross value of industrial output, and an increase of 4.2 billion yuan in profits and tax revenue.

But Shanxi itself remains economically underdeveloped. The gross output value of heavy industry there is lower than that of Guangdong Province, the gross output value of light industry is only 12% that of Guangdong, and its total provincial income ranks 18th among the nation's 30 provinces.

One-third of the state employees in Shanxi Province are engaged in coal production. Working hours are long and conditions are dangerous, with health risks from poisonous gases. The Beijing Mining Board has reported that the average working life of underground workers is only 12 to 13 years. Nor are such severe working conditions offset by better living conditions at home, where those of us who have personally investigated have seen shocking situations.

The Datong Basin lies beyond the Hengshan Mountain in northern Shanxi, and is the biggest coal mining area in the country, with known reserves of 37.6 billion tons. The Datong Mining Board is the largest in China, with 13 productive mines, 15 pairs of pitheads, 131 trained mining teams, 67 excavation teams, 60 exploration teams, two engineering sections, a machinery repair plant, and a coal chemicals plant. The board has 124,000 employees, of whom only 1,587 are engineers and technicians (less than 1.3% of the total). Next to the Board Headquarters is the large Yungang Mining Area at Jiangjiawan (about 20 kilometers from the city of Datong, 5 kilometers west of the famous Yungang Caves).

The Yungang Mining Area has over 10,000 employees, and a total population of 20,000 to 30,000 people including employees and their families. However, there are only 20 brick four-story apartment buildings to house all these people. The maximum reasonable capacity of these buildings is just over 200 households each, and even at double this number, they cannot accommodate even a tenth of the total population. The rest of the people live in shabby clay houses built on the hills or roadsides around the mines. Except for a few apartment buildings at the headquarters of each mine, the whole area is covered with shabby, crowded clay houses, some inferior to the caves built at Yungang 1,500 years ago. It is pitiful to see that workers who have made such an extraordinary contribution to China's economy over the last 30 years have been living in such terrible conditions.

▌ Solar, Wind, and Tidal Energy

China has unlimited resources of solar, wind, and tidal energy, but due to technological limitations they will not provide a reliable source of power within this century. One hope is nuclear energy. By the end of 1985, the United States had 93 nuclear power plants, with a capacity of 7.78 billion kilowatts. However, the problems of safety, waste disposal, construction costs, and public protest have led to a virtual halt in nuclear plant construction there. In the Soviet Union, the nuclear power capacity built in 1984 alone was 2.411 billion kilowatts, but the catastrophe at Chernobyl may make that nation wary of further nuclear projects. China has just begun to build nuclear power plants and, like other alternative sources, they cannot be a major factor for some time to come.

China is rich in hydroelectric power resources, but unfortunately they have not been fully utilized. China has the world's largest hydroelectric power potential (680 million kilowatts). It is estimated that as much as 370 million kilowatts of this could be utilized, to

TABLE 4.2 COMPARISON OF ENERGY EFFICIENCY IN CHINA
AND INDUSTRIALIZED COUNTRIES

	CHINA	INDUSTRIALIZED
General Thermal Efficiency in Iron and Steel Industry	28	55-60
Thermal Efficiency in Nitrogenous Fertilizer Production	25	50
Energy Efficiency in Transportation	6-8	20-25
Efficiency in Thermal Power Generation	28	35-40
Boiler Thermal Efficiency in Metallurgic, Chemical, and Textile Industries	50	about 75

generate 1,900 billion kilowatt-hours of electricity. However, at the end of 1985, actual hydroelectric capacity was only 26.4 million kilowatts, or only 92.3 billion kilowatt-hours of electricity. This was only 7.1% of potential capacity and 4.8% of potential generation. In contrast, the world average level is 20%, and the average level for developing countries is 8%.

Hydroelectricity accounts for less than 7% of the total power generation in China. It requires a large investment over a long period and long-range planning to develop it. But strangely enough, China has adopted a policy of giving priority to the development of thermal power instead. There has not been sufficient investment in hydroelectric power, there is no independent management body for it, and no overall development strategy. Some large projects have been started and stopped by hasty decisions, resulting in protracted construction cycles and giving hydroelectricity a bad reputation.

▪ Transportation: the "Vanguard" That Holds Us Back

Traditionally, the Chinese have regarded transportation as the "vanguard" industry that will pull the rest of the economy forward. But today, China's transportation network is in a sorry state.

Over the last 35 years, China has built 35,000 kilometers of railway track, while the United States once laid 19,200 kilometers of track in a single year. China has only 4% of the world railway, and per capita railway density ranks eighth from the bottom (see table 4.3). Density per square kilometer is only $1/24$ that of East Germany, $1/6$ that of the United States, $1/12$ that of Japan, and about $1/4$ that of India.[10]

To achieve the world average density of railroad, (82.6 kilometers of track per 10,000 square kilometers), China needs to have 80,000 kilometers of railway lines. Existing track covers only 62% of that distance. According to plans proposed by the State Planning Commission, we will reach the world average standard only in 2000, and railroad development lags far behind industrialized countries. To achieve the U.S. level of 0.033 kilometers per square kilometer, China needs 320,000 kilometers of railway track, but currently has only one-sixth of this (it is estimated that China's railway system will not reach saturation point until it has 360,000 to 400,000 kilometers of railway lines, or seven to eight times the current length). Given the current situation, rapid economic development in southern and western China cannot be given serious consideration at this point.

TABLE 4.3

CHINA'S TRANSPORTATION NETWORK (1989)

1. Total length: 122,000 kilometers	6.3 times increase from 1949, but 44.5 times increase in passenger volume, 15 times increase in freight
2. Total length of commercial railway: 53,200 kilometers	1.3 times increase from 1949, but passenger and freight volume increased 10.3 times
3. Total length of operating highways: 1.014 million kilometers	10 times increase from 1949, but passenger and freight volume up by 90.3 times
4. Total length of navigable inland waterways: 109,000 kilometers	10 times increase in capacity since 1949, but volume increased 26 times
5. Locomotives: 13,370	50% steam locomotives, several thousand over 40 years old
6. Seaport handling volume: 490.3 million tons per year	0.43 tons per person per year; world average is 1 ton, Japan is 10 tons per person per year
7. Number of seaport berths: 253 with 10,000 ton capacity	Rotterdam alone can handle 300 million tons
8. Automobile fuel consumption: 8.1 liters per 100 ton-kilometers	5 liters per 100 ton-kilometers for industrialized countries

China's energy problem is related to the problem of transportation, which in turn is linked to overall economic development and the social structure. A good example of how the two weak links interact to further weaken the system is the fact that such a large share of the transportation system is used merely to transport energy. At present, about half of China's railway capacity and 45% of its waterway capacity are taken up transporting coal. In Shanxi Province, 90% of the railway capacity is engaged in coal transportation, but in 1984 30 million tons of coal could not be shipped out of the province. In the first three months of 1986, 13 million tons of coal nationwide could not be shipped from the mines. At the same time, the city of Guangzhou had to spend large sums of foreign exchange to import coal from Australia.

As noted, coal is produced in the remote north, but the consumption center is the southeast. According to the estimates of Transportation Research Section of the National Economic Commission, lack of coal transportation capacity slowed down growth in the gross value of industrial output by 2–3%. As much as 20 million tons of coal was lost due to damaged freight cars and mismanagement, about the same as the annual production of the Kailuan Coal Mines. Such losses alone amount to 600 million yuan a year (not including the 2 million tons lost in waterway transportation).[11]

Agriculture is also affected by the weak transportation system. The northeastern provinces produce 11 million tons of corn each year for export, but can only ship out 3 million tons due to insufficient railway and port capacity. The remaining 8 million tons have to be stored, at a cost of 2 billion yuan, and after three years in storage the grain is spoiled and has to be dumped. In 1983 alone, 60,000 freight cars were loaded a day, but 80,000 cars worth of freight was left waiting. Each year, 20 million tons of goods cannot be shipped out.

Problems relating to transportation, postal services, and telecommunications were the focus of discussion at the 30th Conference on Economic and Social Development Strategies convened in Beijing academic circles on 20 January 1986. Researchers were highly critical of the situation, and pointed out that China's transportation system is incredibly overextended (see table 4.3).

Anyone who has traveled much through China knows that passenger trains are severely overloaded in many places throughout the country. Numerous quarrels break out and people sit hunched up on the dirty floor, with others trampling on them on the way to the toilets. Data provided at the conference confirmed the obvious: passenger trains in China are overloaded by 30% to 50%, or over 100 million passengers a year. There are also 150 million tons of freight waiting to be shipped and it is estimated that current railway capacity can satisfy only 50% to 70% of current needs for freight and passenger transport.[12]

Guizhou Province is one area in the country that has received priority in railway investment, and the capital city of Guiyang is at the center of a railroad intersection. Compared with the national average railway freight flow of 22,500 tons per kilometer and the average railway freight density of 13.82 million ton-kilometers, Guizhou's load is much lower, at 12,000 tons per kilometer and 7.57 million ton-kilometers respectively. Even so, the Guiyang-Kunming, Guizhou-Guangxi, and Sichuan-Guizhou lines are all operating above their designed capacity, and about 2 million tons of coal products cannot be shipped out in time every year.[13] In 1965 there were 4 bottlenecks in the country's transportation network, in 1980 there were 9, and now there are over 20. It is no exaggeration to say that the Chinese railway system is on the verge of collapse.

China's railway system has total assets of 70 billion yuan, one eighth of the total capital assets of state-run enterprises nationwide. However, the profits and tax revenue it earns make up only 1/50 of total state revenue. With 3 million employees, the Ministry of Railway Services makes a smaller revenue contribution than the Daqing Oil Fields.[14] This is adequate proof of its inefficiency. In addition, China's railways are technologically outdated and poorly equipped. Only 1/12 of the network is electrified (about 4,100 kilometers in 1985, projected to increase to 20,000 kilometers by the year 2000, or about a quarter of the total length).

Trains also run at very low speed. At present, most of trains operate at 70 to 90 kilometers an hour, and it is estimated that most will reach 160 kilometers only in 2000. Only 15 to 33 pairs of trains can use each stretch of line daily, and three-fourths of them are steam trains, which even India stopped manufacturing as early as 1971. Internationally, most trains operate at 160 kilometers per hour, with some experimental lines running as fast as 200–300 kilometers per hour. In Japan and West Germany, between 240 and 275 pairs of trains can use each line daily.

Only a few areas like the Northeast and Shanxi Province have developed railway networks. Even important economic areas like the East, the Mid-south, and the South, have yet to develop networks. There has been much publicized discussion of resource exploration in the Northwest and Southwest but these areas have only a few scattered railway lines. It takes more than a month to ship freight the 900 miles from Chengdu to Guangzhou by rail, a distance of only 900 miles, only a two-day run in industrialized countries. This is a graphic example of the previously mentioned difficulty of shipping material from western China.

Several local administrators in Yunnan Province told me that experts from the National Academy of Sciences and Universities have often been invited to help make "Strategic Development Plans," but the old problems still remain. Asked what these were, their answer was simple: "Products cannot be shipped out." Only three of China's 170 railroads run west of Kunming, Chengdu, and Lanzhou. There are only 0.93 meters of railway per square kilometer in the Xinjiang Autonomous Region, and horses are the major means of transport in the Northwest. Some observers have complained that too much priority was given to transportation in the West and Southwest at the expense of the East, but if this hadn't happened, the difficulty of transportation in the West would be unimaginable.

▌ Population Mobility

Another reason China's economy lacks vitality is the low level of population mobility. This lack of mobility is evident from the data in table 4.4, which compares China's population mobility and trans-

TABLE 4.4 POPULATION MOBILITY COMPARISON

Rail travel (in kilometers per person)	Japan	2,696	1983		
	USSR	1,327	1983		
	India	304	1983		
	China	231	1985	270	1989
Air travel	USA	1,734	1983		
	USSR	649	1983		
	India	20	1983		
	World Average	209	1982		
	China	11	1985	16.7	1989
Railway business operating length (in kilometers) per 10,000 square kilometers	W. Germany	1,145	1981		
	USA	308	1981		
	India	206	1981		
	USSR	64	1981		
	China	54	1984	55	1989
Railway business operating length (in kilometers) per 10,000 people	USA	12.5	1981		
	USSR	5.3	1981		
	India	0.9	1981		
	China	0.5	1984	0.48	1989

portation development in 1985 and 1989 with that achieved in some other major nations by the beginning of the 1980s.

Lack of investment and decreasing returns on investment are primarily responsible for China's poor performance. During the first Five Year Plan (1953–1957) investment in transportation was 17.4% of total capital investment nationwide, and it decreased yearly thereafter, dropping to less than 10% after 1981. Ironically, during the same period, several plans to put priority on developing transport were never implemented. In the early 1980s, the cost of railway construction per kilometer went up to three to four times that of the first Five Year Plan period, and it has been rising even faster in recent years. By contrast, the construction completion period is two times longer than during the earlier period. The cost effectiveness of capital has also been decreasing, and the profit return cycle has gone up from 8 to 10 years in the early 1950s to the current 20 years.[15]

Two main difficulties beset railway construction in China. The area east of the Tong-pu and Jing-guang lines has 77% of the country's total population, over 87% of the nation's total value of industrial and agricultural output, and 80% of the country's total railway passenger flow. However, construction in this area since 1949 was only 20% of all railway construction over the same period. Increasing pressure on the railway system and the development of market economy demand major investment in the region. At the same time, despite the high cost and low efficiency, railways must be built in the West, if the gap between the two regions is to be reduced, and the economy of West China developed.

Official plans call for construction of a railway network of six major north-south and six east-west lines by 2000. Additional lines are also planned in South Xinjiang and between Yunnan and Tibet line, but priority is still clearly being given to the eastern area.

▌ Deficient Highway System

Rail is an ideal form of long distance transportation for large volumes of freight, but highways are more suitable for short distances of freight transport. For shorter runs, highway freight is obviously more flexible, quicker, and more direct. Some researchers have concluded that for normal freight transport within 100 kilometers, high-value freight within 200 kilometers, and perishable freight within 1,000 kilometers, highway is more economical than railway. In the United States, highway transportation delivers freight over distances of 500 kilometers, and all freight transportation within 200 kilometers is by road. As a result, 80,000 kilometers of railway lines in the United States were abandoned. In Britain, 40% of the railway network has been demolished.[16] By contrast, a quarter of China's railroads are still serving transportation needs with ineffecient hauls across distances of less than 100 kilometers. This is mainly because the highway system is underdeveloped, with problems at least as serious as that of the railroads.

In an excellent report on the problems of China's highway transport for the Southeast Shanxi Transportation Bureau, Zhao Yu presented some alarming facts.[17] In southeast Shanxi, huge quantities of high grade anthracite produced in 1958 are still waiting to be shipped. About 50,000 vehicles move back and forth on an old, battered 40-kilometer mountain highway. It is impossible to clear accidents quickly, and traffic is sometimes blocked for a whole week. On the eastbound Shi-Tai highway, the traffic flow has increased from 4,000 vehicles a day to the present 10,000, with 15,000 vehicles at the peak, or five times the maximum capacity of a third class highway. In November 1983, there were more than 30 traffic jams, during one of which about 10,000 vehicles were backed up on the Taihang Mountain road for two days.

In the "golden triangle" along the Yangtze River, there is not even a highway from Shanghai to Nanjing that passes the cities of Suzhou, Wuxi, and Changzhou. The existing 300 kilometers of roads are all third or fourth class. The traffic barely gets through, and the average speed is 30 kilometers per hour. One concerned authority estimated that manufacturers lost 1.1 to 1.5 billion yuan in 1984, simply because of traffic jams.

By 1989, the nation had 1.01 million kilometers of roadways, most of them still of poor quality. Road density is only a quarter that of Bulgaria, and 40% of the roads we do have are substandard. First and second grade roads account for less than 25%, third grade roads for 31%, and fourth grade roads for 30%. The remaining 15% do not even merit a grade, as more than 150,000 kilometers of all roads are unpaved. Over 90% of the 620,000 kilometers of local roads run by counties and townships are dirt roads which cannot be used when it rains. Guizhou Province once received major state investment in transportation, but according to a 1985 report, the province has no first grade highways, and only 5 kilometers of second grade ones.

According to the 1990 *Zhongguo tongji nianjian* (China Statistical Yearbook), there were only 244,000 kilometers of top and secondary top grade highway in China, only 24% of the total road length in the country. Many of the nation's major highways had already exceeded their designed life span, and two counties, over 5,000 townships, and 26 villages had no roads at all. There were also 6,000 kilometers of dead-end roads, and over 5,800 dangerous bridges in need of repairs. In 1983, the total length of roadway was 915,100 kilometers, and by 1990 it had only increased to 1 million kilometers.

The automobile industry is also fraught with problems. The Number 1 Automobile Plant built in China in 1953 went into operation roughly at the same time as the Japanese Toyota Automobile Company. Today, Toyota produces several million cars a year, offers a wide variety of models, and has a high reputation throughout the world. By contrast, the Number 1 Automobile Plant has been producing the same "Liberation" model truck ever since it opened and has a yearly output of only 60,000 vehicles. In the 30 years between 1953 and 1984, China produced only 2.3 million automobiles, and the main models have not changed for 20 to 30 years. In the past few years, average annual automobile production for the whole country has been 200,000, only 5% that of the U.S. General Motors Company and 7% that of Toyota.[18]

At present, the most efficient cruising speed of existing vehicles in China is about 50 kilometers per hour. But because of poor roads, the average speed is actually only 30 kilometers an hour, and in metropolitan areas, the normal speed is only 12 kilometers an hour. Wang Zhanyi, of the Ministry of Transportation, has suggested that if the third grade roads were upgraded to second grade (from a gravel to a paved surface), the average traffic speed could be increased by 15 kilometers, and the haulage capacity of vehicles increased by 50%. This alone would increase the nation's transportation capacity 35%–45%. It would also increase the life of tires by over 40,000 kilometers, reduce fuel consumption by 15% to 30%, and increase engine life by 80%. Calculated on the basis of 1,000 vehicle trips a day, it would save 90,000 tires, 110,000 tons of diesel fuel, and reduce the cost of transportation by 20% for every 10,000 kilometers traveled.

According to Li Zhenjiang of the Ministry of Transportation, the profit margin on new model cars is 2 to 5.8 times higher than that on the old models, and fuel consumption per 100 ton/kilometers is 24–28% lower. At present, however about 60,000 vehicles with mileage of over 500,000 kilometers are still in operation. Many old cars have been sold to farmers, and these now constitute one third of all vehicles in the agricultural areas. If the inefficient old models are not taken out of operation, they will continue to damage the economy as a whole.

At present, about 300,000 large passenger buses a year are produced worldwide, each with a capacity of between 100 and 200 passengers. But China only produces 1,200 large passenger coaches annually, a mere 0.04% of world output, and they only have a capacity of 40–60 passengers. China also produces too few heavy trucks. In the United States, trucks with a capacity of over 10 tons made up 84.7% of all total truck tonnage in 1974. To bring even 12% of its trucks up to this standard, China would need to increase truck production by 10,000 a year until 2000—well beyond current production capacity.

Metropolitan transportation is an even more serious problem. Statistics for 241 Chinese cities show that by 1983, passenger flow had increased 59 times, and the total road length increased 67 times compared to the pre-1949 period, but the number of vehicles had only increased 15.8 times. In comparable big cities, the total length of road increased only 1.8 times, but the number of vehicles increase 33 times.

Analysis by Tao Tongshi in "Suggestions for Metropolitan Public Transportation," pointed out that the bus to population ratio is 1:700–1,000 in some cities in other countries, but in China, it is 1:2,000–3,000 on average and as low as 1:4,000–5,000 in some places. Some big cities in other countries have several thousand to over 10,000 kilometers of roads, with 12–15 kilometers of road per square kilometer. In Beijing there are only 2,000 kilometers of roads, and in Tianjin, 800 kilometers, or only 4.7 kilometers per square kilometer, which adds to the congestion, pollution, and inefficient energy use.

In Guangzhou, it can take an hour on a crowded bus to cross the Pearl River, which is only 200 meters wide. Many people in China take three to four hours to get to work and back everyday, resulting in a loss of over 100 million workdays. An even more serious consequence of the overcrowded roads is the high rate of traffic accidents in the cities. The annual death rate from traffic accidents per 10,000 vehicles is 44.8 in Beijing, 60.4 in Tianjin, and 41.5 in Shanghai, compared to 1.12 in Tokyo, 1.38 in New York, and 4.9 in Paris.[19]

In 1986, there were about 4 million registered vehicles on the road in China. In 1985 there were 5.5 million traffic accidents (up 20% on 1984), resulting in 12,042 deaths and an unknown number of injuries.

According to the Traffic Control Bureau of the Department of Public Security, there was a sharp increase in traffic accidents in 1986, with over 40,000 deaths (more than 100 everyday). In 1987, the figures continued to rise. In October alone, there were 24,119 traffic accidents, 4,685 deaths and 15,228 injuries.

∎ Rivers Abandoned for the Railway

China has over 5,800 rivers, with a total length of 400,000 kilometers, only one-quarter of which are navigable. In the 1960s, there were still 170,000 kilometers of navigable waterways, but by 1983, only 110,000 kilometers remained, a total which was fortunately, stabilized through the rest of the 1980s.

One of the major causes of this decline is the construction of dams and sluice gates on the rivers. Of the 4,000 or so dams and sluice gates in the country, 2,600 (65%) do not have navigation facilities. This has reduced the length of navigable waterways by 37% compared to 1952, or to about 50,000 kilometers. Guizhou, for example, had 2,854 kilometers of navigable waterways in 1952, but by 1983, only 1,661 kilometers were left, a decrease of 42%.[20]

Another reason for the decline of water transportation is the misguided passion for those railroads we do build. A typical example is the construction, at a cost of over 3 billion yuan, of the Chonqing-Chengdu line that runs parallel to the Yangtze River. Total investment in the construction of navigation facilities over the last 30 years was only one quarter of the total investment for the Chongqing-Chengdu railroad line and only 1/40 of total U.S. investment in navigation facilities over the same period.

There is still little navigation on the Yangtze River, China's most important waterway, and apart from the pollution, the scene has changed little since the poet Li Bai wrote in the Tang Dynasty that, "a lonely sail disappears over the distant horizon."

In Europe and the United States, an immense tonnage of bulky freight is transported by water. The freight density on the Mississippi, which has comparable navigation conditions to the Yangtze, is 18 times that of a railway the same length. Its cargo capacity and circulation are 1.5 times and 3.7 times those of the Yangtze, respectively. The transportation capacity of the Yangtze is only equivalent to one 3,000-kilometer railway, and its utilization rate is less than 15% of the Mississippi. If the cargo density of the Yangtze reached the level of the Mississippi, its transportation capacity would equal that of 100,000 kilometers of railroad (94% more than the existing railways in the country). The capacity of the main stream of the Yangtze alone could equal that of 14 railway lines. By contrast, hundreds of thousands of yuan are needed to build every kilometer of railway.[21]

Confused policy and bad management have also retarded the development of water transport in China. The actual cost for transportation per ton-kilometer is 20 fen (US$.04) by road, 10 fen (US$.02) by railway, and only 2 fen (US$.005) by water, but strangely enough, the price charged for water transport is twice as high as rail shipping in many places.

The cost of shipping goods from Chongqing to Yichang provides a vivid illustration of this problem. If the average charge for rail transport is 100 yuan per ton for 400 kilometers, the cost of water transport over the same distance would only be 235.2 for coal, 239.6 for ore, 222.2 for grain, and 193.4 for iron and steel. But almost all freight leaving Sichuan Province went by rail (only 1.1% was shipped by water in 1982).[22] Even stranger, goods shipped from Chongqing to Shanghai have to be unloaded at Yichang and reloaded onto ships belonging to the Yichang fleet. Different areas all take a cut of the profits, and the goods have to be shunted around several times before they finally reach Shanghai.

The outlook for sea transportation is not promising either. The biggest problem is the limited handling capacity of China's seaports, which between them is not even double that of Rotterdam (300 million tons a year). Only 135 (less than 36%) of the 380 ships engaged in foreign trade that enter the ports each day can be loaded or unloaded. For every ship being loaded or unloaded, there are 1.8 ships waiting. On peak days, there may be as many as 570 ships each day, three times the ports' current handling capacity. For this limitation, China has to pay over 100 million dollars in penalties every year. Another 200 million dollars are spent renting foreign ships.[23]

On 11 July 1985, 146 ships carrying steel products alone were waiting to be unloaded at each of the ports in Dalian, Qingdao, Tianjin, Lianyungang, Shanghai, and Huangpu. The Port Committee under the State Council held an emergency meeting with the relevant officials at the Ministries of Railways, Transport, and Economics and Trade, the Headquarters of the General Staff, the army's General Logistics Department, and the Navy Headquarters to organize an emergency unloading operation. Such incidents are common in China and reveal both the strong and weak points of the system; the strength being the ability to do a rush job when cost is not a consideration. Unfortunately, the government has always tried to solve long-term economic problems with this kind of semi-military operation, leaving the fundamental problems untouched year after year.

In addition to inadequate facilities, mismanagement, and bad planning, the longstanding problem of silted ports and waterways has also contributed to shipping delays. This is a typical example of how environmental problems like those discussed in chapter 2 can be connected to economic problems a thousand miles away. Mawei Port at the mouth of Minjiang River in Fujian Province originally had a berth draft of five to eight meters, but since the port was constructed in 1974, silt deposits have increased dramatically, and in 1981 the minimum draft fell to as low as half a meter. Originally the Yongjiang River in Zhejiang Province could accommodate passenger ships of between 3,000 and 5,000 tons, but the construction of big sluice gates at Ningbo has caused heavy silting ever since 1959.

In 1983, China built 230 ships with a total tonnage of 517,600 tons. It was estimated that by the year 2000, China's ocean-going cargo fleet will have 2,000 to 2,500 ships, with a capacity of 300 million tons. To match these developments in shipbuilding, China needs to build deep-draft berths in 20 ports capable of handling 100,000-tons, to form an international container shipping center with Tianjin, Shanghai, and Huangpu as the key ports.

In addition, the construction of two inland waterway transportation systems north and south of the Great Wall is one of the key plans which will have to be accomplished by 2000. Then the Grand Canal will have the capacity to transport 100 million tons of freight, and the mainstream waterways of the Yangtze 500 million tons.

The "Ten Construction Projects" completed in Taiwan in 1979 played an important role in Taiwan's economic development, and six of them were transportation projects. China's planners are also keenly aware of the backwardness of China's transportation system, and have always appealed to speed up the pace of development. During the sixth Five Year Plan (1981–85), transportation and energy were made two strategic focuses of development, but in fact, actual investment in transportation was decreasing. The proportion of investment in transportation as a proportion of all capital investment was as follows:

First Five Year Plan:	15.3%
Second Five Year Plan:	13.5%
Three-year adjustment:	12.6%
Third Five Year Plan:	15.4%
Fourth Five Year Plan:	18.0%
Fifth Five Year Plan:	12.9%
Sixth Five Year Plan:	10.0%

One other consequence of backward transportation is severely inadequate postal and telecommunication services. There is a shortfall of 20% to 30% in service capacity on the nation's main postal routes, and a 50% shortage of mail handling space (400,000 square meters). There were only 0.4 telephones per 100 people in 1983, and 0.6 in 1985, only 5% of the world average (12 per 100 people), 0.7% that of the United States (76 per 100 people in 1982), 1.75% that of Hong Kong (35 per 100 people), and 2.9% that of Taiwan (21 per 100 people). Since 1949, China's industry has grown 56 times, but the number of telephones has risen only 7.4 times, the latter increase being only 13% of the former.

Even if the goal of increasing telephone equipment and services eightfold set by the postal service is achieved, there will only be 2.8 telephones per 100 people by 2000,[24] merely 23% of the current world average. This lack of telecommunications is another obstacle to efficiency in energy and transportation. According to surveys in other countries, the use of telecommunications systems to control transportation can increase existing capacity by 50%.

At a time when many people in China have pointed out that energy and transportation are bottlenecks that should receive first priorities in economic development, some experts are actually downplaying their significance. Some have made the astonishing claim that the real bottleneck in China's economic development is not energy, transportation, and raw materials, but capital.[25] As the accumulation of funds depends on developing light industry, it has been suggested that in the near future we should limit the development of energy, transportation, and raw material industries, and use the limited funds, foreign exchange, energy, and raw materials available to develop light industry.

This strange claim implies that the economy develops in logical steps from light industry to funds to energy to transportation, and completely ignores the actual existing situation. The whole country has had an energy shortage for 17 consecutive years: 30% of industrial productive capacity lies idle due to power shortages, and power plants are operating below capacity because the transportation system cannot supply adequate fuel. This has resulted in losses of hundreds of billions of yuan; many cities and towns have no light, and food rots in refrigerators due to constant power cuts. In view of this, any claim that we should limit the development of energy and transportation is incomprehensible and completely unrealistic.

5

PROBLEMS IN INDUSTRY AND AGRICULTURE

▌ Industry Faces Three Challenges

China's industry faces problems no less serious than those in other sectors. The three major challenges are (1) the reorganization of heavy industry to better serve the rest of the economy; (2) the development of consumer goods industries; and (3) the reform of industrial technology and development of a high technology industrial sector.

In a Government Work Report at the Fourth Session of the Fifth National People's Congress, the then general secretary of the Communist Party Zhao Ziyang stated, "In the future the development of heavy industry, apart from producing certain consumer durable goods, should focus primarily on becoming more service oriented. It should extend the range and improve the quality of its services and increase its adaptability, so that it can better serve agriculture and the consumer goods industry, the export industry, and the modernization of national defense."

China's industrial structure was built basically on the principle of giving priority to heavy industry. From 1952 to 1979, gross investment in capital construction was 648.2 billion yuan, of which 349.4 billion yuan (53.9%) went into heavy industry, and only 35.1 billion yuan (5.4%) into light industry. From 1949 to 1979, the gross output value for heavy industry multiplied by 67 times, while the gross output value of light industry increased by a factor of only 18. In the

27 years from 1952 to 1978, the ratio of investment between light and heavy industry averaged 1:10 and during the period of the third Five Year Plan, it was just 1:14.

The biggest problem is that heavy industry constitutes a closed, self-serving system. Of the all steel consumed in production from 1953 to 1979, agriculture accounted for only 13.4%, and light industry only 12.9%. In 1982, national steel output had already reached 27 million tons, but light industry could still not acquire the 2 million tons it needed each year, and had to spend over US$0.2 billion to import the 500,000 tons shortfall. In 1978, more than 80% of the heavy industrial output was used by heavy industry, and in some provinces and cities more than 90%. Heavy industry provided only 30% of the raw materials used by light industry.

China's watch industry, for example, requires more than 90 different types of machine tools, but less than 20 can be produced domestically.[1] Of the 31,000 types of mechanical and electrical goods currently produced, 26,000 (84%) need to be replaced. Over a third of the equipment used by light industry needs to be updated, and 24% should be scrapped immediately. Less than 20% of the mechanical and electrical products made in China match the standard of overseas products of the 1970s.

The major drawback in China's traditional model of industrial production is that the percentage of fixed capital per worker is 40% higher than in most other low income countries, while net output is only 17% higher. In the manufacturing industry the discrepancy is even greater: the percentage of fixed capital per worker is four times that of typical low-income countries and almost as high as that of middle-income countries, although net output is only 50% higher than the former and not even half that of the latter. In addition, the ratio of liquid capital to fixed assets is almost 50% (in most other countries it is 15%).

The structure of the economy is also irrational. It overemphasizes the development of heavy industries that cannot absorb much labor, creating a large labor surplus. Staff and workers are too concerned about job security, even though labor intensity is 30% to 50% lower than in middle-income countries. The Number 1 Automobile Factory in Changchun employs 75,000 workers and staff, 60,000 (80%) of whom have nothing to do with actually making cars.

Factories and enterprises in Shanghai have a labor surplus of 120,000, but the very work units with surpluses still have to employ 60,000 temporary workers a year. According to a report in the *Shijie jingji daobao* (World Economic Herald), the number of extra temporary workers hired in Shanghai has increased by 9% a year since 1984, and already accounts for 5% of the total work force, causing a 25% increase in production costs for the units concerned. The situation is bizarre: the regular workers are dissatisfied with their existing jobs, and hang around doing nothing, but the managers have to get the job done somehow, so they end up hiring temporary workers. This problem will be difficult to resolve without fundamental changes.

No solution has yet been found for the enormous problems industry faces in management and policy. The case of the "650" workshop in Wuhan gives an illuminating example of just how disorganized management has become in China.

In April 1987, news media reported that the Zhongnan Steel Rolling Mill had spent about 10 million yuan to set up a "650" workshop, but seven years later not a single meter of steel had been rolled. Leaders at all levels, from the mayor of Wuhan and the Minister of Metallurgical Industries to the Deputy Head of the State Economic Committee expressed their "deepest concern." Shortly afterwards it was discovered that 87 enterprises in Wuhan alone had had a total of 911 pieces of imported or scarce quality equipment worth 51 million yuan standing idle for long periods. In some cases, the packaging had not even been removed.[2]

What is really surprising is that officials at all levels of the Party and government had been in constant touch with the project for more than seven years, issuing directives and stipulating where expenditures and savings should be made. How was it then that we had to wait until a newspaper reporter happened upon the problem for them to come to their senses? It is hardly conceivable that for seven years no one in any of these government bodies knew what was going on. One wonders how long it might have taken to expose this scandal if the journalist had not happened to go there, and how many people would have been promoted or gotten rich out of the "650" project in the meantime.

All this is confusing enough, but it is even harder to understand why, after these losses of billions of yuan were reported, nothing was said about finding out who was responsible. Instead, all kinds of self-congratulation began, with people talking about "putting unused equipment to use" and "turning waste into wealth." Leaders at all levels developed high-flown theories about "Sounding out the equipment management situation in every system and enterprise" and "Putting it all to use as soon as possible." Vague phrases like this get trotted out every time a problem is discovered, and then the mistake is supposed to disappear, and failure turn into success.

When a system is completely closed off from the real world, "turning a bad thing into a good one" is as easy as kissing your hand.

Even the authorities admit that the "650" project is not an isolated incident. Not long after, another case occurred where large numbers of cars bought with precious foreign exchange were left standing outside and were ruined by the weather. This time we had to wait until foreign journalists reported it before any attention was paid to the matter, and no one ever found out exactly what had gone wrong.

If a country wants to emerge from technological backwardness, it must naturally rely on investment. But it is even more important that it first reform its own work methods and organization, and raise the standard of policy-making and management. At present, increases in investment have outstripped improvements in management and organizational reform.

▌ Consumer Industries Struggle to Survive

While heavy industry is caught in this self-serving cycle, the nation's consumer industries are struggling to sustain themselves under the pressure of the wartime guarantee system, which was discussed in chapter 3.

In the *Preface to a Critique of Political Economy,* Marx said that "without production, there is no consumption, but without consumption there is no production." Many of our managers and policy makers who are familiar with Marx understand the first half of the sentence very well, but very few grasp the second half. For 30 years, the Chinese have been lining up to collect or hand over ration tickets. These long lines have certainly kept consumption down but we did not realize that they were also restricting production.

Terms like "consumer habits" and "the structure of consumption" were practically counterrevolutionary ideas, as were concepts like high quality, attractiveness, nutrition, and entertainment.

China only has a socialist system of "guaranteed" unified distribution and is not supposed to need a market mechanism. In some people's minds, the word "consumption" is almost synonymous with "enjoyment" and "waste." Their whole job is to consider whether they should issue a few more or a few less ration tickets next time around. It is only when supply cannot meet demand that they have anything to do, and the more shortages there are, the more easily they can justify their existence. Nor are they concerned about excess inventories. They assume that in the end even unmarketable products will be in short supply and, besides, as a last resort there is always "paired supply," (where consumers are forced to buy another unwanted product along with their intended purchase).

The distribution of national income in China is peculiar in that the proportion applied to personal consumption is very small compared with the proportion used for investment. In 1981, personal consumption accounted for 58% of the Gross Domestic Product, 26% lower than the level for most low income countries, and 8% lower than medium income countries with average per capita incomes six times higher than China's. Furthermore, savings are 36% of national income (the figure for most low-income countries is 7%, and for middle-income countries only 22%), making it a typical high investment country.

The issue of consumption relates directly to food, clothing, accommodation and transport. Foreign researchers are projecting how people will be living in 2001, but to us all that seems a million years away. For the last few years, except for some coastal areas, many people have been struggling to shake off the image of being a "horde of blue ants," and have been striving to solve basic problems like increasing grain rations and getting everyone at least three or four square meters of living space.

In 1952, China's annual per capita grain consumption was 198 kilograms In 1980 it had risen to 325 kilograms, an average yearly increase of 0.23%. On the basis of five bowls of rice per person per day, that is an increase of only five bowls each per year. The total is stable at about 400 kilograms a year.[3] As noted previously, per capita consumption in 1990, at 372 kilograms, was actually 22 kilograms less than in 1984.

A few years ago the argument was put forward that China has a lot of grassland (700 million acres in the north) and 114 million acres of mountainous terrain in the south that could be used to raise livestock. On the basis of this reasoning it was predicted that by the year 2000, our diet would be primarily meat.[4] But this ignores the fact that the grassland regions are generally at high altitudes and therefore cold, desolate, and dry. The grasslands are also receding, vegetation is being destroyed, and there is serious soil erosion.

Personal consumption is low in China, especially when compared to consumption by collective bodies in business and government. Total fiscal revenue increased almost 2.5 times from 1977 to 1986, but collective consumption increased by 3.5 times. This increase in consumption by business and government exceeds on average the increase in personal consumption. Although machines from the 1940s and 1950s are still grinding away in workshops, more and more luxurious office blocks are being built and expensive cars purchased. Government organizations and enterprises are leading the trend in high consumption and encouraging this kind of prodigality to spread throughout society.

According to a report in the *Shijie jingji daobao* (World Economic Herald) (30 May 1988), between 1977 and 1986 the total purchasing power of Party, government, enterprises, and collectives rose 343%, from 13.47 billion yuan to 46.2 billion yuan. In 1981, only 15,000 small cars were purchased by collectives, at a cost of 340 million yuan. By 1986 this had increased to 115,000 vehicles at a cost of 5.34 billion yuan. Over the last 40 years, the country as a whole spent US$13 billion importing foreign cars, but total investment in the domestic car industry for the same period was only US$3 billion. In 1987 a further US$840 million was invested in an automobile plant in Changchun with an annual output of 30,000 luxury sedan cars. In the same year 59 counties and cities spent 8.3 billion yuan on the construction of luxury buildings.

(This phenomenon is not limited to government departments and enterprises. Even schools are involved. Staff at schools that make extra money by recruiting students who pay high tuition or by renting out school premises may make several trips a semester to hotels at tourist resorts to attend "Working Groups for Cadres" or "Intensive Study Groups for the Department Party Committee." This use of large amounts of productive capital for the untimely enjoyment of high consumption and the pursuit of superficial prosperity is not much different from exchanging silver for opium as we did in the past.)

Many supervisory departments are aware of the problem but turn a blind eye, and some indulge in such practices themselves. In some open areas, like the Pearl River Delta, a standard reception banquet for 10 costs 1,000 yuan, and no one thinks anything of it. One can spend an ordinary person's annual salary on a single meal. But an official who should himself have been concerned with such matters will comment that "it only bothers you because you're not used to it." With state funds being wasted in this way, some cadres have naturally begun to take pleasure in using public funds for private gain.

Policy concerning light industry is also difficult to account for. Capital is vital for economic development, and capital accumulation relies mainly on developing light industry, more than 80% of which is related to consumer industries producing clothing, food, utensils, and transportation for the masses. One observer, Liu Fengchang, pointed out in 1987 that from 1952 to 1983, the state invested 415 billion yuan in heavy industry, but during the same period heavy industry contributed only 815 billion yuan to national capital accumulation, or only 1.98 yuan for every yuan invested over the 32 year period. During the same period, light industry contributed 613.5 billion yuan in tax revenue, an accumulation rate of 10.85 for every yuan invested.

A similar situation exists with foreign currency earnings. For example, in the 37 years after 1949, the state invested US$3.6 billion in the construction of light industry, and over the same period light industry earned more than US$50 billion in foreign exchange, or US$16 for every dollar invested. But for the last 30 years, the development of light industry has been neglected. Investment has been less than one-seventh that of heavy industry, and light industry's share of the total has not increased in recent years. The rate of profit on output has also been steadily declining. From 1979 to 1981 it was 13.39%, 13.01%, and 11.33% respectively. In 1983 it was 9.97%, in 1985 9.86%, in 1986 8.73% and in the first quarter of 1987 it fell even further to 6.75%, which already verges on the break-even point of 5%. The increase in the state's fiscal deficit in recent years is not unrelated to this.

▮ The Demise of Efficiency

The overhaul and updating of industrial technology and the development of a high technology industrial sector are two of the most serious problems the country faces, and the outcome of these efforts will determine the future course of industrial development.

In most developed countries, the importance of scientific and technological advance is considered to account for 60% to 80% of the increases in labor productivity. Various estimates put the level for China at only about 20%, and the nation still relies primarily on huge inputs of capital and labor to expand production.

No one opposes technological transformation any more, but it is still easier to talk about it than achieve it. The depreciation rate in industrial enterprises has long been too low, and they have not been allowed to retain enough of their depreciation funds. A large chemical company in Lanzhou provides a good example. In 1985 it had 34,000 staff and fixed assets of 1.245 billion yuan, but for quite some time the depreciation rate had been only 2.7%, and even after decentralization it was only 3.2%. According to the seventh Five Year Plan, 800 million yuan is required to update technology, but the factory is 400 million short.[5]

The deputy director of Mitsubishi's research institute has presented convincing data showing that industries that produce only one product will have a life span of only 30 years. If we were to make a list of China's enterprises and cross out those that are more than 30 years old and delete only one product, few would remain. Most of our enterprises will soon die a natural death unless they are thoroughly remolded.

By 1983 state industrial enterprises in China employed a total of 35.5 million, of whom less than 1.34 million were engineers or technical staff. The ratio of technicians (only a few of whom were engineers) was on the order of 1:26, a differential far greater than in the advanced industrial nations—and one that will remain quite wide because of the deficiencies in education.

Technical innovation is generally considered to be the only remedy for industrial decline, but unfortunately; China's industrial system does not encourage innovation. A State Planning Commission survey of enterprises in metallurgy, chemicals, mechanical engineering, light industry, and electronics in 1986 revealed that they generally paid high taxes and had a low level of profit retention (an average of only 100 to 140 yuan per person). This lack of capital for self-initiated reform and development stifles enterprises' development.

The Economic Commission has reported that only 15% of large and medium scale enterprises were thriving, 20% showed little sign of vitality, and the other 65% were moribund. Surprisingly, even under these conditions, demand for 48% of the enterprises' products exceeded supply and only 11% were unmarketable, so there was little pressure to innovate.

Another feature of this industrial ecology is that many poor-quality products continue to be produced due to support from influential quarters. In August 1987, the Ministry of Light Industry solicited consumer opinions on product quality and announced its intention to hold an "exhibition of low grade products" (some people called it a Hall of Shame). Despite strong consumer support, letters and phone calls opposing the idea poured in, and ministry staff were bribed by the enterprises involved to transfer letters of complaint back to them. In the end, it was impossible to collect products for the exhibition and it had to be canceled.

One major reason for the lack of innovation in Chinese industry is the absence of incentives. If industry is to innovate, it must be supported by advances in science and technology, but these in turn require some stimulus before progress is made. It must be ensured that those organizations and enterprises which develop and employ new technology reap economic and social benefits.

The economic incentive for industrial innovation usually comes from savings on production costs, profits from the sale of products based on the innovation, and the benefits of shorter production time or improved quality. These in turn affect pricing, investment, borrowing, profit margins, and costs. They are particularly relevant to things like the contingency fund, the incentive fund, and the insurance fund, but none of these things exist in China's economic system, so there is no incentive to innovate. In 1986, labor productivity only increased by 1%, while taxes on enterprise profits fell 1.4%. From 1952 to 1981, China's yearly average industrial growth rate was an impressive 6%, but it must be remembered that the yearly increase in capital inputs was 11.6% and the yearly average increase in the labor force was 2.6%. In terms of total factor productivity (the ratio between output and the quantity of all major labor and financial inputs), China's productivity has actually fallen by 9%. From 1957 to 1978 alone, total factor productivity for developing countries rose by an average of 31%, and in developed countries by 49%. China's performance has been disastrous, with little to show for the heavy investment aimed at improving the composition and technological base of industry.

The deputy head of the State Economic Commission, Zhu Rongji, reported that by November 1987 about US$10 billion had been spent to import technology and plant from abroad. It seems to have disappeared into thin air. In May 1987, *Jingjixue dongtai* (Trends in Economics) reported that in the 1986 budget, capital tied up in finished goods produced by state industrial enterprises was as high as 37.09 billion yuan, or 21.8% more than the previous year. A large portion of these were outdated unmarketable goods.

At the same time, state-run industrial enterprise losses had risen from 10.3% the previous year to 14.2%. In 1987, losses again increased by 4.6%. Total profits realized by state industrial enterprises were 9% lower than the previous year, and of the huge capital investment in over 200 large and medium scale projects, more than half failed to achieve expected results. It must not be forgotten that all this occurred at a time when everyone was stressing the need to increase efficiency.

This situation is particularly evident in township enterprises. By the end of 1986, there were more than 15.1 million township enterprises, with a work force of almost 80 million. Their gross output value exceeded 330 billion yuan, or 20% of GNP, and they paid 17 billion yuan in tax to the state, so they clearly already formed a significant part of the economy.

In 1986 township enterprise profits per hundred yuan of fixed assets, per hundred yuan of investment and per hundred yuan of output value were all down by 25% from the previous year. Even in Jiangsu, where the situation was best, profits fell 20% and there were losses of almost 200 million yuan. In the same year, 25% of township enterprises in Xi'an made a loss, and 30% of them closed down.[6] (I described this in detail in "A Breathtaking Leap" in the January 1988 issue of *Baogao wenxue* [Reportage Literature]).

The reasons for this slide are very complex. First, the vast majority of township enterprises are nominally called collectives, but are in fact controlled by county or village Party and government organs, and a substantial part of their profits are used by these bodies for expenditures unrelated to production. In 1986, 37.8% of the profits made by township enterprises in Yancheng in southern Jiangsu were handed over to the state, and 17.1% (more than 7 million yuan) went to county and village Party and government bodies, while only 10.2% was distributed to individuals. In 1985, township enterprises in Jiyang handed over 47% of their profits (22.26 million yuan) to the state, despite regulations limiting the state's claim to 30%.[7]

Secondly, the township enterprises have been adversely affected by shortages of capital and resources, the low level of technology, backward management techniques, and confused market information. A typical survey shows that in the three years of 1983–1985, average yearly rural per capita income and living expenditures were 309 yuan and 248 yuan, 355 yuan and 273 yuan, and 397 yuan and 324 yuan, respectively, giving a yearly surplus of 62 yuan, 82 yuan and 73 yuan, not necessarily enough to cover increases in production costs for the following year. This indicates that state loans are a major source of capital for township enterprises. Surveys show that the average start-up capital for township enterprises is 302,000 yuan, only 21,000 yuan of which comes from commune or production team savings. Many enterprises are in debt, over 25 of the outstanding loans are already past due, and it is estimated that at least 17% cannot be repaid. Many township enterprises were hard hit after 1985, when the money market contracted.

▌ Managing Agriculture Barehanded

China manages to feed one-fifth of the world's population from less than 1/13 of the world's cultivable land (about 247 million acres). Although, as we have seen in the chapter on ecology, China's cultivable land area may actually be considerably larger than that, this is a truly remarkable feat.

Agriculture in China has always been an arduous business, beset by crises and unforeseen dangers. (Professor Lawrence Klein, winner of the 1980 Nobel Prize for Economics, told some Chinese visitors in Philadelphia in 1981 that agriculture and population were the two major problems facing China's economy, and that if they could be resolved it would be a remarkable achievement. Of course, we were already well aware of this: the difficult part is doing it.)

Making agriculture the foundation of the economy is a key element in basic national policy. According to the Central Committee's plan, agriculture is to achieve two major transitions by the year 2000: the transition from a self-sufficient or semi- self-sufficient economy to a commodity economy; and the transition from traditional agriculture to modern agriculture. Specifically, after five years devoted to thoroughly implementing the responsibility system in agricultural production, the plan calls for a further 10–15 years to introduce specialization and gradually reduce the number of peasants engaged in cultivation to 300 million from the present total of 800 million.

Specialization is the "second major agricultural policy" being promoted at the moment, but thus far the idea of quadrupling output has been so attractive that few pay much attention to the second policy goal. With three-fourths of the population engaged in agriculture, and the agricultural population in 2000 projected at about one billion, about 200 million workers would have to be transferred out of agriculture. The success of this effort will have profound implications for China's modernization and reform, and fulfilling this task will be much more difficult than quadrupling output. In order to understand the problem, we must come to terms with certain aspects of the situation in agriculture.

First, although we have long called ourselves a "resource rich nation," this is not in fact so, or at least not for agriculture. China has a land area of 2.37 billion acres, of which 1.75 billion acres, or 74% of the total, are used for agriculture (not including Taiwan or the 352 million acres of the continental shelf). Of this, cultivable land accounts for about 247 million acres (around 1/10 of this is stable or high-yield land, and about 99 million acres are infertile, dry, or salinated low yield land). The surface water area is 41.16 million acres, and forest, grasslands and mountainous terrain account for more than 1.3 billion acres. Another 7% is urban areas or is used for transportation, and 19% is desert or ice-bound for much of the year.

Moreover, from 1957 to 1977 alone, 72 million acres, or 29% of cultivable land, was commandeered by the state for various construction projects and subsequently abandoned. During the same period, 42.8 million acres of previously uncultivated land were brought under cultivation, giving a net decrease of 29 million acres, equivalent to the combined area of the three provinces of Guangdong, Guangxi, and Sichuan.[8] The average annual decrease in arable land was equivalent to the cultivated land area of Fujian province. Nor does this include the fact that since 1979, 80 million peasants have left agriculture for township enterprises, taking another few million acres out of cultivation.[9] With per capita natural resources below the world average, China is far from being a resource rich country in agricultural terms *(see table 5.1)*.

TABLE 5.1
NATURAL RESOURCES FOR AGRICULTURE IN CHINA COMPARED TO WORLD AVERAGE

	World	China 1982	China 1990 (est)	China 2000 (est)
TOTAL LAND (ACRES PER PERSON)	8.15	2.37	2.08	1.98
AGRICULTURAL AREA	5.44	1.07	0.98	0.91
CULTIVATED LAND	0.91	0.24	0.21	0.2*
FOREST (A/P)	2.55	0.3	0.27	
GRASSLAND (A/P)	1.88	0.58	?	0.66*
SURFACE WATER (CBM/P)	11,000	2,700	2,336	
FOREST COVER (%)	22.0	12.00	12.98	

*Taking the population as 1.2 billion and assuming no decrease in existing cultivated land and grassland (figure is high).

Over 65% of China's territory is mountainous, and consequently should have abundant forests, but as noted, the forested area is only half the world average. Agriculture and forestry are intimately linked, but there is no policy for the management of these regions. When the mountain dwellers are obliged to live off the land, they are forced to take a shortsighted view and clear the ground for cultivation, causing the rapid destruction of mountain forests. The forests are threatened, mountain regions have been unwisely exploited, and lakes have been filled in to create farmland, causing a series of prolonged droughts and flooding.

For the last 30 years arable land per capita in the Tai Lake basin has decreased from 0.36 acre to 0.2 acres. When it drops below 0.12 acres, then only subsistence farming will be sustainable and the commercial grain producing base in the Yangtze River Delta will disappear. In Sichuan province, people are anxious to break out of what they call the restrictive "basin mentality," but if cultivable land continues to decrease at the current rate, in 20 years time the Chengdu plain will have disappeared and that once fertile region will become a land of scarcity.

Shandong has 55,900 square kilometers of mountainous terrain, of which 43,000 square kilometers, or 77%, are already affected by soil erosion. Approximately 200 million cubic meters of soil are lost every year, containing nutrients equivalent to 2.5 million tons of chemical fertilizers. Between 1955 and 1985, cultivable land in the province decreased from 22.7 million acres in 1955 to 17.8 million acres in 1984, an average decrease of 1%, or 200,000 acres a year.[10]

Excessive amounts of fertilizer have been used, and decreasing soil fertility has almost completely exhausted the nutrients in the soil. From 1965 to 1982, fertilizer consumption increased by 12.8% per year, but grain production only rose by 3.6% over the same period.[11] From 1978 through 1990, fertilizer use increased over 160%, while insecticide use grew to 229,000 tons in 1990—over 10% higher than the previous year. The nitrogen, phosphorous, and potassium lost each year due to soil erosion are equivalent to the annual chemical fertilizer output. This is compounded by the great reduction in legume crops and the massive burning of hundreds of millions of tons of straw each year as fuel, which further deprives the soil of fertilizers and organic matter. Less fertile soil means lower output and lower output leads to the cultivation of marginal land, which in turn exacerbates the problem of soil erosion.

The shortage of agricultural natural resources, the decrease in cultivable land, desertification, salinization of the soil, the destruction of the ecological environment, and soil erosion are all increasing dramatically. As noted when discussing the environment, it can require from five to several hundred years to restore the ecological balance, and possibly as long as a thousand years for the natural ecological environment to recover. For the present, however, the environment continues to deteriorate, and it is unclear when a serious attempt will be made to control this deterioration.

One of the causes of the agricultural problem is that investment in agriculture has not kept pace with other sectors. From 1952 to 1981, China invested 700 million yuan in capital construction for agriculture, only 11% of the 600 billion yuan investment in capital construction overall. For several years after this, investment fell even lower to less than 6%. Of this about 60% went to hydroelectric projects, while another 80 billion yuan was spent on operating costs for agricultural departments and assisting communes and brigades.[12] The amount spent was already small, but the state took another 20 billion yuan out of agriculture to provide investment for industry, causing a scissor effect.[13]

These problems are compounded by the fact that investment in agriculture has shown poor results and labor productivity is low. During the period of the first Five Year Plan (1953–57) the rate of fixed asset formation for capital construction investment in agriculture was 82.4%, but the yearly average over the last 30 years was only 65%, and from the 1980s on it has fallen 60%. Moreover, in 1980 the agricultural population was over 80% of the total population and average grain production per worker was less than half the world average. Between 1949 and 1980, the latter rose by an average of only 1% a year. In 1988 the average grain output per agricultural worker was only 1113 kilograms. If this figure is compared with those recorded by Wang Shiduo in the *Yibing Diary*, then it is only half that of the Tang dynasty period (2262) 56% that of the Ming dynasty

TABLE 5.2 COMPARISON OF CHINESE, U.S., AND SOVIET AGRICULTURE

COUNTRY	USA	USSR	CHINA	USA/CHINA
Agricultural pop. as % of total 1976	2.6	21.0	88.3	1:0.029
Cultivable land (acre) per worker 1978	199	24	0.82	1: 241.4
Grain output (kilograms) per worker 1978	140,800	10,712	1035 (in 1988)	1: 125.97
Meat output (kilograms) per worker 1978	7,521	555	27	1: 273.49

(2000 kilograms), and a mere 0.8% that of the United States *(see table 5.2 for a general comparison)*.

China's agricultural development has relied almost entirely on massive inputs of labor and raw materials. It is difficult to exaggerate the backwardness of our agricultural technology. Since the slogan "The way out for agriculture lies in mechanization" came out, counties all over the country have been setting up agricultural mechanization research centers and tractor factories. But in most cases it has been just a question of opening a bank account and spending a lot of money, with minimal results.

In this respect, the shortcomings of the agricultural technology extension system are particularly disturbing. The peasants are anxious about their lack of technology, but technological extension staff seem unconcerned, and stick to their own activities, like running experiments or giving demonstrations. The technicians lack equipment, and apart from their meals, receive little support. Many people have to rely entirely on their own imagination, with the result that all kinds of strange things are springing up with names no one has ever heard of like "Zero cultivation," "Biological cultivation," or "Ecological biology factory."

This state of affairs cannot be blamed entirely on the government. It has been estimated that it would take a trillion yuan just to introduce elementary mechanization into agriculture, not to mention anything more sophisticated.[14] This obviously cannot be accomplished in a short time, and in fact, even before appropriate mechanization can begin, competent technicians must be trained, and employed to develop agricultural techniques.

The money China spends on agricultural research is barely enough to maintain the staff, and there are only 60,000 agricultural extension technicians in the country, an average of one for every 14,000 peasants. Agricultural research institutes have about 20 staff on average.

Over the last 30 years, 730,000 people have graduated from advanced and middle level technical schools, but only 34.3% have stayed in the villages.[15] That is only 248,000 people, or one for every 1,000 acres of cultivated land and every 3,200 peasants. It has also been estimated that many rural cadres have no work experience or knowledge of management, and that a third of them do not really know what they are doing. The low educational level of most peasants, including more than 180 million illiterate adults, is a major obstacle to the introduction of more efficient, environmentally sustainable, and soil conserving farm strategies. One-third of the world's peasants live in China and they constitute a veritable army of illiterates. Poverty and backward production are major factors constraining agricultural reform. They restrict the pace of reform, hinder reform of the procurement, distribution, and price systems, and prevent the use of advanced technology for organizing large scale production.

▌ Agricultural Production May Fall

It is widely accepted that the condition of agriculture is the most accurate reflection of a nation's level of development, and that a strong agricultural sector can only be built up by raising the economic and educational level of peasants, introducing scientific cultivation techniques, and raising productivity. These are the breakthrough points for agriculture.

After the contract and responsibility system was introduced in 1980, China had five or six successive years of bumper harvests. In 1984 grain output reached a high of 394 kilograms per capita, nearing the world average of 425 kilograms for the first time. This should have been a matter for great rejoicing, and it did not occur to anyone that a "bumper crisis" would immediately follow. Nonetheless serious difficulties ensued in storing, transporting and distributing the grain. (Over 30 million tons are still stored outdoors due to lack of storage facilities.) National grain stocks already exceeded 75 million tons, and some peasants had three years worth of stocks. Regions with grain surpluses requested to transfer out 53 million tons, but the regions they were to be transferred to could only accept 7.5 million tons.[16]

The reasons behind this were the poor quality of the grain, inadequate transportation, and the weaknesses and irrationality of the procurement and pricing systems. Of all the factors involved, however, insufficient purchasing power and the excessively low level of consumption were the major ones. Although the urban areas, which comprise 20% of the population, have 50% of the purchasing power, the consumption level of 200 million urban residents was still too low to absorb the output of 800 million peasants. The state insisted the grain be procured at subsidized prices, but Grain Bureau chiefs said this left them a choice between defying the policy (not purchasing the grain) and committing a crime (buying it and then having it rot because it could not be properly stored).

Policy alone is not enough. Our processing technology, market mechanism, and purchasing power simply cannot deal with the situation any more. To take figures for the two years 1979 and 1983 alone, grain output increased by 44 million tons, cotton by 50.1 bales, sugar by 1.27 million tons, and oil by 1.23 million tons. To consume the output of just these four items would cost about 59.4 billion yuan, and according 1983 statistics, urban residents' total retail expenditure on consumer goods was only 95.2 billion yuan. Total retail sales by peasants to non-rural residents were 13.3 billion yuan.

It has been calculated that if this method of subsidized procurement continues, before long 60% of national fiscal expenditure will go on subsidies, and as a result, agricultural output figures are bound to be distorted. For this reason, many people have predicted that the incentives which the policy can provide have almost reached their limit, and other factors have not yet been able to catch up. This leaves us confronting the painful possibility that agricultural production will decline.

This prediction is supported by the forecast that over the next 10 years, agriculture will not only confront unprecedented population growth, and a doubling in demand for fertilizer, but will also face huge water shortages of between 70 and 100 billion cubic meters a year. Even worse, meteorological forecasts predict a concentration of droughts, floods, and cold spells over the next decade. If temperatures fall by an average of just one degree, and rainfall decreases by an average of one centimeter, grain output could decrease by 10% to 15%.[17]

Of course, there are different forecasts. The Meteorological Research Laboratory at the Chinese Agricultural Science Institute has used the method of distinguishing trends and cycles to mathematically analyze the distribution of grain output during the 1949 to 1981 period. The main conclusion was that total grain output is currently going through a period of comparatively rapid growth, and that this is an excellent opportunity, but that for 12 of these years —more than one-third of the period—there was a negative growth of over 10 million tons. As we plan to meet the crisis ahead, it is necessary to consider the possibility of a grain shortage on the order of 15 million tons.[18] In fact, the country already has to import about 15 million tons of grain, and 40% of urban grain consumption is imported (3–4 million are exported). However, it is dangerous just to look at the distribution of grain output over time without analyzing the meteorological forecasts. Turning points in agricultural production are not easy to predict.

In 1982 average per capita grain output in the United States was 1464 kilograms.[19] As noted, in China it was 394 kilograms in 1984, and 362 in 1985, only a quarter of U.S. output, and half that of the Soviet Union. After hitting an all-time high of 407 million tons in 1984, grain output decreased to the 380–390 million ton range, and it was not until 1989 that the harvest rose back to the 1984 level. 1990 was even better, hitting 435 million tons according to official figures. But this bumper crop can only inspire cautious optimism at best, especially with the threat of natural disasters.

Another major issue is the transfer of surplus labor out of agriculture which is already taking place. Five million peasants left agriculture to go into construction in 1984, but the transformation of the structure of China's rural industries and labor force began long ago and it is no longer the case that 80% of the population are engaged exclusively in agriculture and 95% of them are concentrated on the plains of the Southeast.

By 1981 the composition of the agricultural work force was as follows: the five sectors of cultivation, forestry, animal husbandry, sideline activities and fishery accounted for 93.89%, commune and brigade industries for 2.7%, and 1.36% went out as temporary workers. It has been forecast that by the year 2000 the balance will have changed so that cultivation accounts for 30%, forestry 10%, livestock 10%, rural industry, commerce, services and culture 40%, and others (including those who go to the city) 10%. About half the labor force will have left traditional agriculture.

In 1989 the agricultural labor force was about 333 million, and since the implementation of the responsibility system there has been a surplus labor force of about 180 million. Production opportunities are hard to find. If 20 million people are to be transferred out of agriculture each year, inputs of 20 billion yuan (mostly to provide fixed assets) would be required, and to transfer 200 million people over the next ten years would cost 200 billion yuan.

Another perplexing problem is that among a generally ill-educated rural population, the first members of the labor force to leave agriculture are precisely the minority who have some "culture." They are in fact the mainstay of the labor force, and not "surplus labor" at all. It is easy to see that if we implement an ill-conceived reform that involves a massive transfer of the labor force, the results could be disastrous. Modern agriculture needs qualified people, but it may well be the least educated who remain behind to work the land.

It is abundantly clear, as some people have warned, that there will be an unbearable burden on society if peasants abandon farming in large numbers and take up commerce, or if a tendency to undervalue agriculture develops and too big a gap grows between agricultural and commercial incomes. In fact, the disappointing grain harvests are not unrelated to the fact that large numbers of capable, strong young workers left the farms to work in commune and brigade industries.

One further point needs to be mentioned here, which is that in the future, the increasing gap between the Eastern and Western regions of China will be most extreme in the countryside. The middle and lower reaches of the Yangtze River, which account for 20% of the country's cultivated land, produce 35% of the total grain output, while the Northeastern region, which has 17.6% of the country's cultivable land, produces only 5% of the total.

Nowadays, Party branch secretaries in some places in the Pearl River Delta, Liaodong, and Jiangsu are riding around in luxury sedan cars and some counties control a capital of 10 million yuan. But it has not yet been fully realized that China's agricultural development has been uneven. The Jiangnan model, the Wenzhou model, and the Pearl River Delta model that are talked about in the propaganda, are all examples of agricultural workers being transferred to processing industries, and are not models of self-initiated agricultural development. If these models were copied in regions where the economy is underdeveloped, it would inevitably be at the price of contraction or stagnation in agriculture. The Pearl River Delta in particular has special conditions of climate, soil, and people that very few areas of the hinterland could replicate.

Furthermore, it must be recognized that the much-publicized reports in recent years about peasants in the suburbs of Zengzhou and Beijing selling airplanes and pianos, or peasants in villages in Yuanbeiguan wearing suits and buying cars and color televisions are all individual cases, and represent a very small number of people. It must not be forgotten that China's agriculture is a matter of 800 million peasants, not just a few million, and that it concerns 36,000 townships, not just a few hundred villages in river deltas along the coast or on the outskirts of big cities.

According to World Food Program statistics for the beginning of 1985, average annual rural per capita income in some areas was less than 120 yuan, and annual cereal consumption did not exceed 200 kilograms, with the population taken as approximately one billion. One-tenth of the population were below the poverty line and lacked basic food and clothing. Places like Dingxi in Gansu, and Xihaigu in Ningxia are incredibly poor. A survey carried out in Hezhang county in the mountainous region of Northwest Guizhou, found that 10 or 20 thousand people belonged to families with total property worth less than 10 yuan. In 1985 the total value of peasant assets for the whole country was estimated at 700 billion yuan, an average of only a few hundred yuan per head. For 1989, the per capital rural income was only 601.5 yuan.

Over the last few years it was impossible to store surplus grain, but at least 10% of the population had no money to buy it anyway.

Peng Defu of the Land Management Bureau of the Ministry of Agriculture reported in March 1987 that there are still eleven regions of the country, (including 13 provinces, 225 counties, and 6194 townships) that are classified as poor.

In 1983, over 85% of all counties had an average annual per capita grain intake of less than 400 kilograms, and a quarter of all counties had insufficient grain. More than 90% of all counties had an annual average per capita income of less than 200 yuan (an average of less than 0.54 yuan a day), and of these, 56 counties had average per capita incomes of less than 100 yuan (an average of less than 0.27 yuan a day). This report should also have mentioned that outside the 11 regions, even in areas like Jiangsu and Guangdong, there are hundreds of thousands of people with incomes well below 100 yuan a year.

The quality of the labor force and the conditions for agricultural development continue to worsen. There is basically too little land and too many people, and production and management techniques are outdated, all of which is causing the peasants to lose the real initiative in the reforms. If the market mechanism were allowed to operate freely, prices for scarce agricultural products would go through the roof, and many state enterprises that depend on continued state subsidies would be in danger of collapse, as would the huge administrative and bureaucratic organs.

Hu Juren has rightly pointed out that where there is no civilization, there can hardly be any culture, and nowhere is this no more evident than in China's villages. Over the last few years, there has been a rising incidence of theft among the peasantry: theft of lumber, minerals, and even cultural artifacts. Shanxi has many important historical remains at sites in Dingcun, Longshan and Yangshao, but in recent years, 382 ancient tombs have been robbed, and 295 Qin and Han tombs were seriously damaged.

Changsha in Hunan is world famous for its glazed pottery, but since 1986 a series of thefts have taken place which even the government has been powerless to stop, and the peasants of several nearby villages now openly walk off with cultural relics from the site. The law protecting cultural artifacts has become a useless piece of paper. *Beimei ribao* (Beimei Daily) reported (1 June 1987) that 1,700 peasants in Qinghai robbed 2,000 ancient tombs, damaging 330 acres of farmland and carrying off over 10,000 cultural artifacts.

Meanwhile, in some "developed" regions, peasants who have "got rich first" are busy burning incense at Buddhist shrines, praying for divine assistance, and competing to build more and more extravagant tombs for their ancestors. Some of them throw banquets and spend vast sums on marriages, funerals, and betrothals. Some mountainsides in the Wenzhou area are a white expanse of concrete gravestones, many of them costing more than 10,000 yuan. An amazing story in the *People's Daily* on 9 June 1988 told of finding more than 60 "advance" tombs at a famous scenic spot in Yunnan, 12 of which were built for Party members and 8 for cadres.

In the Pearl River Delta area, many peasants flock to hotels in nearby county towns and eat and drink for days on end. They think nothing of spending up to a thousand yuan on a single meal, and no longer consider poultry good enough. A great many of these people have made their money at other people's expense because of the scissor-like effect of policy, but they do not use it to invest, or build up infrastructure. Instead they spend it on luxuries and frivolities that merely serve to expose their own foolish vanity. One family of yuan millionaires in Guangdong actually bought six color television sets, one for every room in the house, even though there were only four people in the family, and the local officials came by to congratulate them.

No one imagined that the bumper harvest of 1984 would end up revealing the weaknesses of the procurement and allocation system and exposing the grave inadequacy of China's rural infrastructure, the backwardness of organization and management, and the fragility of the market mechanism. It was this that in 1985 finally caused the Central Committee to reform the system of centralized procurement and distribution that had been in operation for more than 30 years.

It later turned out, however, that when planned procurement was replaced by contracts, the prices of some agricultural products still could not be allowed to adjust freely. Extreme fluctuations in supply and demand forced the revival of some planned procurement and distribution policies, and price reform was abandoned for the time being. The major causes of this were backward production and the inability of supply to meet demand.

According to a typical survey, the average Chinese peasant household has only about 1.45 acres of land, which is usually divided into nine pieces. Chinese peasants have an average of .29 acres of cultivable land per head, whereas the figure for the United States is 57.7 acres, or 195 times as much. If one calculates on the basis of an agricultural work force of 390 million, that gives 0.61 acres per head, whereas the U.S. figure is 199 acres, or 327 times as much. The seriousness of the problem becomes apparent when one considers that in the commercial grain producing areas, cultivable land per head is only 0.16–0.32 acres or even less.

Chinese agriculture has always been a question of eking out an existence from severely limited resources. In this kind of small-scale production, the death of one cow may ruin a farmer, and the minimal resources available for production are inevitably divided into smaller and smaller units. The problem is exacerbated by increases in the price of materials for agricultural production and the products of rural industry that undercut increases in the price of agricultural products. In recent years price increases for rural industrial products have exceeded the overall income increase over the last 30 years, putting a heavy strain on peasants and urban residents alike.

The result has been to create suspicion of reform, especially among the peasants who are ill-equipped to deal with such pressures. It also puts those who support reform in a difficult position. They want to leave agriculture and attempt other enterprises, but they also know that they cannot withstand the pressures caused by unclear and changeable policies, which makes them very reluctant to risk leaving the land for other occupations.

Moreover, the danger of the strain on the cities that would result from massive peasant migration was the origin of the policy of "leaving the soil but not the village." But this just means that the peasants now pursue two occupations at the same time and do neither well. In fact, since agricultural reform began in 1979, specialization among agricultural households has progressed very slowly, while at the same time between 2% and 5% of the farmland has been left fallow. Many individual peasants do not want to give up their land to create larger units, but neither are they prepared to devote all their energy to farming. This is obviously a serious impediment to the introduction of advanced technology, the organization of large-scale production, and the transfer of labor out of agriculture which is intended to be the next phase of reform.

Many issues are linked in complex ways, and the transfer of rural population is not simply a matter of moving from the rural areas. For example, between 1979 and 1984, about 55 million people left the villages and went into township enterprises. There was no conception of systematic town planning in these county towns, and people built all over the place with no thought to providing the necessary educational, hygiene and cultural facilities. Almost 14 million acres of farmland were lost in the process, more than 11 times what would have been lost by letting the same number of people migrate to the cities.[20]

One important reason why the freeing of prices for agricultural products has been obstructed and peasants have been unable to dispel their wariness of reform is that the system of exchange for rural commodities is chaotic, with no clear regulations or organization regarding ownership, commercial management, and the market. In this situation, small scale producers are unable to sustain the risks involved in market competition and are forced to return to subsistence farming. In some areas, the number of specialized households has sharply declined due to the excessively harsh taxation and restrictive regulations imposed on them.

Moreover, the imperfection of the market mechanism means that speculators are in a good position to profit from unclear market signals, and can make huge profits by doubling the price on certain products. This increases the burden on peasants as far as consumption is concerned, and is a great impediment to reform.[21] This leads to situations like that in 1987 when many large cities, including Beijing, Tianjin, and Shanghai, had reintroduced rationing for sugar and oil. This is the result of the failure of production to keep up with demand, and the lack of clear market signals.

It may fairly be said that agriculture is at the root of the problems in China's current reforms. The greatest question hanging over reform is that there is no rational way to transfer real surplus labor out of agriculture, but reform is also hindered by the circular effect of periodic increases in the price of agricultural sideline products. In 1980 and 1985, the state twice increased the procurement price of agricultural sideline products by a large margin, and this was followed by subsidies, all of which caused a defensive reaction from industry. Bonuses were raised, subsidies increased, and one by one these were added to production costs. This finally resulted in massive annual inflation of the retail price index which occurred in 1988 and 1989.

If the peasants had enough leeway to enable them to respond flexibly to market signals, upgrade technology, and expand production, then they would be able to pull the whole reform out of this wild inflationary trend. But unfortunately they do not have that kind of flexibility: the paltry strip of land they do have is shrinking and deteriorating, and the nutrients in the soil are being rapidly exhausted. The transfer of the labor force has meant the departure of the most productive workers, who also have taken capital with them. By 1985, 70% of all agricultural accumulation capital was being transferred to non-agricultural production.

When a peasant leaves the land and it is contracted to others, these farming contractors further damage the already infertile ground. Because they do not own the land they farm, they use unsound methods, sacrificing the soil to achieve short-term goals. In the vast backward areas of the country, minimal advances in the crude economy are being made at the cost of the serious damage to the environment, the ecosystem, and natural resources. In Guizhou, for example, one of the first provinces to introduce liberal ideas and implement the contract system in 1979, over 180,000 acres of forest were destroyed in the brief three year period between 1980 and 1982—destruction on a scale matched only during the Great Leap Forward.

It is easy to understand that the problem of agricultural reform in China is tied up with the whole culture, and involves education, customs, the level of science and technology, the environment and other basic conditions. It is certainly not a task that can be accomplished overnight. The main difficulty is that the potential of small scale production has been exhausted, while a smooth transition to large scale production has not yet been made. It is essential to go back and build up the agricultural infrastructure.

Practical measures must be taken to concentrate land in the hands of competent farmers. Scientific methods of cultivation must be introduced, and surplus labor must be transferred to agricultural infrastructure projects, including the management of the environment, hydroelectric projects, transportation, and the development of agricultural technology, so that a base can be built up for the next stage of development.

It is essential to realize that China's agricultural development is starting from a very weak base. There are many hidden dangers and the road ahead will be slow and arduous. We must not be carried away by the early achievements of reform, and it must be understood that only hard work, not self-congratulation, can save us.

6

WRANGLING AT THE WINDOW TO THE OUTSIDE WORLD

The primary economic purpose of China's current open door policy is to bring in foreign capital and technology, and it has been the most popular policy in over 30 years. In fact, however, it is far from an unmitigated success.

Importing is not new to China. To say nothing of its long history of importation, the country has already experienced four big import drives since the founding of the People's Republic in 1949. In the 1950s, China imported from the Soviet Union and Eastern Europe, with the famous "156" engineering projects being the major focus. In the 1960s technology and equipment were imported from Japan and Western Europe, but although 84 contracts were signed, the total value of the completed deals was only US$280 million. In the early 1970s imports from Western Europe continued and there was the "43 Plan," which entailed investing US$4.3 billion to import 43 large lines of equipment. The emphasis was still on complete lines of equipment. In 1976 the fourth round of imports commenced, and in 1978 alone, 120 contracts for complete lines of equipment were hurriedly signed with Europe, the United States, and Japan. These included 22 major engineering projects like the Baogang steel works in Shanghai. Of total imports, complete lines of equipment accounted for 89% in the 1950s, 91% in the 1960s, and 95% between 1978 and 1979.[1] In economic terms, the imports of the 1950s were the most effective, even though the Soviet Union later reneged on contracts [following the Sino-Soviet split]. Those of the 1960s were less productive, and those of the 1970s even worse, but the "Western Leap Forward" of 1978 was the most disastrous. The fact that the economic benefits of imports seemed to be declining with each round should have been sufficient to provoke serious reflection, which makes it all the more incredible that after the fall of the Gang of Four, great damage was inflicted on the economy by repeating the same mistake again.

After 1982, at least it was finally understood that we should concentrate on technology imports. Economic targets were set for imports which focused on "High technology, high efficiency, and high foreign currency earnings" and "Making foreign investment, industry and export markets priorities." The "Three Highs" and the "Three Priorities," as they came to be known, were the economic goals of the policy of opening to the world. What actually happened, however, was another matter altogether. China's cultural tradition is like that. Everything sounds beautiful, and in theory it is quite correct; there are no loopholes and it all seems appealing. But actual behavior leaves much to be desired, and the results are far from what was envisioned. When that happens, yet another splendid new theory appears, only to fail again when it is put into practice. Due to the fondness for generalization which is characteristic of Chinese culture, it is not thought necessary to analyze the environment, specific circumstances, and other destabilizing factors that bring about this discrepancy between theory and practice.

But let us turn to some realities. In the six years between 1979 and 1984, China signed 3,605 contracts with various foreign countries, bringing in the equivalent of US$17.2 billion, or 15% of the total national investment in capital construction over the same period. But complete lines of equipment accounted for 80% of this and single items for 17%. Technology imports, which were supposed to be the priority, accounted for only 3%.[2] The US$17.2 billion was used to set up 20 or 30 large-scale enterprises and to reform more than a thousand medium- and small-scale ones. This sounds fine until one considers what kind of projects they were: high-class hotels, expensive bars and nightclubs, luxury consumer goods, amusement parks, and expensive household electrical goods. Consumption. Consumption is still what it is all about.

Historically, China resisted intrusions from outside. This time, however, China has opened the door herself, and events have reached a different stage. This time we have woken up to the lure of modern materialist civilization but, unfortunately, we have immediately turned into worshipers of Mammon, and have exchanged a superstitious belief in a "red" world for an equally unrealistic vision of a "golden" one, substituting our naive faith in spiritual values for an equally simplistic materialism devoid of all human feeling.

It is even more disturbing that in the midst of this great transformation, some people seem to be intent on promoting foreign products at the expense of domestic ones. This has gone so far that even laundries, bathhouses, photo booths, and breakfast stands all compete for the honor of using imported equipment. "Assembled from Japanese Parts" is now the fashionable tag on Chinese-made goods, and it is hard to say whether this is any more ridiculous than "Export Goods for Local Sale," which was the previous free advertisement for foreign products.

China is supposed to be importing technology, but in fact it is importing consumer goods. Imports are supposed to stimulate industrial development, but in fact they merely promote a high level of consumption. In a very short time the goal of the import drive was diverted from production to consumption. Everyone swears they are determined to work hard to catch up with the rest of the world, but in fact their obsession with profit has blinded them to all else. People shout slogans about "modernization" and then go back to making a fast buck. We seem to be prepared to risk everything in an attempt to cure the chronic shortage of consumer goods with huge infusions of imports, but the result has been rapid growth, high investment, a large deficit, and the serious devaluation of the currency.

In this context it is informative to examine the case of Guangdong, a province whose foreign investment accounts for more than half the national total. By 1984, Guangdong had imported 57 video recorder production lines with an annual production capacity of more than 50 million sets, and 17 color television production lines with an annual production capacity of 1.85 million sets, both of which vastly exceeded the market demand.

Another telling example of the trend towards high consumption is the luxury hotels, restaurants, and tourist attractions that can be found all over the province. There are at least 13 "Disney-style" amusement parks alone, all of them established with foreign investment. There are seven just on the road from Shenzhen to Guangzhou, and another billion dollars in foreign exchange has already been spent on others in the pipeline. All these amusement parks are more or less the same. The foreign tourists have seen it all before and are not interested in them; the real target is the domestic market. Yet a visit to the "Oriental Pleasure Park" in Guangzhou, which includes all the various attractions, would cost 50 or 60 yuan, well beyond the range of the average family in the People's Republic.

Currently, many of these luxury amusement parks earn barely enough to pay the engineers and the water and electricity bills. It is also strange that while they are empty much of the time, on public holidays thousands of buses arrive bearing hordes of visitors. A closer look reveals that most are there at public expense. This could be said to be another "Chinese characteristic." It is like a conjuring trick: the state takes money out of one pocket, puts it into another, and then proclaims that "the situation is excellent and we have made a fortune."

In fact, even in the production sphere, Guangzhou has imported more hardware than software, and even less patented technology. Over the last few years, Guangdong's imports have been predominantly equipment, production lines, and assembly lines. They are mostly for processing, and the relevant information and instructions are often lacking or incomplete. All this adds to the real cost of imported equipment and also affects the ability to absorb it successfully into the economy, thereby reducing the benefits.

Fujian province, the second biggest importer in the country, approved 407 import projects in the category of technology imports in 1979–1984, but in fact only three projects—car parts (piston rings), vaccines, and one related to refrigerator production—were true technology imports. The three projects totalled US$3.6 million and amounted to only 1.15% of the total investment in imports.[3]

Over the last few years, Fujian has imported 14 high-frequency electronics production lines, 100 plastic-casting machines, several dozen sewing machine lines, and a similar quantity of refrigeration equipment. This has made the increase in Fujian's total industrial output value the second highest in the country and Fujian the fastest-developing province. However, the situation is not quite as healthy as it appears, and it would be well to restrain our enthusiasm.

One problem which has already come to light is that enterprises based on imported equipment are unable to resell their products overseas and have to depend on favorable currency exchange rates for their profit. When foreign exchange is in short supply, such enterprises either have to continue operating at a loss, stop production and keep paying interest on their loans, or do nothing and wait to go bankrupt.

Fujian researcher Xia Yang's investigation of six factories in Zhangzhou that imported equipment revealed that the Zhangzhou Refrigerator Factory, Washing Machine Factory, Brewery, Preserved Fruit Factory and Number 1 and Number 5 Wireless Factories spent a total worth US$1.63 million on imported equipment.[4] However, the spare parts and accessories needed for production—from transistors and feed wires to soft paper for packaging—all had to be imported, at an annual cost of US$4.98 million. Meanwhile, the products could only be sold on the domestic market.

The preserved fruit factory and the brewery were forced to

borrow to pay off their debts, and ended up owing the bank 1.3 million yuan in loans for equipment on which the annual interest payments are 90,000 yuan. They estimated that it would take 10 years to recoup the cost of the equipment and they still had to spend US$400,000 to stay in production. The refrigerator and washing machine factories found themselves in a similar position. To produce 50,000 machines a year, they have to spend US$3.43 million in foreign exchange annually. Such a situation naturally causes a loss of foreign exchange and adds to the foreign exchange deficit in the area.

This reverse was inevitable, as can be seen from the example of Mitsubishi two-cylinder washing machines that were imported from Japan. At the official exchange rate of 1 to 2.83, each machine cost 510 yuan (US$74.66 paid in foreign exchange). The ex-factory price was 570 yuan, yielding a net profit of 69 yuan and an average profit of 0.8 yuan per U.S. dollar invested. However, if foreign currency is bought at the floating exchange rate, it costs 162 yuan more per machine. This means a loss of 102 yuan on each machine, a loss rate of almost 18% and a loss per U.S. dollar of 1.36 yuan. When enterprises like this claim to be making money, many are in fact relying on handouts from the state.

In 1985, the six factories mentioned above estimated they would need US$4.98 million in foreign exchange to maintain production. On that basis, calculated at the floating exchange rate (of 1 to 5), they lost 4.7 million yuan. They had to stop production and keep paying interest on the loans they took out to purchase the equipment while waiting for the foreign exchange transaction to be approved.

The problem is reflected throughout the country. By October 1984, there were already more than a million video recorders stored in warehouses nationwide, and the market for calculators, refrigerators, and washing machines was more or less the same. The situation for color televisions was even worse. The Commercial Bank of China estimated that in 1984, 41 assembly plants nationwide had imported 37 color television production lines. With them all in operation, the yearly output would be 5.55 million sets, but in early 1985, the Ministry of Commerce had already ordered 2 million color televisions from abroad. So in 1985 an estimated 5 million televisions hit a domestic market with a demand for only around 3 million.[5]

Currently, more than a hundred color television production lines have already been imported nationwide. The black and white television production lines that had just come out did not even get a foothold before they were pushed out of the market by color sets, and the transition from black and white to color televisions took place in record time. However, one should note that in Shanghai, for example, it costs US$100 to produce one color TV and US$50 million to maintain plant production for one year. Of the 20 production lines in the whole of Shanghai, only seven were running in 1987, because of a shortage of foreign exchange.

A great deal of the technology that is imported is not put to efficient use. We have already seen how Wuhan imported a "650" steel rolling workshop (see chapter 3) and then let it stand idle for seven years, and how a factory in Nanjing spent around US$2.5 million to buy two machine tools and then left them in storage for eight or nine years. In 1984, a factory in Beijing imported a US$6.6 million silicon chip production line which was scrapped as soon as it went into operation, and another factory spent US$3 million on a press, and then only used one month's capacity each year. Two-thirds of the color television and refrigerator assembly lines imported nationwide have been left unused, and the utilization rate of other imported large machinery and computer systems is even lower.[6]

The nation's leaders are not unaware of the situation. Former Communist Party General Secretary Zhao Ziyang reported to the party's central committee in 1985 following his personal inspection of the Pearl River Delta area, that "importing equipment and raw materials to produce 'foreign goods' and then selling them at a profit on the domestic market, is not the right way to go, and the profits to be made by using large quantities of foreign exchange to import luxury consumer goods will not last. Trade protectionism is rearing its head all over the world, competition is stiff, and there is little chance of being able to resell processed goods abroad to pay off foreign debts either." From this one can appreciate the seriousness of the problem.

It is not only in the open coastal regions that imports are taking the wrong direction. The most striking example is the massive importation of automobiles. No objection can be made to importing vehicles for production-related purposes, but all kinds of institutions and enterprises pride themselves on having imported sedan cars. In 1987, an automobile engineer who attended the People's Congress stared in amazement at the rows of Japanese Hondas lined up outside the Great Hall of the People and remarked, "Before, we always used to drive Chinese-made cars, but at the last three congresses we have been driving foreign ones."

As many foreign cars were imported in 1985 as in the whole period from 1950 to 1979. By 1986, almost all Chinese-made cars had been replaced by foreign imports. In Jiangxi province alone, 1,500 sedans worth US$6 million were imported in the 18 months prior to September 1985. More than 5 billion dollars was spent on importing cars between 1982 and 1986: four times the total investment in the domestic auto industry nationwide. According to a report in the *Zhongguo laonian bao* (China's Seniors)(14 June 1989), China had already spent a total of US$13 billion importing 1.3 million automobiles.

▌ Imported Technology Is Hard to Absorb

The painful consequences of the rash import drive lie all around us. The problem is that modern imported equipment needs an appropriate and equally modern technological environment, but we have overestimated our own ability to absorb and utilize it. The skills, management, and the whole social system itself match the backwardness of our old, outmoded equipment. For too long there have been no strict requirements concerning quality, efficiency, and large scale production, and because we do not have the conceptual basis for absorbing and utilizing the imported equipment, much of it stops functioning properly as soon as it falls into our hands. Add to that difficulties with energy supplies and transportation, and the poor quality of the social services that accompany them, and it is inevitable that we should to come grief.

The preserved fruit factory and the brewery in Zhangzhou which imported equipment originally had contracts to pay for it using four years' worth of products, but because the equipment did not function properly and there were changes in the international market, the products could not be sold abroad, and they were forced to break off their contracts. Three electrical power plants—Zouhe in Tangshan, Dagang in Tianjin, and Yuanbaoshan in Inner Mongolia—imported equipment from Japan, Italy, and France which was of 1970s standard and worked regularly. Under Chinese management, however, coal consumption for every kilowatt-hour of electricity produced reached 353.7 grams (the corresponding figure for domestic plants is 471 grams), considerably higher than in countries like Japan or the Soviet Union.[7]

China imported a complete line of ethylene manufacturing equipment from Japan with an output capacity of 300,000 tons. In the same installation in Japan, one operator can produce 337 tons, but in China one operator produces only 144 tons. This is not surprising, because the technical level of workers in China is far below the standards of the industrialized nations.

Imported technology also strains the energy supply. A steel-rolling mill in Wuhan that imported equipment but could not get the energy supply to operate has become an international joke. There was a similar case in Sichuan, where equipment was imported from Japan and around 700 million yuan invested in a vinylon factory, but the diversion of all the natural gas used by the Chongqing steel works was still not sufficient to meet even half its production needs.

Imports are often made without consideration of the marketability of the product. Pingdingshan in Henan province invested a billion yuan to import a curtain material factory with an annual production capacity of 13,000 tons, but so far there is no market for the product. The Jinling Hotel in Nanjing was set up with foreign investment, but no one dared to take it over because its annual occupancy rate was less than 50%, even though it was the only hotel serving foreign tourists and overseas Chinese visiting Nanjing.

Poor management is also a major factor in the inability to absorb foreign technology. Among the vast number of enterprise managers in China, many are incompetent amateurs who waste time arguing over trifles and use outdated management techniques. Staff are also poorly trained, while overstaffing is common. In the United States, for example, a chemical fertilizer plant with an annual capacity of 300,000 tons of synthetic ammonia has a staff of only about 50, whereas a similar plant in China employs almost 2,000. One electric power station in China using imported advanced technology employed 1,112 staff, of whom only 193 were operators and 387 were administrators and managers or worked in construction and agriculture. Furthermore, after the modern equipment was introduced, the number of staff increased rather than decreased.[8]

Sophisticated imported machinery requires fewer staff and a high level of performance, but the low-wage, high-employment policy which tolerates low efficiency levels is still in place. Failing to recognize our own limitations, we are now left with imported equipment that our outdated system of management cannot absorb.

Attempts to introduce foreign management techniques are not always successful either. Because it was said that many large overseas firms use the technique of "specialization and coordination," this method was incorporated into reforms in China without proper consideration whether it was appropriate. The Daqing chemical fertilizer factory, which imported equipment from the United States, reorganized according to the principles of specialization and coordination, and reassigned all the backup workshops and cultural and service units to the parent Daqing chemical factory. The original staff of 1,520 was reduced to 315, but after a year, production had fallen and problems developed. There was too much specialization and not enough coordination, and the factory had to return to the old system.

Political and military factors are the first consideration when deciding where to locate industries in China, and after that everyone expects a share of the pie. If 13 chemical fertilizer plants are imported at the same time, then one goes to each province, and narrow ideas about equality are satisfied at the expense of efficiency.

At the government level, too, the management of imports is very strange. The science and technology development plan is set by the Committee for Science and Technology, but specific technology imports are proposed by the Economic Commission and the Planning Commission. What passes for "management" is really just an approval process. It is not an appropriate system for absorbing the technology, let alone an effective framework to enforce appropriate regulations.

Most of the large delegations sent overseas to evaluate foreign technology are either on sightseeing or shopping trips. *People's Daily* (16 June 1985) reported that the staff of one government ministry had made more than 4,000 trips abroad by June 1985. "Buyers" who are allowed to spend large sums of foreign exchange to purchase foreign goods—they could probably even get away with buying door handles or bed pans—fail to provide the financial or personnel help needed to utilize and maintain the imports.

It would be fine if these buyers lived up to their names, but unfortunately they cannot even manage that. In 1985 for example, Shanghai imported beancurd processing equipment and technology from Japan, and we actually sent a special "Beancurd Evaluation Mission" to France, apparently without even realizing that beancurd is quintessentially Chinese. Not surprisingly, the result was high prices and inferior quality. Another of the many strange examples of foreign trade is the factory in Xian that found a pair of calipers marked "Made in China" among some new equipment imported from England. They were actually made in Shaanxi and sold at a domestic price of only 63 yuan, compared to the import price of 400 yuan which they fetched when imported back to their country of origin.

Everyone agrees that we should have our own Chinese way of adapting ideas from outside, but when it comes to imported equipment, the crucial question is whether it can be effectively absorbed. The early success of the Japanese did not depend merely on importing, but rather on investing considerable capital in absorbing what they bought. It is useless to harp about the need for "Chinese characteristics" unless we are prepared to dedicate the time and energy necessary to create our own special style.

■ Foreign Investment: A Difficult Partnership

A famous American strategic research institute once calculated that the maximum amount of foreign capital China could safely absorb would be around US$100 billion. The danger point would come around US$150 billion, and going beyond that would put the nation on the path to a debt crisis like that of Poland or Brazil. In fact, from the time of the proclamation of the "Foreign Joint Investment and Enterprise Management Law of the PRC" in September 1979 until 1985, the total of foreign investment was only US$21.6 billion, with only 44% of agreed investment directly invested. Much of it came in during the hectic period of liberalization between 1984 and 1985. In 1986 only US$3.3 billion was invested, down 50% from 1985, and only in 1989 did it rise back near the 1985 level.

Furthermore, most of the foreign investment came from Hong Kong. (In 1989, Hong Kong still accounted for over 60% of all foreign investment.) According to statistics for the period up to June 1984, over 80% of the 370 firms that entered the People's Republic during six years of the opening up policy were from Hong Kong. However, the return on investments was poorer than in South America, and even further behind other regions of Asia. In 1987, 50% of the joint ventures and jointly operated ventures were in the hotel sector.[9] The others were mostly small scale, labor intensive industries. Investment in major ventures related to production, information, or technology were comparatively rare, as were investments by non-Chinese firms.

Despite the huge domestic market, the removal of most obstacles to investment, and what are considered to be very liberal tax regulations, China has still not managed to attract investment from major financial consortiums. One reason for this is that the generous tax benefits for foreign businesses are not of much practical use because many foreign investors have to compensate for the tax breaks and special treatment in China by paying more tax in their home countries.

But the main difficulty lies in the goals of potential foreign investors and the risks involved in investing in China. These two topics provoked some interesting responses at an international academic conference on the use of foreign investment held in Hangzhou in March 1985. At that meeting, Chu Baotai, deputy director of the Foreign Investment Management Bureau of the Ministry of Foreign Economic Relations and Trade said, "It is in the common interest of both Chinese entrepreneurs and foreigners who invest in China to take advantage of the foreign investment available and ensure that all foreign investment is profitable."

Chu Baotai's comment was a very fine-sounding generalization but unfortunately it disguised the main point, which is that although both parties aspire to profit, their methods are in fact mutually contradictory, which makes it hard for them to get along. What foreign investors want is access to China's domestic market: they come to make money. But China wants them to bring in technology, management, and capital to help earn foreign exchange. These are contradictory goals which are difficult to reconcile. It presently looks as if China will eventually have to adopt a policy of exchanging market access for technology. In fact, most foreign-invested enterprises have already started to adjust their operations automatically in response to the fact that overseas sales are less profitable than domestic ones. This is a dangerous trend, but it is not clear whether the government has yet found a policy to deal with it.

At the same conference on foreign investment, a Chinese scholar declared that "of all the developing countries, the noneconomic risks of investing in China are the lowest. No other country can compete." This reflects the belief of many Chinese experts that as soon as the opening policy was declared, noneconomic risks would melt away. In fact, China's investment environment is difficult, and it is likely to continue to deteriorate for some time, because although China is taking measures to improve the investment climate, the pace of these reforms will lag behind that of liberalization.

Foreign businessmen operating in China may encounter the following risks: ignorant and arrogant bureaucrats who undermine the investor's control by excessive interference in the management of the business; the inability to predict changes in the availability of external factors like energy, transportation, materials, and engineering; the inability to cope with policies emanating from numerous different sources which impose restrictions of a non-market nature; the controversial problem of repatriating profits; lost opportunities due to the excessively slow decision-making process; the low competence of technicians and workers, which results in decreased productivity and increased production costs; the dearth of specialized technical staff, and the lack of competent middle-level managers.

It has to be admitted that the noneconomic risks involved in investing in China are greater than those in North America, Western Europe, and certain regions of Southeast Asia. Only when we recognize this can we make a determined commitment to improve the investment climate in China. Obviously, an urgent task for this decade is to learn how to do business with foreign firms in a sincere, fair, and economically intelligent manner.

■ The Export Situation

If the import drive has been unproductive, then China's performance with regard to exports has been even more incomprehensible.

Consider the example of Guangdong, supposedly the leading province in foreign trade. Since 1979, Guangdong's foreign trade has doubled each year—hardly a bad performance, and no one expected the good times could end. Starting in 1981, however, the cost of foreign currency grew yearly and losses in foreign trade mounted steadily. In 1980, the exchange rate was less than 2.8 yuan per dollar,.but a year later it had risen 5.7%, and by 1983 it was 32.8% higher than in 1980. The result was that increased exports only meant higher losses. Export losses in 1982 were 9.7 times higher than in 1981, and 90% higher again in 1982. That resulted in the forced restriction of exports, and from 1982 to 1984 the value of exports decreased yearly by 2.02%, 13.46%, and 34% respectively.[10]

In 1984 China's total exports constituted only 1.25% of the total value of world exports, far below what would be expected for such a large country.[11] The fundamental problem was the poor quality of the products and the small range of goods available. Prices were low but goods were still not competitive, and outdated equipment and technology were coupled with bad management and lack of adaptability. The unified state procurement and distribution system was too rigid, and resulted in production units taking the profits because the state itself paid the production units higher prices than their goods would fetch on the international market. Moreover, after decentralization of the authority to engage in foreign trade, provinces and cities saw cutthroat competition for export contracts, and Guangdong alone reduced prices 34% due to this.

The management situation became even more strange: the number of loss-making exports greatly increased (60.8% in 1982, an increase of more than 21% over 1979); the yearly capital turnover rate fell (it was 1.4 in 1983, 0.35 times less than in 1981),[12] while the number of intermediaries grew. Fewer contracts are met, scant attention is paid to market research, and the bureaucracy continues to swell. The incompetence and irresponsibility of some officials, and the pervasive influence of bureaucratism and self-interest can hardly be exaggerated. This is compounded by an oppressive tax policy (more overtime means higher taxes and less pay overall) and the fact that exporting finished products is less profitable than exporting semi-finished products and raw materials.

Agricultural raw materials and manufactured products (including textiles) have long constituted about 32% of total exports, and oil, chemicals, machinery, transportation equipment, and other export goods account for only about one-fifth of the total. According to some foreign forecasters, the relatively slow growth of China's agricultural production and the need to raise domestic living standards will restrict the growth of exports for quite a long time to come.

But the Chinese never work on the basis of a comprehensive analysis of all the factors involved, preferring instead to imagine the situation as they would like it to be. Statistics published in 1985 predicted that over the following six years the total value of foreign trade would grow by an average of 23.5%, of which exports would grow by 27% and imports by 21%.[13] Exports did in fact increase from US$27.35 billion in 1985 to US$51.69 billion in 1990. But this performance is not as impressive as it appears. China exports mostly middle- and low-grade products, light industrial and agricultural products, and traditional goods like textiles. Heavy industrial goods, and new or expensive product lines continue to account for a much smaller proportion of the total. [In 1989, according to official reports, power and special industrial machinery comprised only 1.2% of the value of China's exports. By contrast, raw materials and agricultural products accounted for 28.7% and clothing alone was 11.7%.]

Here is a telling example. Heilongjiang Province produces 32,000 tons of flax annually, but has only one flax mill which can absorb 7,000 tons of raw hemp annually in the production of fine linen cloth. The remainder of the flax is bought by the state at high prices of 4734–4997 yuan a ton and then exported at low prices of 1466–2258 yuan. In this way 2739–3307 yuan is lost on every ton exported, and every year the province as a whole loses 70 or 80 million yuan. At the same time, there is a national shortage of linen cloth, which is imported at the steep price of US$8.4 per square meter. If the flax were not exported, 2000 meters of linen worth US$16,800 could be spun from each ton. As it is, the import price is more than 10 times that of the export price.[14]

Such situations are common knowledge, and criticisms are made, but the situation simply seems to get worse. According to media reports, in 1983 Shanghai imported 200,000 tons of steel billet at US$211 per ton, and exported 200,000 tons of processed steel products at US$202 per ton. The loss from the difference between the import and export prices was US$1.8 million, and the financial subsidy was more than 30 million yuan. Apart from this, energy costs for transporting the steel were equivalent to 100,000 tons of coal, and 500,000 tons of harbor handling capacity was taken up, not not to mention the use of water resources and the pollution involved. These are the incredible losses the country was forced to bear just for the sake of an *apparent* increase of 1.2 billion yuan in the value of industrial output.

As a result of uncontrolled imports, the ineffective export policy, and the sharp decline in foreign exchange reserves, there was a foreign trade deficit of US$13.78 billion in 1985, equal to over 52% of total exports.[15] In 1985 the foreign trade deficit reached US$14.9 billion. In 1988 it was $3.4 billion, in 1989, $6.5 billion. In addition, the reckless pursuit of rapid growth whipped up by the slogan of quadrupling output increased the pressure on the raw materials and semi-finished products, which in turn stimulated demand for imports. At the peak of the opening policy, from 1984 to 1985, 70% of China's foreign exchange was lost.[16] In his book, *Zhongguo waimao fanying de yanzhong wenti* (Serious Problems Reflected in China's Foreign Trade), Hong Kong scholar Chen Wenhong analyzed many facets of the situation and made the acute observation that the strategy of import-driven industrial development has already become "imported industrialization."[17]

It was all this that led Chen Muhua, Director of the People's Bank of China, to announce the devaluation of the yuan by 15.8% in July 1986. It was hoped that this sizeable devaluation of the currency would stimulate exports and stem the foreign exchange deficit. It remains to be seen whether higher exports will continue to mean higher losses. According to the Foreign Trade Ministry's plan, the value of imports and exports should quadruple by the year 2000, reaching US$160 billion. (It reached $US84.05 billion in 1990.) That is an average yearly increase of 7.5%, but if nothing is done about this strange practice of exporting "suicidal products," one shudders to think what is in store.

The export problems are related to the insufficient number of bases, outdated infrastructure and equipment, and the dearth of skilled personnel. Up to 1986, China had established a total of 132 export processing zones, and 198 specialized factories and workshops producing industrial goods for export, but these could only provide about 30% of the total annual exports. In addition, inadequate transportation, communications, and living quarters have hindered the ability to sign and fulfill contracts, and resulted in late delivery of goods, in price reductions, and in enforced domestic sales. Few foreign trade experts have been trained in China for a long time, and now they are scarcer than ever. Those there are have not been evenly assigned to different sectors of the international market, which means that many markets have not yet been exploited and it is even more difficult to set up multinational companies overseas.

▌ The Big Dispute over Special Economic Zones

In 1979, on hearing for the first time that the so-called Special Economic Zones (SEZs) were going to be set up, most Chinese were rather startled. But the concept has had a history of over 400 years.

Since the town of Leghorn on the northwestern coast of Italy was designated as a "free harbor" in 1547, up until 1980, there had been at least 350 such setups around the world. A dazzling variety of names had been invented for such places as well, ranging from free-trade zones, free-tax zones, processing and export zones, investment enhancement zones, to free-border zones, etc.

The slogan in China then for the SEZ was "new styles for new businesses; special policies for special circumstances; maintain the old principles; completely rejuvenate the methods." The intent was quite laudable. But it must not be forgotten that over the first 30 years of the history of the People's Republic, every single slogan that was put out had been based on some laudable intentions. And in the end we suffered from the empty emphasis on spirit, intent, and imagination; and from complete oblivion to conditions, methods, and sequences. Shenzhen, as the leading model among the new SECs, has been essentially launched forward in a style resembling the same grandiose hype, so prevalent in the past, that involved paying dear prices only for the embellishment of some shiny images.

The skyscrapers of Shenzhen, when they first sprang up from the ground, looked so chic, so proud. Shenzhen's efficiency, its speed and its people, suddenly became the vogue. All around the country, men and women, young and old, tens of thousands in number, rushed to Shenzhen by every possible means. Not a small number of them were once pious pilgrims, with their little red books, traveling north to Dazhai, the famous model agricultural community that emphasized strict egalitarianism and collective action. Now they are packing into what was once a tiny little village in the south, in big hordes, looking to exchange some foreign currency and take a few deep breaths of the perfumed-filled air that drifts over from the other shore, the gold-plated island of Hong Kong. I don't know whether there is any other country in the world that is willing to incur, from the pockets of its own state treasury, the expense of sending tens of thousands of people to tour either a wretchedly poor village in the mountains, or to view some new skyscrapers that line but two or three streets.

In May 1984, Liang Xiang, mayor of Shenzhen, made a report on the accomplishments of his city at the Second Plenary of the

National People's Congress. Headlines hit the newspapers all around the nation with the following title: "In Four Years, the Total Assets Have Surpassed the Aggregate of the Last 30 Years!" According to the report, the total value of industrial production in Shenzhen, as of the year 1983, reached 673 million yuan, which amounted to 10.7 times the total value for the entire 29 years prior to the initiation of the SEZ.[18] In other words, every one of the four years hence produced the equivalent of 310 times each one of the 29 years prior! Seemingly another "unprecedented miracle" was in the making. The chorus of the new "Shenzhen Model" was getting louder. But if economic development were such a simple matter, humanity would have been spared considerable sorrow.

Late in that same year, at a conference for the development strategy of the SEZs held in Shenzhen, this author discussed with many other participants of the conference the hidden dangers behind the ongoing "model craze." Unfortunately at that moment the nationwide hail of the "tremendous Shenzhen success" was in full swing. And within the Chinese cultural context, to utter a "no" at such moments would be quite unseemly.

Granted, between 1978 and 1983, the total value of industry and agriculture in Shenzhen expanded five times, and among those two sectors the value of industrial production multiplied by a factor of 12. But it would be simplistic to gasp in awe and call it a "miracle." The expansion had been a fantastic result of the juxtaposition of a series of circumstances, timing and conditions, all of which were highly artificial. The logic behind the spectacle bore resemblance to a fairyland, something only the modern Chinese, so bent on creating gigantic propaganda models, could produce. Over the last few decades, whenever a certain "model" was in swing, who could dare a "no" and avoid the wrath of collective indictments?

It was beyond all belief that there could be a complete reversal of mood so shortly after. In just a few months, a big debate hit the floor on "whether the Shenzhen experience signifies a success or a failure."

The first one to raise the issue was Dr. Chen Wenhong of Hong Kong University Asian Research Center. He gave a large list of disturbing statistics and exposed a series of severe questions in his article "What Is the Problem with Shenzhen?" *(see table 6.1)*

First of all, the speed of Shenzhen's development was largely propped up by increased investments in the sector of construction. As of 1983, for example, of the total 720 million yuan in industrial production, almost 600 million was accounted for by building construction.[19] Over the five and a half years of Shenzhen's development, the total industrial production minus the value of the construction

	1978	1979	1980	1981	1982	1983	1984—1st 1/2
Total value of Output	170	146	189	340-370		870	
Total Industrial Ouput	60	61	84	243	362	720	555
Total Agricultural Output	87	86		105	135-141	150	
Investment in Capital Construction		50	125	270	633	886	603
Real Investment of Foreign Capital (mil. HK$)		120	250	590	880	1,130	590
Fiscal Income of the Locality	20	35	55	118-130	163	296	190
Foreign Exchange Income of the Locality		28	48	40-61	56	67	105
Total Retail Sales	117	148	220	350	554	1,251	861

sector amounted to a mere 230 million yuan, of which the year 1983 alone took up about 100 million. It is not such an impressive record.

Secondly, the total value of the consumer products sold in Shenzhen repeatedly surpassed the total value of the production, in both agriculture and industry. In 1979, the first figure was only 2 million yuan over the second figure, or less than 1% over. Not much change in that discrepancy occurred over 1980–82 period, either. But in 1983 the first figure surpassed the second by a daunting 380 million yuan, or almost by 50%. If the comparison is to be made between the total consumption and the total industrial production alone, the discrepancy was in favor of the total consumption by 530 million yuan, or 74%. The first half of 1984 showed the same discrepancy by about 310 million yuan, or 56%. There are other sources which indicate that, despite the significant development of industry in Shenzhen as of 1984, the total industrial production was still well below 1/4 of the total production of all sectors.[20] That was a major departure from the original intent of "relying mainly on new industries."

As of the year 1983, the per capita total annual sale of consumer products in Shenzhen (including the floating population of about 300,000) came up as high as 4,170 yuan. That was much higher than the same per capita for the same period in other major cities: 912 yuan for Shanghai; 896 yuan for Beijing; 504 yuan for Guangzhou. The miracle of the huge sales had been created essentially by the constant inflow of tourists, of the type portrayed earlier, from other inland areas, standing anywhere from 10,000 to 20,000 per day. The superficial prosperity of Shenzhen was thus generated by the consumption expense by people from other parts of China, based on the commercial advantage secured by special regulations and policies. It should be quite clear to everyone that this type of growth is by no means sustainable.

Furthermore, the figures show that the spending in the construction sector has not been composed primarily of foreign investments, as originally hoped for. In fact, the comparative ratio of foreign investments was 30% or less, and has shown a trend towards gradual decrease. As of 1983, the enterprises established jointly with other cities and provinces in China made up 82% of the total value of industrial assets. The weight of the domestic investment is much heavier on the scale.[22]

The interesting irony is that, even though attracting foreign investments was at the very core of the original intention for the SEZs, out of the 166 billion yen in loan provided by the Japanese banks, we had utilized only 3.2 billion by the beginning of 1982. For this we have been obligated to pay the delayed usage fee of 800 million yen to the Japanese side (the equivalent of US$400,000).

The total value of exports for Shenzhen in 1983 was approximately 59 million yuan. That was only 1/12 of the total value of industrial production for the city. And those products exported were mostly foodstuff and vegetables. The share of manufactured goods was small. Even including the products from other parts of the country exported through Shenzhen, the figure was merely US$120 million. But the total value of imports into Shenzhen was US$640 million. The deficit was US$484 million. Obviously the prediction of "relying primarily on exports" has not stood. According to another report, between 1979 and 1983, the "industrial production" of Shenzhen (severely tilted) increased 10 times. Over the same period, the Chinese import from Hong Kong increased 9.6 times.[23] This is a very interesting contrast.

If we allow that due to various circumstances, the earlier figures on Shenzhen might contain haphazard elements, by 1987 we were surely getting more reliable figures. According to these newer reports, over this five-year period the building construction investment was 6.4 billion yuan, of which the direct state investment was 3%; investment from various ministries and provinces, 11%; domestic loans, 30%; state plan allocated funds or loans, 13%; domestic funds raised by the municipality alone or jointly with other municipalities, 23%, and finally, the foreign investments much courted after came up to a meagre 20%. Thus, for every dollar of foreign money that was lured over, China had to spend four dollars out its own pocket.

What absolutely defies comprehension was that, up until August 1987, at a seminar on development strategy run by the University of Shenzhen, a local official commented during the opening ceremony: "You have all seen with your own eyes, the central government only gave us 200 million, barely enough to fix the barbed wire along the border. The rest is the proud achievement of the open policy!" Being personally present at that seminar, it was difficult to refrain from reacting to such cavalier statements.

Even more fantastic was the fact that, of some products sold on the streets of Shenzhen, such as electrical appliances, nylons, fashion clothes, umbrellas, etc., quite a number were originally exported to Hong Kong by other provinces, and were then sold back to Shenzhen through some magical price differentials. Some folks from Shanghai went to Shenzhen and bought folding umbrellas, and then discovered that they were first sold from Shanghai to Hong Kong and then back to Shenzhen. Folks from Shanghai were happy, saying that they spent a bit less that they would have in Shanghai. The folks from Shenzhen were happy that they made a few bucks. And the Chinese product dealers in Hong Kong were happy as well, because they, too, made a few bucks. So where the devil did the profits come from? The money invested in Shenzhen from Hong Kong, as it turned out, was frequently from companies originally set up in Hong Kong with money from the PRC. The wheel of fortune in Shenzhen consisted of moving money from one pocket into the other on the same jacket.

On a stretch of wasteland, at the price four times the investment actually obtained from overseas, was built the glib new city of Shenzhen. The original intent of "relying primarily on industry, primarily on export income, and primarily on foreign investment" has been summarily dashed. Are we going to open up our entire coastal region on the basis of this model, when there are major questions about the efficacy of the whole idea?

■ Careful Preparations Are Essential

The establishment of Special Economic Zones (SEZs) has been an important part of China's attempt to build up its export industry. It is interesting to observe, however, that when addressing the question of whether a zone like Shenzhen has been a success or a failure, the authorities have tended to fall back on the idea of "paying for experience."

In 1985, when Li Hao became mayor of Shenzhen, a Hong Kong newspaper published an article headlined "Beijing official comes south to take care of special economic zone," in which a Guangzhou journalist asked Mayor Li outright whether Shenzhen was a success. Li's response is worth quoting here: "As the establishment of special economic zones by socialist countries has never been tried before, and since the Shenzhen Special Economic Zone is still an experiment, the whole country can learn a great deal from it. . . . It may be regarded as the price of experience. . . . If our destination is a hundred miles away, and we have now only covered 10 miles, can that be called a failure?"[24]

This speech sounded very familiar. Simply substitute the words "Great Leap Forward" or "People's Communes" for "Special Economic Zone," and it becomes the old tune that we have already heard quite enough of in the past. These experiments, among which even the Cultural Revolution may be included, were all things which "had never been done before." They were always said to be good in the beginning but by the end they were all chalked up as the "price of experience."

It is obvious that the Shenzhen Special Economic Zone stays alive on transfusions; by making money out of the hinterland. To put it simply, we have learned a much needed lesson, but we paid too high a price, and from the standpoint of the goal we originally envisioned, this stage of the experiment was a failure. Mayor Li's speech was actually an indirect admission of the fact that the first stage of the course had failed.

It is easy to proclaim to others that "failure is the mother of success," but it is rather more difficult to admit our own real failure. In fact, however, to say that the Shenzhen experiment was a failure is not at all to declare that the whole idea was mistaken, but rather that the methods used, the first steps, and the choice of pace were wrong. When we started the Great Leap Forward and the People's Commune movement, the intention was also good. It was just that the methods were foolish and unscientific, and of all the policy mistakes, the worst has been not allowing people to comment from the start: even if something was blatantly wrong it could not be criticized.

The shortage of skilled personnel has been a major obstacle to the success of Shenzhen. A professor who has made many evaluation trips to the area has pointed out that the crux of the problem is that the cadres cannot keep up with the pace of development. When we established the SEZs, we did not train nearly enough cadres, and in view of the enormity of the task, cadres and workers in Shenzhen are poorly qualified.

Only a few days mixing with people in Shenzhen are needed to encounter some very surprising situations. A general manager informed one graduate student that "we don't need modern Chinese or history and we have even less need for philosophy," and a deputy general engineer in charge of planning Shenzhen's technological development said at a research meeting held for the whole province in 1983, "We are not worried about a shortage of capital because we can borrow as much as we want from the fishing villages. . . . We won't rely on Shenzhen University either, or we would have to wait forever!"

By 1986 Shenzhen's debt was almost equal to the total value of its agricultural and industrial output (around 5 billion yuan). This is a profound reflection of the problems Shenzhen was experiencing at the time. Everyone knows that Shenzhen will damage the market in the interior, that the currency is in chaos, and that there is a huge black market in foreign exchange, but no move has been made to solve the problems.

Some people have charged that Shenzhen is just a big Disneyland where Hong Kong residents to go to rest up or amuse themselves. By 1987, there were 10 major tourist attractions, and more than 40,000 hotel beds on the route from Hong Kong to Shenzhen. But although the hotels compete to provide luxury accommodation, most of the visitors make a short stay, and the occupancy rate for the hotels is usually only 20% or 30%, most of which is taken up by local Chinese on business trips. Only the bottom five floors of the 50 story International Trade Center, for which capital was raised nationwide, are actually used as a trade center. The place had been open for three years when I visited in 1987, but one-and-a-half floors were standing empty, still without floorboards or wallpaper. But construction had begun right next door on another building over 50 stories high.

Then look at Zhuhai, a great expanse of empty tower blocks. There are 20 luxury hotels and inns with more than 5,000 empty beds and unused entertainment halls everywhere. The place throws another dark shadow over the SEZs, and the investors' enthusiasm is cooling rapidly.

The SEZs were intended to be independent. In April 1979, in the early days of the SEZs, Deng Xiaoping said, "The central government doesn't have any money, so you will have to find it yourselves, and carve out your own path to success."[25] In 1982 Hu Yaobang also declared, "The special economic zones must not be dependent on the central government or on the other provinces."[26]

Unfortunately that was not how things turned out. The fastest construction teams in Shenzhen came from Jiangxi, the best roads were laid by teams from Liaoning and the Ministry of Metallurgy, and the best enterprises and factories were run by the Ministries of Aeronautics, Aviation, and Armaments. Even military engineers from the People's Liberation Army were officially transferred to Shenzhen. By 1985, Yao Yilin said in reply to questions from Hong Kong and Macao journalists that Shenzhen "needed the support of the whole country."[27]

However, all the human resources, materials and capital that other provinces and ministries have invested in Shenzhen do not so far seem to have produced many results. Researchers lack information and equipment, and different disciplines work at cross purposes. Capital is also poorly utilized. According to calculations made by Hu Dun'ai of the Hong Kong Baptist College, the figures for investment in capital construction and investment in fixed capital as percentages of the newly increased national income are 50% and 23% lower in Shenzhen than the national average. At the end of 1986, many overseas business people thought the investment environment in Shenzhen did not even compare with that of Dongwan County in Guangdong.

The first stage of the SEZs did not fail just because over-investment in the early days caused changes in the original targets. Although high investment became an established fact, some enterprises that did have higher a technology level than most still failed due to lack of technical and financial support. Many developing countries have also encountered this kind of situation: although they achieved some prosperity by bringing in foreign investment, they soon fell behind because they were unable to build up the research capacity to develop it properly. They also suffered from outdated management, lack of coordination, poor control over production and marketing, and insufficient market information. When these happen to coincide with the deadline for debt repayment, domestic and external pressure combine to force underlying problems into the open.

From the vital standpoint of efficiency, the original siting of the SEZs seems questionable. What the state has actually done is to suppress the vitality of highly productive regions by taking a high proportion of local revenue, setting high tax rates and retaining conservative old regulations, and promoting the economic development of less productive regions by taking a low proportion of revenue, reducing taxes, increasing profit retention rates, and using new liberal policies. This has distorted the balance between inputs and outputs, with the inevitable result of reduced productivity throughout the whole economy.

The question is whether pouring money into low-productivity regions can compensate for the losses incurred by depriving the highly productive regions of inputs. A comparison of Shanghai and Guangdong presents the clearest picture. Even today, Guangdong's economic productivity cannot compare with that of Shanghai. In 1987, 70% of the 4,600 Taiwan-invested enterprises nationwide were in Guangdong. But only one of the 10 best-rated enterprises in the country that year was in Guangdong, while four were in Shanghai. Since the reforms and opening policy began, the proportion of income handed over to the center by Guangdong (2 billion) and Shanghai (20 billion) has remained at proportions of one to ten. During the sixth Five Year Plan, capital inputs in social infrastructure reached 58.8 billion yuan for the whole of Guangdong province and only 41.3 billion yuan for Shanghai (about 30% less).

It is particularly noteworthy that much of Guangdong's capital came from bank loans (more than 30 billion yuan), and from the difference in price of transferring foreign exchange bought with high subsidies, and imported raw materials and commodities to the inland regions (about 4 billion yuan), which brought in considerable capital from outside the province.[28] Yang Lin, writing in *Tequ jingji* (SEZ Economies) (February 1986), mentioned that Shenzhen actually received only about half the 574 million in foreign exchange income from exports that was reported for 1985, and this is undoubtedly not the only example of false reporting of foreign currency earnings.

Given this situation, it was only natural that Guangdong sprang into life while Shanghai could barely maintain its position. Throughout the period of the sixth Five Year Plan (1981–85) the gross value of industrial output grew by an average of 10.8% annually. Guangdong's growth was as high as 16.2%, while Shanghai, which would have been expected to make a bigger contribution, averaged 7.1%. By the time economic adjustment was carried out in 1986, the situation was even clearer: with the exception of Guangdong, the annual growth rate of the gross value of industrial output for all the nation's five other industrial centers had fallen below the national average of 8.56%. Shanghai was only 4.85%, Jiangsu 3.94%, Liaoning 0.16%, Shandong 0.68% (Guangdong was 10.3%). The development of Guangdong's regional economy was at the expense of other regions, and affected the economy as a whole.

It should be noted that in the provincial capital of Guangzhou, skilled workers in industry and enterprises make up only about 5% of the total workforce, the lowest figure for the 10 largest cities in the country. Yet investment in Guangzhou was highest. Meanwhile Shanghai, with its relatively high proportion of skilled workers, has had to turn over 70% of its wealth to the state, resulting in the deterioration of infrastructure and a decline in its investment environment. A third of its industrial processing capacity was unused and economic productivity fell. This happened because during the sixth Five Year Plan, investment in fixed assets in Guangdong grew by as much as 48% annually, while the increase in industrial output for the same period was only 16%. National income grew by more than 17% and the gross value of exports by 13%, not even 28% of the increase in investment.[29] It is hard to see how such a high rate of investment and such low productivity can possibly be a model for anything.

From 1978 to 1987, the amount of currency entering circulation in Guangdong increased progressively by over 26% a year, 9% more than the annual increase in revenue. As a result, the total money supply increased 10 times in as many years. This forced inflation of over 118% in Guangdong's retail price index, 16% higher than the rest of the country. The value of the yuan also fell 46% more than in the rest of the country. Given the sharp fall in grain production and the fact that the whole province has over 50 billion yuan in unused potential purchasing power and an expanding consumption fund, inflation will continue to worsen.

A look at achievements only is bound to produce an optimistic view. But a look at the actual results of the investment, makes the problems readily apparent. This is precisely why Guangdong, the Pearl River Delta, and Shenzhen cannot serve as models and why they are of little significance for the rest of the country.

The only valid explanation for choosing Guangdong as the window to the outside world is its geographical position. But we have always been critics of geographical determinism and there seems no reason to suddenly replace traditional political economy with an economics based purely on geography. If we now call the Dazhai-style strategy "ideological" economics, then it is clear how much we are going to suffer if we just leap straight from that to another extreme. The center of the whole "open economy" is consumer industries, and so the only really rapid development has taken place in that sector. As a result, the whole structure of the economy is tilting towards consumption and is becoming distorted. Consumption is rapidly expanding, but basic industries and heavy and chemical industries are still developing slowly. Policy-makers cannot afford to take the consequences of this too lightly.

7

QUESTIONS OF PACE AND REGIONAL DEVELOPMENT

▌ The Trap of Over-Rapid Growth

In the end, all the economic trials that China has experienced over the past few decades come down to the problem of speed. Our political leaders and theorists have held some extremely strange views regarding the pace of China's economic development. The most typical are those of Mao Zedong himself.

As early as 1949, Mao said: "The pace of China's economic development will not be slow, but may rather be quite rapid. A prosperous China is well within sight and there is no foundation for pessimism about China's economic revival."[1]

In 1958, we embarked upon the Great Leap Forward, which amounted to a race against time. In that year alone, investment in capital construction increased by 87.9%, and the rate of accumulation leapt from 24.9% to 33.9%. In 1959 the latter jumped again to a staggering 43.9%. From 1958 to 1960, a deficit of almost 20 billion yuan built up, and in 1960 a massive 8.18 billion was added to this. Meanwhile, agricultural production fell by an average of 9.7% annually for three consecutive years starting in 1959. By 1961, the government was forced to make adjustments, and the whole economy immediately entered a period of contraction.

In 1962, in a speech to an enlarged Central Committee work meeting, Mao immediately put forward a new idea, saying that "Fifty years may not be enough to build up a strong socialist economy in

China. It may take one hundred years, or even longer." Unfortunately, only two years later, in December 1964, when going over a "Government Work Report" prepared by Zhou Enlai, Mao again remarked, "China will experience a Great Leap Forward," adding, "We must break all norms and make every effort to use advanced technology to build our nation into a powerful modern socialist state within a fairly short historical period." As a result of this, when the plans for the fourth Five Year Plan (1971–75) were in progress, the quota for steel output was set at 35–40 million tons. This led to an unprecedented high in staffing levels, wage outlays, and grain consumption which came to be known as "the three breakthroughs."

In 1978, after the fall of the Gang of Four, Mao's Great Leap Forward speech made a comeback as the slogan "Great achievements within three years," which was used as an ideological weapon and widely broadcast for the second time. And so another leap began, this time a "foreign" one, involving our opening to the outside world. In that year investment in capital construction leapt by 32% over the preceding year, and the rate of accumulation rose from 32.3% the previous year to 36.5%. In the wake of this, a balance of payments deficit of 29.8 billion yuan appeared between 1979 and 1980, and the government was again forced to make adjustments. Considering that the country was still nursing its wounds after the trauma of the Cultural Revolution, it is not surprising that this attempt at forced-march development brought out many underlying problems. The high quotas and rapid pace left huge inventories, many products had to be scrapped, and there were heavy losses. Once again we paid a stiff economic price for our mistakes.

Incredibly, many people are still over-optimistic, and are not aware that abnormally rapid growth is really a disaster. The most recent of these risky experiments took place in 1984–85, when we fell victim yet again to the perils of excessively rapid growth.

It began in the last quarter of 1984, when the nation was suddenly swept by another bout of wild economic enthusiasm. In that year, following the decision to carry out economic reforms, capital construction investment rose sharply by more than 34% over the previous year, and in 1985 it again increased by 22%. The banking system immediately followed the expansionist trend, and in October 1984, it was announced that the following year's lending quota would be based on total lending for 1984. The specialized banks immediately started lending furiously in order to expand the amount of credit they could give the following year, and began the practice of linking lending quotas to deposits, which fueled savings. The result was that national credit swelled and premature consumption broke out again. The balance of payments deficit increased rapidly, and there was a large foreign trade deficit. With the pressure of market demand mounting, the banks frantically printed notes (afterwards they announced publicly that they had issued an extra 8 billion yuan in currency).

In that year, the total money supply reached 26.23 billion yuan, the highest figure since 1949. The amount of money put into circulation in 1981 was only 5.01 billion yuan, in 1982 it was 4.78 billion yuan, and in 1983 it was 9.066 billion yuan, and by 1986 the total money supply had increased to 121 billion yuan.[2] Finance Minister Wang Bingqian, in his report to the Seventh People's Congress, announced that the national budget deficit in 1987 was 8.03 billion yuan and the estimated deficit for 1988 was 8 billion yuan. According to statistics for the past 10 years, the accumulated deficit already exceeds 100 billion yuan.

Major adjustments had to be made for the third time and we entered a phase where the rapid pace of economic development was sustained by high inflation. This was a typical Keynesian policy which has been successful in other countries. The problem in China was that there was no mechanism for controlling the money supply at the macroeconomic level, and it was even harder to stem the inflation of credit caused by increased deposits.

In fact, these trends had already begun as early as 1982. The planned increases in industrial output value for 1982, 1983, and 1984 were 4%, 4%, and 5% respectively, but actual growth was 7.7%, 10.5%, and 14%. The planned increase for 1985 was 8%, but in the first four months of that year actual growth exceeded 23.3%.[3] This was far higher than the previous record of 18% set during the first Five Year Plan. To meet the official target of quadrupling output by the year 2000, gross industrial output value would only need to rise by 5.7% for the first ten years and 9.5% for the second ten years, so we appear to be overshooting the goal.

The explosion in investment is even more typical. In 1982 national fixed capital investment rose to 84.5 billion yuan, a record high since 1949. The upward trend continued in 1983, and despite stringent government measures to reduce it, by the end of the year total investment had still reached 95.2 billion yuan. In 1984 total fixed capital investment increased yet again, reaching 116 billion yuan, 21.8% up from the previous year. Of this, investment in capital construction was 73.5 billion yuan, more than 123% of the 1983 figure.[4] The central government repeatedly called for restraint, but to no avail.

In June 1985, the economic fever reached its peak. In that month, fixed capital investment increased by 100 billion, 56.6% higher than the same period in 1984, and industrial output still rose 20%, heading for a record high. But the reality behind these impressive figures was an endless stream of duplicated projects, policy mistakes, unproductive investments, extended production time, and poorly coordinated engineering projects, with little to show for all that was invested. In 1985, the rate of investment in construction projects (50.7%) and the fixed capital utilization rate (68.2%) were also down from 1984 levels (54.1% and 71.8% respectively). From 1982 to 1986, investment in capital construction increased progressively by 10% a year, but only one-third of the capital invested was actually realized in fixed assets.

Moreover, the surge of investment in capital construction provoked a shortage of energy, transportation, and raw materials. Electric circuits were overloaded and faulty electrical generators continued in service. The country had to use foreign exchange to import materials to maintain production, causing foreign exchange reserves to drop sharply to the critical point of just over 40 billion.

The prices of scarce commodities rose several times and the quality of many products declined sharply. Costs increased and the increase in inventories of finished products exceeded the increase in production. The value of rejected mechanical and electrical products alone reached 15.3 billion yuan—one-quarter of that year's inventories. The macroeconomy was out of control again, and the result was that when the brakes were put on in early 1986, the industrial growth rate immediately fell to 5.6%, a remarkable slide of 15% in the space of six months.

Another side effect was inflation. According to an article by the director of the State Statistical Bureau, Zhang Yigeng, in *Jingji yanjiu* (Economic Research) (May 1985), the purchasing power of 100 yuan in 1984 was the equivalent of 97.3 yuan in 1983, 85 yuan in 1978, and 69 yuan in 1952 (only 58 yuan for urban residents). In addition, urban residents spending 100 yuan on food in 1984 had the equivalent of only 40 yuan at the 1952 rate, and for non-food items, only 37 yuan. The retail price index continued to climb after that, reaching an official inflation rate of more than 18% in 1988–89. [This inflation contributed to the unrest which culminated in the events of 4 June 1989].

It should be borne in mind that the Engel coefficient (expenditure on food as a proportion of total income) for China is probably between 0.6 and 0.8, or possibly even higher. This means that people spend 60% to 80% of their income on food, and for those to whom food is especially important, the Engel coefficient may be close to or even more than one. From this we can see how the devaluation of the yuan has affected the standard of living.

There is less exaggeration and empty talk these days, but the fervor of the "surpass the West" movement and the Great Leap Forward has not entirely dissipated.

Progress in economic affairs is like progress in other areas: it is a scientific problem which requires strict planning in accordance with the facts. Planning for healthy growth must also be consistent with people's psychology and capabilities, and in accord with the society as a whole. The huge swings in the China's foreign trade, and the difficulties surrounding the Shenzhen question, are all related to the inappropriate pace of development.

▌ Theories Distilled from Myths

When it comes to economic problems, we often see only the mistakes of decision-makers and let their "advisors" off the hook. Keynes once said that the frenzy of politicians is "distilled" from the theories of economists, and it is certain that many theoreticians and advisors bear partial responsibility for China's previous economic spurts, and particularly for the investment craze.

According to figures comparing the Gross National Product in various nations from 1973 to 1983, the Soviet Union had the highest economic growth rate in the world, surpassing even that of Japan.[5] Nor is the Soviet Union alone. When the *Statistical Yearbook of China* for 1983 published the most complete statistical data on China since the founding of the PRC, it showed that the annual average industrial growth rate over a 30-year period also exceeded that of Japan and was the highest in the world. Even taking just the 17 years from 1966 to 1982—which included the Cultural Revolution (now condemned as total chaos) the country shows an average annual industrial growth rate of 9.5%, still higher than Japan's (7.4%) and followed Romania as the second highest in the world. The gross output value of industry from 1985 through 1989 more than doubled. Statistically, the Chinese appear fortunate indeed, but unfortunately, the unreliability of China's statistical data is also world famous.

At first it seems natural that a bigger population would mean a higher output value. But many harsh realities are disguised by this simple figure. Many economic indicators contain misleading elements, statistical analysis may be superficial, hiding what lies beneath the surface, and there may also be over-optimistic projections for the future, all of which need to be carefully scrutinized.

For example, it is difficult to determine how to remove the

padding from inflated figures for output value, and prices and inventories are also unrealistic indicators. According to a World Bank report, in 1984 China's GNP ranked eighth in the world, but per capita national income ranked 129th on a scale of 151 countries and regions, and was equivalent to only 2.6% that of the United States. According to statistics comparing 1979 with 1952, national income had increased 5.7 times, and the labor productivity rate for all workers in industrial enterprises increased 2.8 times, but salaries for staff and workers rose by an average of only 58%.

In 1987, Yang Qixian of the National Committee for the Reform of the Economic System further pointed out that between 1953 and 1978 the value of total national fixed assets increased 41 times (40% of national expenditure went on construction), while total national economic revenue only increased 4.5 times (in the official statistics gross output value increased elevenfold, which shows how inflated the figures can be).

Fifteen to 20% of the nation's enterprises have been generating losses for a long period, and more than 90% of the increase in production was maintained by inputs, as opposed to actual increases in productivity. If we consider that the fixed capital formation rate was only one-third of the capital invested, then over the last 30 years, capital inputs have increased 135–40 times (an average of about 5.6 times per year), but the rise in the standard of living does not even remotely correspond to this huge increase.

This situation has existed all along, but unfortunately many of our theoreticians have not been willing to face up to such simple facts, preferring instead to promote the myth that economic development is proceeding at a flying pace. Chinese commentators are infamous for making exaggerated claims of socialist success and achievement, and substituting fantasy for reality. At the same time, these mythmakers resolutely refrain from mentioning the failures and shortcomings, such as ossified economies, huge economic swings, and inflated statistics for gross output.

Lu Yi published an article in the *Shijie jingji daobao* (World Economic Herald) (February 1988) entitled "What the Chinese Race Needs Most Urgently Is Global Citizenship." This was one of a very few specialist articles to appear in China that addressed the crisis. Because it excited a lot of enthusiastic discussion, its premises deserve some further consideration here.

Above we mentioned the question of GNP, and the discussion of "global citizenship" makes the same point. In 1955, China's GNP was 4.7% of the world total. At that time, Japan's GNP was 2.4%, only half that of China's, but by 1960 China's GNP had fallen to 2.5% of the world total. In 1960, China's Gross Domestic Product was the same as Japan's, but by 1980 it was only a quarter of Japan's; in 1985 one-fifth, and in 1986 it had dropped to only one-sixth. Although the changes in the relative values of the yen and the yuan are factors in these figures, they cannot account entirely for the startling and disturbing nature of this downward slide.

In 1980, China's per capita GNP (US$300) was only 3.3% that of developed Western nations (US$10,000). Even allowing for the distortion caused by the official exchange rate, it still would not be more than a tenth. If we assume that per capita GNP in developed Western nations grows by an average of 2% annually starting from 1980 and that of China by 5%, using the official exchange rate it would take China 121 years to catch up with the developed nations. If the developed nations' per capita GNP grows by 3% annually and China's by 4%, then it would take China 363 years to catch up.

In our discussion of development strategy we must also mention the question of participating in the "international circulation" *(guoji xunhuan)* raised by Wang Jian. This idea has become extremely widespread because it received the approval of senior members of the Communist Party Central Committee. The plan envisions a strategy of importing raw materials and processing them for resale overseas, and hopes to transfer 200 million agricultural laborers into labor intensive industries and to capture export markets left by the four Asian Newly Industrialized Countries (NICs) (Taiwan, Singapore, Hong Kong, and South Korea). In particular, exports are hoped to increase to US$150 billion by the year 2000, and create 60 million jobs.

Wang Jian's article first appeared in an internal publication on 1 November 1987, and was approved by the Central Committee three days later. Three months later, a communique published by the Fourth Plenary Session of the Central Committee Politburo (6 February 1988) announced: "The development strategy recently proposed for the coastal belt will not only push the nation's open coastal region into the world market to take part in international exchange and competition, but will also certainly be effective in promoting the economic development of the central and western regions. This is an extremely important strategy for the overall construction of the Four Modernizations. It must be implemented resolutely. This opportunity must not be bungled."

It is very unusual in China for the proposal of an individual researcher to be acknowledged so quickly and almost immediately written into high level policy. Unfortunately, this also demonstrates the lack of thorough analysis at the highest level of policy-making.

First of all, it is not at all clear what this "opportunity" is. The four Asian NICs were able to take advantage of the longest period of continuous prosperity ever in the Western capitalist world, which lasted from the 1940s to the early 1970s, and by the end of the 1960s they had established a base for their export industries. But after the mid-1970s, and particularly in the 1980s, the Western developed nations entered a long period of slower economic growth; competition between developing countries for the export market was fiercer than ever before; worldwide inflation caused market contraction, and trade protectionism increased. It may therefore be the case that the chance to take advantage of prolonged economic growth in the developed Western nations has already passed us by.

Secondly, the NICs, or "Four Little Dragons," only have a combined population of just over 50 million, and even including Thailand they would still number only 100 million. It is indeed strange for a country with a population of more than a billion to choose them as its competitors, and to anticipate creating jobs for 60 million people by competing with these nations and filling the gaps they have left in the market is utterly simplistic.

Third, according to the two-to-one subsidy for exports, it would require US$300 billion in subsidies to achieve exports of US$150 billion, which is almost 88% more than the 80 billion originally planned, and just happens to be the current total annual investment figure. Wang Jian thinks an extra 10 billion a year will do the trick, but it should be remembered that 10 billion is almost half the total education budget for one year. If exports alone require that amount, it would put an enormous strain on other aspects of development. Furthermore, China only has foreign exchange reserves of about US$12 billion, and at the beginning of 1988 the foreign debt was already US$24 billion, a good part of which was short term loans calculated in Japanese yen. The pressure of debt repayments will come at almost exactly the same time as the need to spend large amounts of foreign currency to import raw materials, meaning that we could well face a serious crisis at that time.

Fourth, it is also questionable whether the domestic investment climate, equipment, the quality of labor (especially the rural work force), and the level of management can meet the requirements of the international market. Close investigation reveals that most of our economic achievements in recent years have been achieved by the sheer vitality of the primitive economy and the transfer of labor to crude processing industries. In fact, when it comes to competing for labor-intensive industries that require some technology, we are not even a match for Thailand. In 1985 Japan set up 127 direct investment projects in China, worth US$470 million. But in 1987, there were only

111 projects worth US$297 million. In 1988, Japan's overseas investments grew enormously but the direction switched to locations like Thailand and Malaysia.

Fifth, economic competition throughout the world is now primarily for quality, efficiency, design, service, innovation, and marketing. It is no longer merely a question of cheap labor. Not many years ago, the percentage of labor in industrial costs in the United States was 23%. Now it is only 18%. In this sense too, we face a crisis. There is the danger, as a Japanese observer remarked, that in 10 years' time as automation increases, China's pool of cheap labor will be no advantage, and she will be left behind.

Apart from this, in implementing the international market plan, there is also the question of whether the central government can control the macroeconomy, how much authority will be given to the coastal region, and the growing gap between the eastern and western regions of the country. It is still not clear whether the international market theory will turn out to be a new myth, but hopefully it will not sprout another theory of "rapid development." No good will come of handling real economic development problems by switching from one slogan to another. It would be far better to research a strategic theory for overall development.

■ Peacocks Fly Southeast

Until recent times, the history of China was one of a migration from west to east and from north to south, but these days there is even talk of a strategic shift west, and for the long term, the crux of China's whole development strategy lies in developing the West.

China's western regions are incredibly poor. The depths of this poverty have been vividly shown in some contemporary films and novels. The famous sociologist Fei Xiaotong wrote of the profound impression made on him by a 1984 visit to a poor peasant's hovel in Dingxi in central Gansu: "In a mud hut containing nothing but a *kang* [a large stove made of dried mud or brick] and an empty cooking pot, a middle-aged peasant told me tearfully that his wife was sick and he had no food or firewood. Apparently, at that time about a third of the peasant families were also unable to secure the basic necessities of life."[6] Dingxi was the most inhospitable place on earth, and to its people the bare essentials of grain, firewood, and water constituted a livelihood.

In their book *Furao de pinkun* (Abundance of Poverty) (Sichuan People's Publishing House, 1986), Wang Xiaoqiang and others described several equally distressing scenes. In the Shanzhuang district of Yuzhong County in Gansu, the annual average per capita grain intake was only 20–50 kilograms, and of the 49 production teams in the whole district, 48 had an average per capita income of less than 40 yuan. In some production teams, three people shared a bed quilt, and at the house of a veteran volunteer of the Korean war, a family of six slept under a worn old quilt he had brought back from the battlefield years before. Another family of three slept on two cement sacks. Of the 7,000 people in the whole district, over 4,000 either had no padded pants, or the ones they did have were already threadbare.

In 1982, Guanling County in Guizhou was one of more than a hundred "advanced counties" that announced a doubling of the gross value of agricultural and industrial output, but average per capita grain intake in 1983 was still only just over 175 kilograms. More than 210 production teams had an average personal grain intake of 138 kilograms, an average per capita income of 39 yuan, an average of 1.6 sets of clothes per person, and only one quilt for every six or seven people. There were also several hundred families in which each member had only one set of clothes and where there was only one bed quilt between five or six people.

In 1984 more than 8 million people in Guizhou were living below the poverty line, and more than 3 million of them had an average yearly income of less than 80 yuan. In Ta City and the Alatai region of Xinjiang, 216 production teams had an annual per capita income of less than 60 yuan in 1981. In North and South Xinjiang, more than 30,000 households had no tents or lived in threadbare ones, and in winter they had to sleep on mud which had been warmed by the fire.

How many places like Dingxi, Hezhang, Yuzhong, Guangling, and Alatai are there in the west of China? The area is covered with bare mountains and peaks, drifting sands and rocks. The high elevations are cold and dry, plagued by drought, water loss, and soil erosion. The threat of desertification increases daily and the environment is trapped in a cycle of steady deterioration. Transportation is inconvenient, agriculture and livestock raising is unproductive, and the structure of industry is irrational.

In 1980, output value realized for every hundred yuan of fixed capital investment in the Northwest was 65.17 yuan, only 56% of the national average, and the illiteracy rate was 27%. The five provinces of Shaanxi, Gansu, Ningxia, Qinghai, and Xinjiang cover an area of approximately 3.07 million square kilometers, or almost 32% of the whole country, but in 1983 the combined value of agricultural and industrial output was only 5.1% of the national total and average per capita income was 20% below the national average.[7] The cities of Xining in the Northwest and Changzhou in the East both had a population of about 400,000 in 1982, but the former had a combined agricultural and industrial output value of only 845 million yuan, less than one-fourth that of the latter.

The gap between East and West continues to grow. For example, if we compare the average per capita value of industrial and agricultural output for Xinjiang with the national average, the figures for 1949 were 96 and 86 yuan respectively, with Xinjiang 12% higher. By 1981, they were 575.6 yuan and 751.8 yuan respectively, with Xinjiang 23.4% below the national average.[8] In Ningxia, the average per capita value of industrial and agricultural output was 69.5% of the national average in 1982, and some projections show the gap widening in the 1990s. To achieve the target of quadrupling output by the year 2000, the country as a whole only needs to maintain an average annual growth rate of 7.2%, but the Northwest must grow by 8% a year.

The situation in the Southwestern region comprised of Yunnan, Guizhou, Sichuan, Guangxi, and Tibet is more or less the same. Tibet should be considered as a separate case because of the terrain and various other differences. In 1984, Tibet's gross industrial and agricultural output value was 6 fen (0.06 yuan) per square kilometer, or 8% of the national average.[9] Even excluding Tibet, the population of the four southwestern provinces in 1984 was 19.5% of the national total, but the value of industrial output value was only 9.4% of the national total and the value of agricultural output 17.3%. The region accounted for 13.4% of national income, students in higher education were 11.7% of the total nationwide, and the value of retail sales 13%, all lower than the percentage of the population.[10]

A further comparison can be made between the 11 territories of Inner Mongolia, Gansu, Ningxia, Qinghai, Xinjiang, Shaanxi, Yunnan, Guizhou, Sichuan, Tibet, and Guangxi that make up the Western region, and the other 18 provinces and autonomous cities (which we will take as the East). In this division, the West covers 64% of the total land area, has 31.6% of the total cultivable land (7.6 million acres), and an annual grain output of 98.3 million tons, which is 25.4% of total national grain output. In terms of unit yield, 10 of the provinces that fell below the national average in 1984 were in the West. The amount of grain produced by one agricultural laborer in the West is only 69% of that of the East (1426.5 kilograms). The average yield per acre in the Northwest (144.5 kilograms) is only 63% that of the East (226 kilograms), and cultivated land per capita in the Southwest (0.19 acres) is even further below the national level. In the same year, the total revenue of township enterprises in 10 Western provinces (excluding Tibet), was 15.67 billion yuan, only 10.2% of the total earnings of township enterprises nationwide, just over half that of the township enterprises in Jiangsu, and about the same as the figure for Shandong.

That year, the value of total national rural fixed assets was 96.6 billion yuan, of which the ten Western provinces accounted for only 17.5 billion yuan, or 18% of the total. The annual per capita incomes of the agricultural population in the East and West in 1982 were 211 yuan and 160 yuan respectively. In 1984 they were 365 yuan and 229 yuan. The absolute difference had increased from 69 yuan to 164 yuan, or 2.2 times in two years. By 1985, the gap had increased by a further 170 yuan, and the difference between the annual per capita value of industrial and agricultural output had increased by 1,098 yuan. Tens of millions people in the West are still living below the poverty line, with average yearly incomes of less than 200 yuan, and because the West's rural population grew by 9% between 1978 and 1984 (as opposed to 3.4% nationwide and 2.1% in the East), the pressure continues to build.

To illustrate the kind of extremes in income which exist, Guizhou, the poorest province, saw its per capita income increase only 100 yuan, from 365 to 465, from 1985 to 1987. Shanghai, the richest, grew by 433 in the same period, from 3,384 to 3,817. Just the increase in the Shanhainese income almost equaled the entire per capita sum in Guizhou.

There are a number of dramatic success stories of large numbers of people rising above the official poverty line of 200 yuan. For example, 6.05 million people in Shaanxi were living in poverty in 1985. By 1991, 96% were reported to have risen past the poverty line with per capita income multiplying 2.5 times, to 495 yuan. However, even this increase falls far short of the level needed to eliminate all the environmental and development problems so severely aggravated by poverty.

Whenever the issue of developing the West comes up, the enthusiasts mention a whole string of advantageous conditions, while underestimating the difficulties. In agriculture, for example, the West has an apparent advantage over the East in terms of the cultivable land, with 0.43 acre per person in the West, 73% higher than the 0.25 acre per person in the East, but they rarely mention that the quality of the soil and natural environment in the East is generally superior, therefore making comparisons of gross acreage completely meaningless.

Historically, the Northwestern Plateau (Huangtu Gaoyuan) consisted mostly of forests and wooded grasslands, but it has already fallen into a cycle of ecological decline. Since 1958, exhaustive cultivation of the area has rapidly depleted the soil, leading to further expansion into fresh ground. Fuel and fodder gathering, coupled with the shortage of fertilizers, have seriously depleted many resources, and the policy of extensive cultivation has resulted in a pitifully low wheat yield per acre of only 45–61 kilograms. The area of cultivable land lost by desertification has extended from .46 million acres in 1961, to 1.32 million acres in 1983, an average of 39,500 acres per year, and soil erosion affects an area of more than 26,000 square kilometers, with more than 5,000 tons of soil lost per square kilometer. Agriculture reduces the pastureland and the desert encroaches on agriculture, with disastrous effects for agriculture, forestry, and animal husbandry. To this must be added the dramatic population increase, the imbalance of agricultural activities, the destruction of vegetation, the decreasing size of livestock farms, and the reduced fertility of the soil.

Guizhou is a province rich in natural resources, and its environmental conditions are better than in many other provinces. Located on a crossroads in the railroad network, it also has at least seven water routes connecting it with other provinces. It enjoys a high concentration of construction projects from the "Third Front" period. But economic development is severely retarded. In 1978 it ranked second from last in the country in terms of average per capita income, and it had slipped to last by 1987.

The 1950s saw a bout of Northwest fever, when the strategy was the very basic one of oil drilling, coal mining, livestock farming, and opening up the desert to cultivation. But 30 years later, although the situation compares favorably with before, the gap with the East has grown even wider.

Between 1952 and 1982, the country invested 220 billion yuan in construction in the West (an average of 7.1 billion a year), and from this, fixed capital of 130 billion yuan was created. But the realization rate of investment in fixed capital [i.e. the amount of investment that actually formed fixed assets] was low. For example, between 1950 to 1983, Guizhou only achieved a realization rate of 65.1%, while the corresponding figure for the whole country was 71.8%. In 1983, output value realized per hundred yuan of fixed capital (original value) in Guizhou enterprises was only 50.44 yuan (95.13 yuan for the country as a whole), and the profit realized was only 6.5 yuan (13.44 yuan nationwide).[11]

Between 1980 and 1983, the state invested a total of 95 billion yuan in the ten eastern provinces and cities, and obtained 276.5 billion yuan in taxes on profits—more than four times the investment. For the same period, total state investment in the western region was 30.8 billion. The state received 31.8 billion yuan in taxes, but at the same time its subsidies to the West amounted to 29 billion yuan.[12] Investment per ton of steel output capacity was 1,000 yuan in the coastal regions and 3,000 yuan in the newly developed areas of the interior. The construction of the two railroads between Chengdu and Kunming, and Xiangyang and Chengdu cost 3–4 million yuan per kilometer, between four and eight times the cost for equivalent length of track in the Eastern coastal region. In the 20 years after 1953, the investment output coefficient (the net increase in output over the period divided by the accumulated amount of investment over the period) for the coastal region was 0.973, for the interior 0.414, and for the "Third Front" region only 0.256. According to a calculation made in 1978 for 28 provinces, autonomous regions, cities, and districts (excluding Tibet), most of the six provinces and cities with a capital utilization rate above 30% were in the East, the 12 with a utilization rate between 15% and 30% were mostly in the central region and the ten with a utilization ratio of less than 15% were mostly in the West.[13]

Among all the unfavorable factors currently facing the West, the worst is the lack of qualified staff and the drain of trained personnel to the East. The West, which makes up two-thirds of the nation's territory, has only 10% of its skilled personnel, and between 1982 and 1986 alone, 22,000 skilled people migrated to the East just from the four provinces of Gansu, Ningxia, Qinghai and Xinjiang. In the past few years, Qinghai, Gansu, Ningxia, Yunnan, Guizhou, and Guangxi have lost many talented people. Between 1983 and 1985 alone, 111 teachers left Lanzhou University, the most reputable in the West, 60% of whom held senior or middle level posts. The drain continues, and it is difficult to bring in qualified replacements.

It is rarer still for anyone to move voluntarily to the West. To understand why, one only has to consider what happened to those young scholars who, full of enthusiasm and altruism, volunteered to trek to the outlying regions in the 1950s. Worn out by a lifetime of toil, they return to the East only to find that they have to pull strings to transfer their residence registration, and ask friends to help get them rations. They have to struggle to have their children admitted to school and they have to wait endlessly for housing allocations. These living examples are sufficient to discourage anyone who might be considering the same path.

The West's personnel problem is exacerbated by poor organization, the over-concentration of people in certain areas, and irrational backlogs and deployment of staff. As a percentage of the total population, its 700,000 professionally educated personnel is not a particularly small number (96.6 for every 10,000 people—actually higher than the national average of 74.7). But almost 35% of these are attached to enterprises under central government departments. Of the 700,000 technicians, 43% are engineers, 16.7% teachers, and only 7.8% agriculture technicians—only one for every 260,000 acres of prairie. More than 35% of Xinjiang's skilled people are concentrated in Urumqi, and 37% of Shaanxi's engineers are employed by the defense industry. One survey even indicates that up to 1987 only 20% or 30% of the educated people in Qinghai and Gansu were actually serving a useful purpose.

More than 200,000 skilled people are backlogged in the West. Meanwhile technical personnel in regional town enterprises account for only 0.5% of all staff. What is even more difficult to understand is that some regions have a strict rule against transferring jobs within the region, and that those who can manage it must transfer out of the area, which has the effect of forcing people to leave.

Anyone who harbors ideas about a strategic economic shift towards the West around the end of this century would do well to consider that the natural tendency to migrate East will continue. It is clear that the gap between the eastern and western regions of China will continue to grow until the year 2000.

The worldwide trend toward regional economies can also be felt in China. Regional rather than central administrations control a large share of some basic resources of the nation, with 70% of the concrete, 40% of the timber, and over 25% of the iron ore. The percentage of extra-budgetary capital controlled by the autonomous regions as a proportion of national income has risen from 8% under the first Five Year Plan, to 18% under the second Five Year Plan, and 26% under the fourth Five Year Plan, to more than 50% in recent years.[14] The strategy of trying to make every region self-sufficient in steel and grain is out of date. The age of regional economies must come to China, and we will meet with a whole series of thorny problems in this respect. The loss of control of the macroeconomy and the excessively rapid growth rate in recent years have mostly been caused by the failure to deal with the emergence of regional economies.

The Eastern coastal region of China covers only 14.2% of the country's total area but it has 41% of the total population, and accounts for 57.5% of gross industrial and agricultural output value, and 62% of industrial output value. The gross value of industrial and agricultural output of 16 entire counties in Guizhou province is only a little over 100 million yuan, but many individual counties in Jiangsu and even some villages in the Pearl River Delta have an output value that high.

Given this disparity, the emergence of regional economies will further increase the gap between the regions and also confront the state with the nasty dilemma of whether to concentrate investment in the East and aim for higher returns at the cost of allowing the gap between the two regions to grow, or whether to invest in the West, and pursue balanced development at the cost of overall returns. For the moment, the government has chosen the former, but it is also preparing to shift the focus of its strategy to the West at the turn of the century.

The first half of this plan is feasible, but the second half may turn into yet another bout of rapid development fever. Looking realistically at the gap between the two regions, and at trends in world development, the focus of China's development strategy for the foreseeable future should remain in the East, where it should push its way into the Pacific bloc and prepare to welcome the Pacific age. The basic task for the West has nothing to do with any shift in the focus of development strategy but is rather a question of working diligently to build up its infrastructure. It should spend a long time gradually consolidating its wealth in schools, roads, communications, environmental protection, and other necessary infrastructure, and not allow it to be wasted on bureaucracy.

In terms of cultural background, traditions, and the general environmental conditions, a regional shift in China would be more difficult than it has been for the United States, the USSR, or Japan. The shift of the U.S. economic center from the Northeast to the West and Southwest has actually been taking place for 200 years, spurred by factors like favorable climate, agricultural potential, siting of military bases and defense plants, and even fortuitous events like the Gold Rush. The Soviet Union's continuing policy of shifting towards its thinly poplated eastern regions has been in progress for about 60 years. The pressure of Japan's long narrow geography and its developed transportation network were factors in that nation's economic expansion from its eastern coast up into the sparsely settled northwest and Hokkaido island, while the flexibility of market mechanisms and the decentralized structure of government also played important roles. It must also be remembered that these three countries were shifting their focus from one coast to another, while China aims to expand from its coast towards "the roof of the world" and an empty expanse of desert.

With the pressures caused by the earlier development and continued priority given to the East, it was inevitable that western China would face a serious development crisis. Moreover, if China cannot keep pace with the world revolution in technology, the western region will become less of an advantage. Because of the huge growth in the significance of technology, information, and knowledge, the sheer possession of natural resources will never again be the prime guarantor of economic health that it was in the past. Development policy must constantly and carefully investigate the ramifications.

For the present, the most important issue for China's West is successful institutional and organizational reform, which should be implemented more boldly and thoroughly than in the East. In this respect, a piece of research by Bai Yijin and others (1987), is worthy of attention. They point out that elements still exist in the social and economic system of the West which are hostile to a commodity economy. Administration and management systems interfere with smoothly running economic operation and tend to work as a force for inertia, manifested in irrational controls and mechanical opposition to action.

A huge bureaucracy has been set up on an extremely weak economic base. The whole of Tibet, for example, has an industrial output value of only 0.13 billion yuan, and investment in capital construction is 80 million yuan, less than that of a single county in the Pearl River Delta, but it still maintains scores of provincial level administrative offices, bureaus, and committees. The administrative cost for every one yuan of investment in basic construction is 0.83 yuan, which must be one of the highest in the world. This "density of institutions" in the economy can only be maintained by transfusions of capital because the institutions are incapable of maintaining themselves.

In the long history of China's feudal past, there are many facts which illustrate the complexity of the relationship between the outer regions and the central government. An excessively strong or weak center will produce both chaos and the division of the nation. Relations between the two have become an important factor in determining the ability to maintain order, and one which affects the prosperity and indeed the very survival of the nation.

Since the Song and Ming dynasties, the basic form of the Chinese state machine has been a high concentration of power in the central government. But in fact, unification is only superficial, and regional concerns and power have always been separate and worked against each other. This is one of China's terrible legacies from the past. At the moment it would be unwise to predict how this tradition will work itself out in the age of regional economies which lies ahead, but it must be recognized that it will be difficult to avoid conflict between the regions and the central government in the future. In fact after the central government started to decentralize authority and revenue retention, and promote urban economic reform in the 1980s, a situation arose where many rights which should have been assumed by enterprises have been retained by local governments, such as the authority to make investments, allocate materials, set prices, make loans, etc. The economic powers of regional governments have increased enormously, and this has hampered the formation of a competitive and unified market. Concern with the pursuit of regional development and reconstruction has caused a dearth of investment at the national level and has intensified inflation.

At present, the financial boundaries between the central government, the regions, and enterprises are very unclear, and if this problem is not addressed, the consequences could be serious, with an inflation of regional economic power and a vacuum of fiscal power at the center. As the economist Li Fan mentioned to a group of journalists, some people joke that there are now more than 20 "independent kingdoms" and 2,000 "marquises" in China. Finding a correct and effective balance between the two extremes of unification and decentralization is a question to which policy-makers must give their concerted attention.

8

EDUCATIONAL DILEMMA

Education is obviously an important factor in development. In modern society, progress and the expansion of production are inseparable from science and, consequently, from education. This is why most industrialized countries have given high priority to education in the post-war period. Without the technical expertise, the new cultural attitudes, and the broader view of reality gained through education, China will continue to suffer from backwardness in industry, agriculture, and attitudes toward population control.

Since the founding of the People's Republic of China 42 years ago, we have established the largest educational system in the world. This accomplishment cannot be denied, but our overall situation is still far from ideal, and a huge gap remains between educational standards in China and those in developed countries. Unfortunately, China has tended to see education as a tool to serve political ends, and this has influenced policy.

China's investment in education ranks very low on the world scale: only 100 billion yuan were spent from 1952 to 1980.[1]

Every year, propaganda claims that investment in education has increased in absolute terms: in 1978 it was 7.01 billion yuan; in 1981, 10.1 billion yuan; and in 1982, 11.4 billion yuan. But in fact, the proportion of national expenditure allocated to education in 1982 (9.75%) was less than in 1981 (10.2%), and the yearly increase in the absolute amount budgeted to education has failed even to catch up with population growth. In 1988, total expenditure was 263.45 billion yuan, of which 25.39 billion yuan, or 9.6% of the total budget, was for education.

In proportional terms, this was the same as in 1987, and appears to be keeping pace with development, but in fact that is not the case. This is because the number of students and schools has increased, and administrative expenditures have risen. Pensions and office expenditures have also gone up, and salaries have increased following professional evaluations. As a result, real funds for education have shrunk. [In 1989 it was announced that funds for education had increased by 15%, but with inflation at over 18%, it can be seen that real investment in education did not keep pace.]

A comparison with education spending in some developed countries in the 1970s and 1980s reveals a huge difference between their education budgets and China's *(see table 8.1)*. The general world level for education spending as a percentage of total national expenditure is 15.2%. Japan reached a high of 22.3% in 1975, but China has not even reached 10%. The proportion of per capita national income spent on education generally averages 5–8% in the developed nations. In China, however, it is only around 2% (in 1987 it was 2.5%), among the lowest in the world.

Currently, annual expenditure on education worldwide is second only to military spending as a public expenditure. The total population of the industrialized countries is only one-third of the world population, but education expenditure in those countries is at least 10 times that of developing countries.[2] China has over one-fifth of the entire world population, but education expenditures in China are only about 1/30 of all spending on education worldwide.

UNESCO statistics from 1978 showed that the proportion of GNP invested in education put China 130th among the 149 countries for which statistics were available. In 1976, China ranked second from the bottom in this category, higher only than the Yemen, where spending was a mere 0.6% of GNP.[3] In 1976, the corresponding figures for Thailand were 4.1%, and for Singapore, 2.7%.

Granted, in the past 30 or so years, China's teaching force has multiplied by 36, and there are more than 17 times as many secondary school graduates, but investment in education in 1976 had increased only 8.8 times over its 1952 level. The gross value of China's industrial output multiplied by 16 from 1952 to 1978, expenditures multiplied by 11 times, and investment in construction increased by almost as much, but investment for education went up only by a factor of 7.30.[4] The education budget was just over 20 billion yuan by 1984, and reached 32.7 million in 1987, according to UNESCO data.

The picture is very different overseas, especially in the history of countries as they developed through this century. In the 55-year period between 1905 and 1960, capital investment in Japan increased only

TABLE 8.1 COMPARISON OF EDUCATION SPENDING IN CHINA AND SIX OTHER COUNTRIES

COUNTRY	YEAR	% OF GNP	% OF NATIONAL INCOME
China	1975	1.7	2.0
	1980	2.4	2.5
	1985	2.7	2.7
	1987	2.4	2.5
Japan	1975	5.5	6.6
	1987	4.9	
USSR	1975	7.6	8.8
	1987	7.5	
West Germany	1975	5.1	6.4
	1987	4.4	
France	1975	4.0	5.0
	1987	5.5	
UK	1975	5.0	7.6
	1987	5.0	
USA	1975	7.4	
	1987	6.8	

seven-fold, labor power multiplied by only 1.7 times, and personal income increased by 10 times, but investment in education went up by a factor of 23.[5] In the 15-year period between 1960 and 1975, Japan's investment in education again increased eleven-fold, almost three times the four-fold increase in the GNP for that period. In 1977 and 1978, the rate of investment in education grew from 6.7% to 7.06%, respectively, of the total national investment.

In 1900, investment in education in the United States was 63 billion and by 1970 it was 815 billion—a thirteen-fold increase in 70 years. From 1965 to 1970 U.S. investment in education increased by 75%, while GNP rose only 45% over the same period. In recent years, education spending in the United States has been $120 billion or more per year.[6]

In per capita terms, education spending in China is also incredibly low compared to other countries. In 1985, Qian Jiaju noted that

China ranked 149th among 150 countries in terms of per capita expenditure on education.[7] In 1978, there were 7.37 times as many secondary school students in China as in 1965, but the budget for secondary schools was only 3.14 times greater. Per capita spending for every secondary school student fell from 112 yuan in 1953 to 88.98 yuan in 1965, and to 39.81 yuan in 1977. In 1978 China had 213 million students and the average expenditure per student was only 33 yuan. The drop in educational spending almost exceeds the rise in the price index! Per capita funding for elementary school students also fell from 20 yuan in 1965 to 16 yuan in 1978. [8]

The situation has not improved in recent years. In 1980, per capita spending on education in China was US$2.7, and average spending for secondary school students was only US$13. This was not even as good as India's 1975 expenditure levels of US$3.9 and US$27 respectively. According to 1982 figures, China's per capita expenditure on education was only 11.2 yuan: not even half the cost of a school desk! Of the 14 countries in the world with per capita expenditure on education below US$5, China was the lowest.[9]

In the 35 years after 1949, China invested a total of 134.85 billion yuan in education, an average of only 3.85 billion yuan per year. This is only just over half the amount spent in 1976, when China ranked second lowest in the world.[10] Over the same 35 year period, 16.3 billion yuan was invested in capital construction for education, an average of only 470 million yuan a year.

As a result, the schools are still desperately short of equipment and teaching materials. In some places, primary and secondary schools do not even have buildings, and a shocking number of school buildings are dangerous. In 1978, 17.2% of the school buildings in Gansu province were considered dangerous, including 77% of all elementary school buildings. Elementary and secondary schools there needed 60,000 desk lamps and 1.7 million square meters of space, which would have cost a total of 180 million yuan.[11]

In the same year the Central Committee announced: "Let us make sure that within three or four years, no school has dangerous buildings, every class has a classroom, and every student has a desk lamp." But three or four years have long passed and Gansu, like other places, still has elementary schools with clay desks and classes held in darkness.

Even in the visible city center of Guangzhou, radio and television appeals had to be made for help from the community to purchase classroom desk lamps. In Beijing, chalk is rationed and in some village elementary schools, instructors are only provided with one piece of chalk a week. Some villages have begun a system of "students supporting their teacher."

In 1985, Liu Dazai, a member of the Education, Science and Culture Committee of the National People's Congress, criticized one province for constructing more than 580 high-rises in the last two or three years primarily for office use, but building only one elementary school.[12] Beijing has built scores of high-rises in recent years, but there has been little improvement in the shabby buildings, playgrounds, and laboratories of the capital's secondary and primary schools.

In 1987, China was 75 million square meters short of classroom space, and had 45 million square meters of dangerous school buildings. In 1988 there were repeated reports from Jiangxi, Tianjin, Zhejiang, and other areas of students being crushed to death by collapsing school buildings. Professor Qian estimated that it would have taken approximately 20 billion yuan merely to repair all the dangerous school buildings in China, which would have equaled the entire education budget in 1980.[13]

The cause of all this is very simple. The majority of China's education budget goes to support teachers and their families: salaries alone take 85% of the total. Little remains for other expenditures. And although teachers receive this share of the total education fund, they are woefully underpaid, while their profession commands little respect— a situation which is bound to reduce educational quality. The budget allotted to physical education for each elementary school student is only 20–30 fen (6–10 U.S. cents)—which for the typical class barely adds up to enough to pay for the gym teacher's regulation uniform. The budget for art classes is equally miniscule. Given such circumstances, there is little chance for a well-rounded curriculum.

∎ Mismanagement

The present structure and organization of the educational system is responsible for enormous waste of both resources and talent, because the relative weight of different parts of the system is not determined by the needs of occupational fields with a view to economic development, but rather by arbitrary decisions of academic departments or scholars. Consequently, the workforce produced by China's educational system does not coincide with the needs of the economy.

The most obvious example of this is the great demand for middle-grade technical personnel in agriculture and light industry. For too long we have concentrated our energies on producing ordinary university students and have neglected the needs of economic reconstruction, which makes it difficult for graduates to find employment. Many students have to change professions as soon as they graduate, which is a great waste. According to a random survey of university graduates carried out by the Ministry of Education, 12.3% of the undergraduates surveyed did not use their specialization after graduation.[14]

The problem is even more serious in China's higher education system. A large-scale survey organized by Shanghai municipality found the following problems to be widespread:[15]

1. There is a shortage of graduates trained in mechanics, electronics, construction, chemistry, and similar specializations, making it difficult to meet the need to update technology.

2. There is great demand for experts in international trade, finance and management, but even in Shanghai, only 7% of finance and accounting staff have a higher education, and only 2% of the personnel in statistics departments have received professional training at an institution of higher education.

3. There are still too few high-level medical science experts.

4. The emphasis on heavy industry over light industry continues. Due to a shortage of trained manpower in the consumer goods industries and related fields, they have lost considerable advantage in the market.

5. There has been a rapid increase in the output value of municipal collective enterprises, and they are growing in scale, but they still cannot get enough trained staff assigned to them.

6. People in the humanities are strangely absent from many professions, and there is almost no one working in some specializations like Political Science, Sociology, Resource Management, record keeping, secretarial skills and so on.

For many years, the principle guiding education in China has been that schools serve specific industries and train specialists for them. This has caused a shortage of trained individuals for the many positions that do not fit the standard categories. For example, there is a shortage of trained medical specialists for non-hospital positions, and a shortage of chemistry specialists to work outside the chemical industry. As a result many workers either have to be retrained or end up in fields where they are not actually qualified. This is a sad waste of scarce resources.

The quality of the education is often substandard, as confirmed not only by anecdotal material but by test performances. Not long ago, results of exams given to young staff and workers in different professions and industries all over China, indicated that their educational level failed to correspond to the length of time spent in school.

In Shenyang, for example, 93% of staff aged 35 or younger scored below junior high school level on the test, even though most of them had received a junior high education. In 1981, Shenyang municipality did a random survey using the lower levels of the junior high curriculum to set questions. In the four subjects of language, math, physics, and chemistry, only 8.58% of those who took the exam passed. In the mining, light industry and textiles, and public utility systems, only 1–3% of the young people passed.

The knowledge level of high school graduates is not much better than the junior high school level, and the situation in elementary schools is just as serious, with the result that a great deal of remedial education is required, wasting precious resources. This situation has persisted for over 30 years, and is a problem in itself, unrelated to other issues, like the fact that much of what is taught is already out of date.

China's education system is not geared to serve the majority of students. For years, secondary schools have functioned largely for the benefit of students who go on to the next grade level: a mere 3–4% of the total. The situation at universities is the same. The ratio of university students to vocational college students in most developed countries is 1 to 10 or 12, but in China it was 1 to 3.1 in 1953 and 1 to 1.1 in 1980.

Second, specializations do not reflect the needs of the economy. Even today, institutions of higher education throughout China offer more than 450 specializations in science and engineering, but only 46, or 10.2% of all specializations are geared toward light industry. Since 1949, a total of 2.24 million students graduated in science and engineering, but only 70,000, or 3.1% of all graduates, specialized in light industry. Currently, there are approximately 18,000 students of finance and economics, only 2.6% of all students in higher education, but China has 400,000 industrial transport and communication enterprises.[16]

When graduates from higher education were assigned jobs in 1981, a joke went round that China's institutes of higher education offered over 845 specializations but there was a shortage of trained people in 353 of them (or 41.7% of all specializations), a shortfall of 190,000 students. There was also a surplus of 10,000 graduates in 157 specializations (18.5% of all specializations), and a total of 214 specializations had shortages.[17]

Third, the teacher-student ratio in higher education has been widely criticized. Currently, the average for universities worldwide is 1:14; in England it is 1:8; at state universities in the United States it is

1:20; in France it is 1:20; and in Japan it is 1:19.3. But in China the ratio of teachers to students in higher education is 1:4.3 and for universities under the Ministry of Education, 1:3.3. If one includes both teachers and staff, the ratio is 1:1.97, because the ratio of teachers to staff is 1:1.5 (in developed countries the teacher-staff ratio is 2:1 or 3:1). There is clearly a large waste in terms of excess personnel at the university level.

The teacher-student ratio in secondary schools is 1:19.1, and in primary schools it is 1:24.3. The overall average teacher/student ratio at all levels in China is 1:22, and if staff are included it is 1:12.1. If one does not consider the quality of the teachers (a problem addressed below), this more closely approximates international levels.

Table 8.2 gives a summary of the situation in China's educational system based on the most recent, formal reports issued by the government.[18]

The table shows that China has already established 1 million schools of different types, and that approximately 200 million people have studied at them. Teachers number approximately 10 million. Over 6 million students have graduated from institutes of higher education in the last 35 years. From the development perspective, branch schools and ordinary secondary schools have increased most rapidly, while elementary schools have increased comparatively slowly.

The table gives a complex picture of higher education. From the 1985 statistics, it appears that there were 17.25 million students that year, of whom 2.085 million were regular university undergraduates, and 15.16 million were vocational school students.[19] In addition, China had sent 25,000 students overseas to study, 15,000 of whom have already graduated and returned to China.

China currently has over 10 million teachers—the world's largest teaching force—and the teacher-student ratio in secondary and primary schools doesn't differ significantly from the general ratio for industrialized countries. Unfortunately many teachers in China are underqualified. The teaching force swelled most rapidly during the Cultural Revolution, when a group of policy-makers put forth the preposterous requirement that high schools be universal.

When their campaign came to an end in 1978, there were 65.5 million secondary school students, an increase of 56.1 million over 1965.[20] In 1983, there were almost 44 million students, an increase of 1.5 times. That same year there were 3.18 million secondary school teachers, 2.72 million more than in 1965. In 1983 there were 2.96 million teachers in the entire secondary school system, still over 220,000 more than in 1965. Of these, only 210,000 or 7.7% had graduated from teaching colleges. The other 92.3% were promoted from primary schools, secondary-level normal schools, or recruited among high school students.

In 1978, the situation in primary schools was similar. That year, there were 146 million elementary school students in China and 5.22 million primary school teachers, an increase of 30 million students (25%) and 1.37 million teachers (35%) over 1965. About 33% of all teachers (1.25 million) were secondary school graduates, while the remainder were locally hired (and less well qualified).

By early 1978, the distribution of China's 8.77 million teachers was as follows:[21]

- 5.87 million teachers were assigned to primary schools and of

TABLE 8.2 CHINA'S EDUCATIONAL STATISTICS 1985

	# of schools (1)	# of students (10,000)	Teachers/ Staff (10,000)	Graduates/ New students (10,000)	End of 1983 Graduated (10,000)
graduate students (including scientific research units)	698	80,553 individuals			
ordinary institution of higher education	1,016	170.31	34.43/52.6	31.64/ 61.92	411.02
adult higher education	1,216	172.50	6.93/ 7.41	34.70/ 78.78	200
total for higher education	2,232	350.84	41.36/ 60.04	66.34/ 140.7	611.02
ordinary secondary school	93,200	4,705.96	259.7 (1983)		17.160.2
technical secondary school	2,529	101.29	12.80/ 18.51	26.16/ 45.36	
secondary teaching school	1,028	55.82	4.60/ 4.41	16.71/ 21.47	
vocational secondary school	8,070	229.57			1,639.8
secondary school for adults	49,322	546.96	14.7/ 11.24	284.27/ 413.53	
subtotal	154,000	5,639.6	291.8/ 34.15	327.14/ 480.36	
primary school	832,300	13,370.18	611.83		23.210
adult primary school	278,450	833.81	7.17/ 4.02	493.82/ 532.18	
subtotal	1.1 million	14,204	623.12		
total	1.27 million	200 million	1,050.5		
pre-school	17.23	1,479.7	41.52/ 22.2 (1982)		

these, 3.53 million (60%) were hired locally.

- 2.6 million teachers were assigned to secondary schools, including vocational secondary schools. Of these, 1.27 million (49%) were locally hired.
- 230,000 teachers were assigned to universities.

A quick comparison with the United States shows that in the same year there were 2.5 million primary and secondary school teachers in the United States, only 30% of China's total figure. But that country had 700,000 university teachers, almost three times as many as China.

The method used in China to solve the shortage of primary and secondary school teachers during the Cultural Revolution was absurd. One estimate from that period concluded that 86% of middle school teachers were unqualified, as were about 50% of the high school and primary school teachers. As a result of this, institutions of higher education are now being confronted with a further fall in academic standards. Statistics from 1983 show that 16.5% of the secondary school teachers and 49.3% of the primary school teachers were unqualified local hires *(minban)*; only 40.4% of the high school teachers had an undergraduate education or more; only 21.2% of the middle school teachers had a vocational high school, junior college or higher training; and only 56.1% of the primary school teachers were high school graduates or higher.[22]

All along, the most difficult issues for teachers have been their low salaries, the nature of their work, and their living conditions. The situation has not changed today. China's teachers must still toil under conditions that would astonish faculty in other parts of the world.

In 1980, wages for primary school teachers were the lowest of all professions in the country, and secondary school teachers' wages were the second lowest.[23] University teachers often earn less than their children and their students. Teachers have relatively low social esteem, and in many areas they are discriminated against, receiving poor, cramped housing and inferior benefits.

In higher education, many teachers do not enjoy a position commensurate with their qualifications. A 1981 survey at Jiaotong University in Shanghai revealed that 54 out of 65 professors (90%), and 198 out of 230 associate professors (86%), held positions that did not match their qualifications. Forty-six of them held positions one grade lower than appropriate; 62 were two grades lower; 42 three grades lower, and 48 were four grades lower. Of the 1,046 lecturers at Jiaotong University, 962 (92%) held positions not matching their qualifications. Two-hundred-five were one grade lower, 548 were two grades lower, and 204 were three grades lower.[24] This situation persists to the present day.

Another major concern for teachers is that students are forced into studying in a system which emphasizes examinations while failing at career preparation. According to 1983 data, for every 10,000 people in China, the number of students at various schools was as follows:[25]

1)	students in higher education	21.2
	— students at ordinary institutions of higher education	12.0
	— adult students in continuing education	9.2
2)	students at vocational high school/ junior college	11.4
3)	ordinary high school	62.7
4)	ordinary junior high school	375.4
5)	agricultural junior high school	12.2
6)	primary school	1352.0

There are over 30 times as many students in middle school as in agricultural middle school and 6.5 times as many students in high school as in vocational high school/junior college *(zhongzhuan)*. The ratio between university, high school, and primary school students is even more out of proportion. When considering these figures, one must also come to terms with another reality: there are no careers for China's secondary school graduates. As a result the vast majority try to carry on to get a higher degree, and Chinese students are all constrained by entrance exams for the next level of school.

In fact, very few have the chance to go on to higher education. According to 1981 statistics, only 68.3% of the primary school students were accepted into middle school, 31.5% of middle school students made it to high school (the latter figure for Japan is over 94%), and fewer than 5% of the high school students get into university. As a result, failing exams is a common experience for Chinese students.

By 1983 only 21 out of every 10,000 people in China were at university, while the figure for the United States in 1975 was 520, Japan, 210 (1976), and the Soviet Union, nearly 200 (1976).[26] In 1983, 454 out of every 10,000 people in China were in secondary school, while in figure for the United States in 1975 was 962, in Japan, 818, and in West Germany, 638.[27]

The Chinese educational system inculcates knowledge with the aim of producing a certain type of scholar. From start to finish, students are caught in the trap of grades. They take notes, memorize them, regurgitate them in exams, and then throw them away when it is over. They learn a lot but have little real knowledge, and their high grades are no measure of ability. A great many qualities, like perseverance, cooperation, creativity, research and organizational skills, verbal ability, and community spirit cannot be measured by standardized tests.

This educational rut has a long tradition. It started in the feudal period when candidates for the civil service were required to write the famous "eight-legged essays," and the goal of study was an official career. Being an official meant being obedient and avoiding risks and responsibility. Officials did not presume to make decisions; they just had to take orders and tow the line. This cultural tradition is the most basic cause of China's backwardness, and even today its influence is pervasive, especially within education. As a result, Chinese students are typically reserved, conservative, and submissive.

This educational tradition has led the entire nation to emphasize natural science over the humanities, and industry over commerce. The mind set of the entire society is to encourage gifted youth to pursue an easy and comfortable career and to discourage them from following a path of independent development or advancement.

■ A Ton of Pressure

China's educational system is also coming under greater and greater pressure at all levels.

First is the problem of preschool education. Every year between 17 and 18 million [20 million by 1990] children are born in China and approximately 60 million three-to-five-year-olds should enter nursery school. But in 1983 only 11.4 million children, not even 20% of the total, entered preschool. In Guangdong, a region that is considered advanced, only 7.45% of children in the appropriate age group entered preschool in 1982 and in many places none did. The increase of one-child families, and improvements in the economy and living conditions are bound to heighten demand for preschool education in the future. It goes without saying that the problems of training teachers and providing adequate facilities will become more acute as a result of this.

The number of three-to-five-year-olds receiving preschool education is quite high in many other countries. In 1980, for example, 50.2% of children in that age group in the Soviet Union went to nursery school. In the United States in 1975 it was 49%, and 87–92%

for children five years of age. In France in 1980, 45% of the two year-olds, 90% of the three year-olds, and 96.6% of the four and five year-olds went to nursery school.[28]

Elementary education is equally inadequate. During the Cultural Revolution, elementary education throughout China suffered a terrible reverse due to the absurd policy of advocating universal high school education. As we have seen this involved a massive transfer of primary school teachers to high schools, a move for which many were not qualified. As a result, primary education was neglected, and many schools lost their staffs.[29]

Education in rural areas will be a key problem. With the economic development of China's rural areas, the peasants will increasingly demand better production technology, more material comforts, and education and cultural activities. If the 80% of the population living in the countryside is left behind in China's development, China's modernization is simply inconceivable.

In 1983 there were 822,300 primary-level schools in rural China, comprising 95% of the total. About 94% of the children of the appropriate age were entering schools, but the pass rate was only 20–45%. Of the 6.06 million teachers,[30] 56.1% of secondary school teachers were high school graduates, but only approximately one-third were actually qualified.[31] This string of figures explains many problems. Compared to the pre-1949 period, the number of students had quintupled, while the number of schools has only doubled.

All this exacerbates the immense problem of illiteracy alluded to in previous chapters. A 1987 survey of the Ningxia Autonomous Region showed that the illiteracy rate among 12-to-14-year-olds in the region was 36.8% and in the 15–40 age group it was as high as 50.9%. If births continue at the present rate, the current capacity for 135 million students will be sufficient, but, as we have seen, quality will be sacrificed.

Making universal elementary education a reality is the first major challenge. In 1982, the new constitution of the People's Republic of China stipulated universal, compulsory elementary education, but many difficulties remain and many areas have not yet been able to implement it. It is obvious that the state will not have the resources to remedy the situation for some time to come, and local demand may cause the development of elementary education to proceed on a regional basis, along with the economic development of each area.

The trend toward regional development is already evident in Jiangsu Province, where on 27 June 1984, the Sixth Plenum of the Second Jiangsu Provincial Congress was the first to pass a temporary resolution for the implementation of compulsory elementary education throughout the province.

But development is very uneven. In some places the percentage of students entering primary school has actually fallen, and many students drop out of school. Recently it was reported that about 2.7 million school age children fail to start school each year, and that 2.24 million or 84% of these are girls. In 1987 the percentage of children starting primary school in eleven provinces and regions was 95% or lower, and in some areas the rate for girls was only 40–50%.

In Ningxia, 56.9% of the Moslem children aged six to eleven are unable to attend school, and in 1986 over 15,000 children in Gansu were unable to go to school, 83.6% of whom were girls. Among the Miao minority of Guizhou only 20% of the students are female, and in the Yao Autonomous region of Guangxi it is more or less the case that "boys study and girls raise pigs." Some schools there do not have a single female student.[32]

Most of the world's nations have already made elementary education compulsory, and it cannot be long before the trend to act on secondary education spreads to China.

By the end of 1983, China had 98,703 secondary schools, of which 3,090 were vocational secondary schools. Technical schools, agricultural middle schools, professional middle schools, and adult middle schools comprised 10,121, for a total of 109,685 schools. The ratio between ordinary middle schools and vocational middle schools is 31.2:1, whereas prior to the Cultural Revolution it was 2.5:1. There are 22.6 times as many ordinary middle schools as before Liberation in 1949, and only 3.97 times as many secondary-level vocational schools.

In the same year, there were a total of 44.765 million secondary school students in China, 43.977 million of whom were ordinary secondary school students, an increase of 29.4 times over the pre-liberation figure. Vocational secondary school students numbered 688,000 in 1983, 8.9 times as many as before 1949. The ratio between the number of students at the two types of schools is 64:1 and the ratio between their rate of increase is 3.6:1. In 1982 the ratio of ordinary secondary school students to vocational secondary school students was 83.5:1.[33]

Even if an average of only 20 million people are born each year in China, the secondary school age group will still number 100 to 120 million, but the number of students actually in school is only 41–44% of this figure. Since 1949, the average percentage of primary school graduates entering the next grade level has been 67.3% (in 1982 it was

66.2%). The percentage of middle school graduates getting into a higher grade was only 35.5% (in 1982 it was 32.3%). Conditions in many middle schools are not much better than those in the worst primary schools.

When it was realized that the blind development of secondary schools in the 1970s had been a mistake, an attempt was made to solve the problem by drastically cutting them back. By 1983 the number of ordinary middle schools in China was 66,000 fewer than in 1978, a 40.7% drop, and the number of students in school had been reduced by 21.506 million, or 32.8%.

In the same year there were 130 million people between the ages of 12 and 16 but only 40 million persons (31%) in this age group were in secondary school. In 1983 only 67.3% of the primary school graduates, and 35.5% of the middle school graduates went on to the next grade (including those who went on to technical schools), far fewer than in many countries.[34]

This state of affairs will make it difficult for China to realize its ambitious modernization goals, and to meet its development needs while salvaging its environment during the final years of this century. In particular, we must consider that the students who are entering secondary education now will be entering the workforce in 10 years time, when China is at the most critical juncture in the effort to quadruple economic growth.

■ Higher Education

Of all the problems that confront education in China, the most complex is still that of higher education. In terms of quality, quantity, teachers, facilities and other requirements, higher education is unable to meet the huge development needs of modern society. The failure to train personnel to work in agriculture, education, management, law and other fields is especially glaring.

Higher education in China has a history of only just over 90 years, a relatively short period compared to other major countries. In 1949, China had only 205 institutions of higher education, with 117,000 students in attendance. By 1965 there were 434 institutions, and 674,000 students, but during the Cultural Revolution the number of schools fell to just over 300, teaching came to a standstill, and college education suffered a major reverse.

By 1977 the number of institutions of higher education had been restored to 404, and 625,000 students were in attendance. Two years later, there was an enormous rise in the number of schools to 633 with 1.02 million students, an increase of over 110 schools per year and close to 200,000 students. After that, came a yearly average increase of 56 institutions of higher education for several consecutive years. By 1983 there were 805 schools (of which 97 were "key schools"), and over 1.2 million students.

By the end of 1985, there were 1,016 ordinary institutions of higher education and 1,216 institutions of higher education for adults. There are another 52 ordinary institutions of higher education still seeking formal approval to start construction, but it is not clear how many of these exist in name only.[35] Many are just glorified technical middle schools with no dormitories, professors, equipment, or books.

One survey of 35 local universities found that an investment of 50,000 yuan and the recruitment of a few dozen students are enough for a school to be considered an established university. Twelve of the 35 schools surveyed had liquid assets of less than 100,000 yuan. Twelve of them had less than 2,000 square meters of space for teaching, and eight had practically no buildings at all.[36] This is not real development, but a hollow façade that serves no one.

To put it bluntly, some people have written flattering essays about the growth of higher education in order to further their careers and win political credibility. Today, of course, money has also become a factor, and the unauthorized issuing of university diplomas for a fee of 1,000 or more yuan is common. Surprisingly, this practice receives a great deal of support from the community. In 1985, one company spent over 100,000 yuan to get 30 individuals admitted to the People's University, most of them the children of the company's officials.

The sheer percentage increase in students can be made to sound impressive, until it is more closely examined. For example, in 1982 Jiang Nanxiang noted that in the 32 years between 1949 and 1982, the number of full-time university students increased by an average of 8% a year. During the 17 years prior to the Cultural Revolution, the average yearly increase was 11.5% and from 1977 to 1981 it was 18%. In the United States the average yearly increase between 1946 and 1976 was 5.33%, and in the 1960s, it was 8.2%. Between 1965 and 1975 in Japan, the average yearly increase was 6.3%, and for the same period, the average yearly increase in the Soviet Union was 2.4%

In light of this, Jiang Nanxiang believes that higher education has developed rapidly in China, and although some critics are concerned that only 4% of the high school students go on to attend university, Jiang does not consider this a problem.[37] He argues that the 18% increase since the pre-Cultural Revolution period is a better reflection of the true situation. On this basis, we are number one in the world again!

In fact, this figure is so distorted that it is not worth publishing. For six years during the 1950s, the number of students accepted into universities exceeded the number of high school graduates that year! For the remaining four years, the percentage of high school students accepted was 89% or higher. In the 1960s, the percentage of high school students accepted into university was 30–40%. From 1965 to 1980 the number accepted leapt from 165,000 to 281,000, an increase of 75%.

During the Cultural Revolution, the number of high school graduates who skipped grades rose sharply from 360,000 to 6.16 million, an 18-fold increase. High schools expanded 24 times as fast as higher education, causing the acceptance rate to fall quickly from 45% to 4%, so the meager 4% entering university is more indicative of the real problem than the figure of 18%.

One aspect of this problem is that the abnormal development of education in China, with its great upswings and downturns, has created chaos. This is the origin of many of the serious difficulties in higher education today. The surges and declines in schools and students have dragged other things behind them: teachers, capital, facilities, research, and people's attitudes to education have undergone similar swings, and the quality of the entire educational system has suffered from these fluctuations.

Compared with other countries, China has too few schools. The United States, with a population about one fifth that of China, had 3125 institutions of higher education in 1979, 4.9 times as many as China. In relation to the population, the United States has more than 20 times as many institutions of higher education as China. In 1979 the United States had 10.3 million college students, about 10 times as many as China had in 1984, and in relation to its population, almost 50 times as many college students as China.

Every year 2.5 million students, or a third of the college age population, are admitted to institutions of higher education in the United States: almost 10 times as many as in China.[38] In relation to the population, the admission rate is over 40 times higher in the United States, and 53% of all Americans in the 18–24 age group attend college or university, and 40% in Japan. There is no way China's figure of 4% can stand up to this comparison, or be dismissed as if it were not a problem. The discrepancy is too great.

New developments in science and technology obviously mean that in the future, education and scientific research will be the most important factors determining a society's collective potential. According to some recent preliminary calculations, about 14–15 million specialists with vocational high school, university or higher education will be needed to build a basic economic foundation for China. But in the 1980s, China's universities and vocational high schools only had the capacity to train 7–8 million.[39]

The country must make major adjustments in education policy regarding the right to establish schools, teacher training, student recruitment, the distribution of labor, teaching requirements, facilities, and the overall distribution of schools, all of which must be modified in order to meet the challenges ahead.

9

NATURE'S UNGRATEFUL CHILDREN

In 1987 I published a journal article entitled "China's Ecological Crisis," which warned about the serious threats to China's forests. The publisher was sensitive to the issue and emphasized that the crisis could erupt at any time. The words "any time" are important, because it is extremely difficult to make precise short-term forecasts about any crisis. Unfortunately, the warning did not provoke the concern it should have.

Less than two months later, a devastating fire broke out in the Daxinganling forest in Heilongjiang. Over 2.5 million acres, including 1.75 million acres of forest, were burned. 850,000 cubic meters of stored timber were destroyed, the county seat of Mohe, home to 60,000 people, was razed to the ground in a single night, and there was serious looting on several hundred kilometers of land along the railroad from the Ta River to Gulian.

The fire took a heavy toll, destroying 67 bridges and culverts, 483 kilometers of communication lines, 284 kilometers of electrical transmission lines, 325,000 tons of grain, 614,000 square meters of buildings, and 193 human lives.[1] The loss of forest, life, and property made this the most serious fire since the founding of the People's Republic of China.

Fires have always been part of the forest ecosystem, serving the function of clearing forest debris. Every year, approximately 200,000 forest fires occur worldwide, most of which are extinguished within a few hours or days. Few fires cause serious destruction, but among those that have, the conflagration in China was the most devastating.

It has been conjectured that the great forest fires that occurred worldwide in 1987 were related to the reversal in atmospheric pressure on the east and west of the Pacific. Canada, the United States, and the USSR were all hit by serious fires. But the fire in Alaska at the same latitude as Daxinganling destroyed only 62,500 acres of forest, 1/28 of the area devastated in the Daxinganling. Canada had four consecutive large forest fires, but each destroyed only 55,000 acres, and although a conflagration in the Soviet Union's Baikal region raged for over a month, it destroyed only 20,000 acres.

Why was it then, that in China, where 58,000 troops dug a 500-meter-wide fire break, the raging flames could not be prevented from sweeping across? The major reasons were excessive logging over a prolonged period, a large build up of forest debris, mismanagement, and outmoded fire-fighting equipment.

From 1950 to 1975, forest fires in China affected an area of 21.6 million acres, or one-third of the reforestation and conservation area (which was about 10% of China's total area). The conflagration in Heilongjiang in 1987 destroyed a forested area equivalent to the total reforestation and conservation area of the province for a five-year period.

As we have seen from the discussion of environmental destruction in other chapters, forest fires are only one symptom of serious environmental damage in China. As noted, destruction from the felling of China's forests has already reached danger point. (Sustainable forest cover should be over 20%, but in China it is only 12–13%). One-third of China's grasslands have turned to desert; the decrease in arable land is already at a dangerous level, and water resources are threatened.

Having discussed the ecological damage to grassland, forest, topsoil, and surface water, we must address three remaining issues: the plight of China's marine fishing grounds, which have been damaged almost to the point of annihilation by pollution, the deterioration of the drinking water supply, and air pollution.

According to reports from various sources, oil pollution in the Bohai Sea and the Yellow Sea already exceeds standards by close to 50%.[2] Yellow croaker, hairtail, herring, seabream, and other fish in the Bohai have already sustained serious harm, and prawns are now rare. Croakers have virtually disappeared from the Yellow Sea, and little trace remains of the silverfish and fresh water crabs that were once famous far and wide.

Beijing residents are allotted four kilograms of fish per person annually. However, 75% of the fish for the capital comes from areas which have reached crisis point due to prolonged excessive and reckless fishing, worsening pollution, and the practice of netting spawn. The Qiandao, Fenlan, and Milu fishing grounds make up the Zhoushan region which is famous as China's largest fishing ground and accounts for one-third of the total salt water catch in China. At present, the region is experiencing a crisis that shows no sign of abating.

In 1986, the quantity of fish caught at the Zhoushan fishing grounds was 100–150 million kilograms less than 10 years before. In the 1960s, the same fishery provided 60 million kilograms of large yellow croakers, 25 million kilograms of small yellow croakers and 35 million kilograms of cuttlefish. In 1986, the catch was only 200,000 kilograms of large yellow croakers and 250,000 kilograms of cuttlefish. There are almost no small yellow croakers left, and the quantity of salt water crab is down from 30 million kilograms to around 750,000 kilograms. The tragedy of Zhoushan is at least as shocking as that of the Daxinganling forest.

More than 50,000 fishing nets are already being cast in China's marine fishing grounds and the number is increasing rapidly. Day and night without pause, thousands of fishing boats make their rounds, casting nets into a polluted sea. Every year, 3 billion tons of contaminated water are dumped into the ocean from Shanghai, Hangzhou, Ningbo, and other cities. This will probably double by the year 2000. The oil, copper, zinc, mercury, lead and other elements present in the water of the fishing grounds already exceeds standards set in the industrialized nations, and the pollution index continues to rise.

▌ Dumping Poses a Serious Threat to Drinking Water

According to statistics from the World Health Organization, at least 80% of disease in the world is water related. Approximately 50% of the 18 million child deaths in the world each year are related to the poor quality of drinking water. As a consequence, the United Nations designated 1981–1990 as the International Decade for Clean Drinking Water. The decade has already passed, but the pollution of China's water sources continues to intensify.

Managers in the manufacturing sector rarely take into account that even at China's current level of industrialization, huge quantities of water are required. To extract a ton of coal 1–1.5 tons of water is needed; smelting a ton of steel requires 20–40 tons of water; manufacturing a ton of paper, 200–250 tons, and producing a ton of chemical fertilizer, 500–600 tons. It takes 1,200–1,700 tons of water to produce a ton of synthetic cloth, and 400 tons to make a car. Moreover, every acre of crop land consumes water during the growing period. Cotton requires 2,000–2,400 cubic meters of water, wheat 3,000 cubic meters—2,500–3,000 tons of water are required to grow a ton of grain.

Due to increases in population, and industrial and agricultural development, more and more water is being drawn from the ground. In particular, increases in irrigation and other processes that consume large amounts of water have reduced river levels in the lower reaches where waste water is diluted. Drawing large quantities from ground water sources obviously increases the concentration of chemical elements in drinking water. In short, industrial waste, sewage and recirculated water from irrigation constitute the three main sources of pollution threatening China's water supply.

Moreover, industry is dumping all sorts of new complex chemical pollutants which are causing a rapid deterioration in water quality. Many of these substances do not readily break down: acetone, benzene, 2-phenylthiazole, isocyanic acid, methyl chloride, styrene, and other wastes are extremely damaging to drinking water. When water from irrigation returns to rivers and the aquiferous layer, it contains considerably more soluble solids, including sodium sulfate, cyanide, and other substances that cannot be eliminated by normal biological or natural processes.

Even more frequently than industrial waste, sewage is dumped into water supply sources. Bacteria, viruses, algae-breeding nutrients, and suspended and soluble solids all produce strange, foul-smelling substances which are pouring into water sources in large quantities.

Currently, 80 million tons of contaminated industrial water are discharged every day in China, and 80% or more of the industrial waste water enters rivers, lakes, and the ocean untreated. Furthermore, in China, thermal power plants discharge approximately 10 million tons of coal dust into rivers yearly, and industry discharges over 300 million tons of waste residue each year.

The pollution of urban water sources is even more intolerable. Not until 1980 did China have its first water treatment plant, in the eastern suburbs of Beijing. And in 1983, when China's urban population neared 200 million, there were only 35 small-scale water treatment plants in operation. By contrast, in the United States, sewage has been treated for decades, and billions are spent on it annually. The United States has not been able to solve the problem of second generation pollution, like eutrophication, toxic substances, and carcinogens, but for China, it is almost futile to begin to discuss the problem of second generation pollution: we suffer from much more fundamental problems.

Shanghai has the greatest technological capability in China, and of the 5 million or more tons of polluted water discharged daily there, only 200,000 (4%) tons can be treated. The sewers in Shanghai were installed in the 1920s and 1930s and long ago became inadequate. They cannot withstand the pressures of the growing population, and the situation is so serious that large quantities of sewage are starting to spill out onto the streets. Although Shanghai estimates that 100,000 individuals in the city are either unemployed or dissatisfied individual entrepreneurs (getihu), the government claims that there are no workers to repair the sewers.

The quality of the water in the Huangpu River was already starting to deteriorate in 1958. Today, the river's water is fetid for at least 165 days in the year. It is particularly bad from November to February, when the level of the river falls, impeding the flushing out of the polluted water. But drinking water is constantly drawn directly from the Huangpu. As a result, even cooked vegetables have a foul odor—and the quality of Shanghai beer is inferior to that of other Chinese beers.

Along the banks of the Shanghai's Suzhou River there are over 70 dilapidated old factories that were built in the 1920s and 1930s. The Suzhou River long ago became a stinking sewage ditch, from which all living things vanished decades ago.

In addition to the vast quantities of polluted water, there are also 8,000 factories in Shanghai that burn a total of 18 million tons of coal a year. The amount of dust falling each month has already reached 44 tons per square kilometer. Despite this horrendous situation, Shanghai did not establish an office for environmental protection until 1980.

In 1985, several researchers from Nanjing University carried out research on the organic pollutants in Nanjing's tap water. Preliminary investigations indicated the presence of 73 pollutants in the water, including DDVP, BHC, and diethylether. The long-term damage to drinking water from such toxins is very great. Fourteen of the 73 pollutants in Nanjing's running water are among those named by the U.S. Environmental Protection Agency as major pollutants, and four are carcinogens.

In addition, a survey of the ground water of 47 major cities in China has revealed that 43 of them suffer from pollution. Of 18 cities in the North that rely on ground water as a primary water source, 17 have been polluted. In nine cities the pollution is serious, and it is worst in Beijing, compared to which the level of pollution of Nanjing's water is considered only average.[3]

Groundwater is also polluted by the vast amount of garbage in China's cities. The quantity of trash is increasing annually by an average of 10%, doubling every seven years. (By contrast, East Germany's annual rate of increase is 3–4%, while in England and France, it has doubled every 18–20 years). (Zhang Shaoguan has made a detailed study of this problem.)[4] In 1985, 51.9 million tons of garbage and 35.5 million tons of excrement were generated by over 300 cities in China per year, but only 3.6% of all urban garbage and sewage is decontaminated. Large amounts of untreated garbage and human waste are dumped in the outskirts of the cities or into rivers. According to photo surveys by the Chinese Air Force, there are approximately 5,000 garbage heaps in the districts around Beijing, covering an area of 1,400 acres. Beijing produces 9,000 tons of garbage per day. Urban household garbage alone totals 70 million tons a day.

West German research suggests that one garbage dump can pollute the water sources around it for 50 kilometers in any direction. If that is the case, 250,000 square kilometers of land around Beijing will be polluted in the future. In fact, the districts around Beijing cover an area of only 17,000 square kilometers, so it is inevitable that their water reserves will all be thoroughly polluted. The Shanghai municipality generates over 12,000 tons of garbage per day. The land available for burying garbage in nearby districts has been sharply reduced. In the past, Zhejiang Province and Jiangsu Province disposed of 30% of Shanghai's garbage, but by 1985 it had fallen to 5%.

Another tricky problem is that 60% of China's urban garbage takes the form not of paper, or large pieces of metal and plastic, but of ashes from coal burning, mixed in with large quantities of brick dust, dirt, and vegetable waste. This kind of waste easily damages the soil, making it gritty and sandy, and harming the crops. The 34,500 acres of crop land in the districts around Beijing receive an average of over 40 tons of garbage per acre annually. Some fields already have a rubble content of 25–50%, forming a layer of garbage in the soil that destroys the soil structure and so seriously reduces its capacity to retain water and fertilizer that many farmers will no longer accept unprocessed refuse. It also enables bacteria and insect larvae to propagate in the fields. If areas like this could clean up their fields, it is estimated that 10–30% of the amount spent on transporting vegetables to China's cities could be saved.

Considering the extent of pollution, it should be easier to understand why China suffers from such a high incidence of hepatitis and other liver diseases. A study done in 1986 indicated that of the approximately 250 million carriers of hepatitis B worldwide, 100 million were in China. Out of the 250,000 peo' cancer worldwide, 100,000 are Chinese, a far hi China's one-fifth share of the world populatio the major outbreak of hepatitis in Shanghai i

■ A Clean River? What's Tha

A new tendency that gives cause for concern is the rap environmental pollution from the cities to more than 50,00 China's towns, and to many villages as well.

Shaoxing in Zhejiang Province has long been famous for its pure mountain water. In the last few years, Shaoxing established over 80 small printing plants, and a few electric power stations and small-scale paper mills. In some places, there is now no clean water left for drinking. (This also makes it difficult to maintain production of the famous Shaoxing wine.) Shaoxing and the much touted Gong County in Henan Province, are classic examples of areas that now believe in "getting rich first," which really means "getting dirty first."

According to incomplete statistics on 798 cities and towns in 10 river valleys throughout China, 78 million cubic meters of polluted water are dumped directly into bodies of water every day without being treated in any way. (This is 28.5 billion cubic meters annually.) Industrial waste water makes up 81.2% of the total, and human sewage 18.8%. There are at least 18,600 kilometers of river with excessive levels of phenol, cyanide, arsenic, mercury and chromium. Of these rivers, 12,600 kilometers can no longer be used for irrigation, and 2,400 kilometers of water in China no longer have any fish or shrimp. In the Lanzhou section of the Yellow River the amount of phenol and arsenic exceeds standards by more than eleven times.[5]

Recently, the deputy director of Shanxi's Provincial Science and Technology Committee, Zhong Jixue, carried out a survey in Qinxian, Tunliu, Xiangyuan, and seven other districts of Nanwu Township in Pudong. He discovered that the water of the famous Zhang River is already severely polluted. Along its banks are the 10 largest provincial and municipal mining enterprises, and a string of provincial-level chemical fertilizer plants, paper mills, and power stations whose waste water and residue is dumped directly into the river.

Waste from these industries has turned the river black, and many dangerous substances are suspended in the water. Oxygen-depleting chemicals exceed standards by 100%, and living organisms that consume oxygen by 50%. The ammonium nitrate content is over 66%

standards; volatile phenol over 16%, and fluorine, 20%. ₁o drink water from the river notice a strange taste, which is ₁rising, and 40% of them are troubled by chronic intestinal ₋ms, diarrhea, and tooth decay.[6]

According to another study in Jiangsu in 1986, 80,000 small ₋tories discharged 670 million tons of waste water annually, only ₁0% of which underwent rudimentary treatment. The remainder ran directly into the soil and polluted at least 65,000 acres of farmland. In parts of Zhejiang, numerous textile dyeing factories, electric power plants, and brick, cement, and paper factories have made the sections of the rivers near cities black and foul. The quality of water in the major rivers, the Qin, the Fenghua, and the Yao, has sharply declined.

In 1986, a survey of eight counties and one city in the Langfang region of Hebei Province found that 4,237 town enterprises were polluters. Of these, 1,689 were serious offenders. The 350 electroplating plants in the region use 28,000 kilos of chromium anhydride and 26,000 kilos of cyanide a month, but the vast majority of them have no equipment for treating waste gas, waste water, and industrial residue. Waste water is "treated" by letting it seep into a hole or flow out slowly. This has contaminated ground water down to 40 meters below the surface, and explains why people or animals that accidently drink the waste water die on the spot. Even well-water 300 meters down is seriously polluted.

As yet, China has found no solution to the continuing deterioration of drinking water. Recently, some cities have built high rise apartment buildings where open, roof-top water tanks are lined up next to chimneys belching foul, smokey dust: their residents face yet another direct threat to their drinking water.

The pollution of several rivers is so serious that many Chinese don't even know what a "clear river" is. The once-beautiful Songhua River is already filthy, and the famous large carp of the Yellow River have more or less vanished due to pollution. The Yanguoxia Chemical Factory on the Lanzhou section of the river alone has consumed 100 tons of mercury annually since 1971 and allowed huge quantities of liquid mercury to pour directly into the Yellow River.

The Huai River has succumbed to the same fate. Its tributary, the Kui, has become a sewage drain. Every day Xuzhou's 124 factories discharge an average of 70,000 tons of industrial waste water and 20,000 tons of human sewage into the Kui. The stench is overwhelming, and pollution poses a serious risk to the health of the 600,000 inhabitants on its banks.[7]

The network of rivers that make up the Pearl River area in Guangdong Province is so polluted that it is difficult to find a suitable water source. The quality of the water in the Mei, Bei, and Lian rivers has already seriously deteriorated. The Fen River (near Foshan) is nearly fetid, and the ammonium nitrate content of the Guangzhou section of the river is five times the standard. Guangzhou's eight water plants were all transferred to Dongjiang and Xijiang because of the pollution of the Pearl River but there is nowhere to transfer the water plants of Foshan, Jiangmen, Zhongshan, Dongguan, and other cities. (In October 1987—a few days after I wrote a long article warning about the danger of this situation, a synthetic textile plant in Guangdong unexpectedly discharged large quantities of cyanide into the Mei River, causing extensive damage and public outcry throughout Guangdong.)

If the Tang poets Li Bo and Du Fu were to travel to the Yangtze today, they would find little inspiration for poetry. A green plume of murky water gushes from a paper mill on the river's banks at Yibin, spreading a layer of foam over the surface of the river. Passengers traveling by literally hold their noses and frown. At all of the ports on the Yangtze, from Chongqing and Wuhan to Shanghai, the surface of the water is covered with dust and coal particles.

The city of Ganliu on the banks of the Yangtze discharges 16 million tons of polluted waste water into the river every day.[8] Even if this does not increase, by the year 2000 the entire basin of the Yangtze River will have 30 billion tons of polluted waste water discharged into it every year. On the basis that a ton of waste water pollutes 20–30 tons of clean water, 60–90% of the Yangtze River, which constitutes 34% of China's water resources, will be polluted. The population of the 20 or more large and medium-sized cities of the Yangtze River basin, or almost one-third of China's population, will be affected.

At least 54 of China's 78 major rivers are already polluted, according to official statistics, and so are approximately 70% of their 50,000-plus tributaries. Fourteen rivers are severely polluted. A recent government survey of over 1,200 rivers found that over 850 (70%) were polluted, more than 230 of them severely. The amount of fresh-water fish caught nationwide fell from 600,000 tons in the 1950s to 400,000 tons in the 1960s to 300,000 tons in the 1970s. This decrease continues to the present day.

The National Environmental Protection Office announced that in the last 10 years, the annual rate of increase in polluted water was 7.9%, close to the combined rate of growth for industry and agriculture. If pollution levels continue to rise in proportion to China's target for quadrupling output, by the year 2000, the amount of polluted water discharged would exceed 125 billion tons, and 2,500–3,800 billion tons of clean water would be polluted. This already exceeds the total amount of fresh water resources in China (approximately 2,700 billion tons).

In 1985 China released the first set of detailed data on the state of environmental protection work. The data shows that the percentage of industrial waste water treated has only increased by 2–3% per year. At this rate, it will take another 40 years before all water undergoes rudimentary treatment. The introduction of other forms of pollution control is equally slow.

▌ Protecting the Skies

Not long ago a United Nations inspection committee brought a set of instruments to China to study pollution levels. As soon as they turned on their instruments at Beijing Airport, the needle swung right off the dial, and the instrument stopped working. This incident has become an international joke.

Many of China's towns and cities suffer from smog, especially where industry is concentrated, or during the winter months in the north. The national standard for airborne particulate matter is 6–8 tons per cubic kilometer per month, but nearly every city in China is in the 30–40 ton range, with some as high as 100 tons, and some even exceeding 1000 tons. The smoke is like a black dragon dancing in the sky and spitting black rain, while we long to see a blue sky and golden sun.

An environmental protection delegation from the United States measured airborne dust in four major cities in China and estimated the health hazards based on risk assessment data used in their country. The results are shown in table 9.1.

Air pollution is a major cause of disease in China. In 1985 a Chinese government office made a study of a small carbon steel factory in the city of Maoming, and found 156 cases of chronic pharyngitis, 47 cases of allergic rhinitis, 11 cases of chronic bronchitis, 8 cases of tuberculosis, and 9 suspected cases of pneumoconiosis. There were also numerous other illnesses, most of which are related to the excessive amounts of toxic airborne particles around the factory. Another investigation of an iron-smelting factory in Chaozhou revealed that the workshop environment was toxic and about half of the staff and workers suffered from illnesses related to air pollution.

In 1985, in Liuyang County in Hunan Province, an investigation of lung disorders around coal mines in four rural towns revealed that the density of dust particles was 17 times higher than the national

TABLE 9.1 AIRBORNE DUST AND ITS HEALTH IMPACT

	Value for airborne dust (microgram/per cubic meter)	Highest value for airborne dust (microgram/per cubic meter)	Annual loss of working days (in 10,000)	Estimated annual deaths directly linked to the pollution
Beijing	80	160	2,500	550
Shanghai	150	200	4,000	1,300
Wuhan	170	400	2,200	3,500
Guangzhou	190	190	2,000	1,700

standard. The rate of pneumoconiosis among staff and workers was in the range of 14–24% and the average accumulated working years of those afflicted was 19. The statistics were quite consistent for all the mines and for all types of work. Hunan's Zexing Mine Bureau tabulated the years of service of mine workers and found that the annual average attrition rate increased each year from 1950 to 1982. The average age at the time of attrition was only 36.4 years, while the average number of years of service was only 11.8.

Liaoning Province made an on-site investigation of female workers at the Liaoyang Petrochemical Company engaged in operations where the benzene and dimethyl benzene levels exceed national standards. The miscarriage rate for 68 of the women was significantly higher than that of the control group. Workers in other places are exposed to high temperatures, high humidity, and radiation, and there are continuous cases of mercury, cadmium, arsenic, and polychloride benzene poisoning.

These threats to workers' health provide vivid examples of the vicious cycle of environmental and economic problems. Pollution decreases productivity while increasing medical expenses, which in turn depletes the capital for the modernization needed to improve efficiency and develop better pollution control systems.

Every year 14 million tons of ashes are emitted into the air in China (approximately 14% of the entire world emission of 100 million tons), and 15 million tons of sulfur dioxide (approximately 10% of the total). Not long ago a survey of 30 major cities in China revealed that the average quantity of airborne dust is 0.6 milligrams per cubic milligram of air, 10 times more than in Japan.[9]

According to state planning, by the year 2000 China will consume 1.2 billion tons of coal, not to mention other pollutants. If existing methods of combustion continue to be used, this means that in the year 2000, 240 million tons of coal dust will be produced, 40 million tons of smoke and airborne dust, and 24 million tons of carbon dioxide.

When sulfur dioxide, nitric oxide, and sulfuric and nitric acid are spewed from power stations, factories, and cars, they combine with rain, snow, and fog to produce acid rain. By 1986, China already ranked third in the world in industrial sulfur dioxide emissions, but as yet no serious attention has been paid to the problem of acid rain. In fact, the east, the Mid-South and the Southwest are rapidly becoming acid rain regions.

A study of Shanghai alone from 1980 to 1983 showed that in three years acid rain had increased by a factor of six. And since the early 1980s, the level of acid rain in Chongqing has already been approaching that of Europe during its worst period in 1966. One need only look at the corrosion of Chongqing's large bridge over the Yangtze to understand the severity of the problem. In 1986, 18 cities between Yibin and Shanghai already suffered from acid rain.[10]

The increased use of fossil fuels, the destruction of forests, and urban growth are causing carbon dioxide to accumulate in the atmosphere, creating a "greenhouse effect." Researchers are currently debating whether the earth's temperature will increase an average of 3–5°C over the next 30 years, causing warm areas to become deserts and polar ice to melt making the oceans rise several meters. China is obviously responsible for part of what could prove to be a threat to the entire planet. Regarding the future effects on the climate, Professor Yang Huairen, a well-known scholar at Nanjing University has actually asserted that it is inadvisable to invest further in coastal areas of China that are less than four meters above sea level, and that for areas below one to two meters above sea level a long-term plan must be made for moving the inhabitants.

TABLE 9.2 STATISTICS ON ENVIRONMENTAL POLLUTION IN CHINA 1981–1983

ITEM	1981	1982	1983	Quantity per capita (1983)
Industrial waste water (10,000 tons)	2,379,272	2,394,396	2,387,744	23.3 tons
Total for 75 cities	1,125,050	1,070,735	1,011,350	
% of waste water treated	15.00%	17.00%	20.60%	
Total for 75 cities	15.60%	19.10%	23.60%	
Discharged industrial particles (10,000 tons)		1,346.00	1,048.00	10.22 kilos
% of industrial particles collected		40.50%	50.80%	
Sulfur dioxide (10,000 tons)	1,421.40	1,327.40	1,256.80	12.26 kilos
Nitric Oxide (10,000 tons)	440.10	413.80		
Ash (10,000 tons)	1,519.10	1,413.20	1,334.10	13.02 kilos
Chromium (VI) (ton)	3,616.58	2,019.80	2,030.31	2 grams
Lead (ton)	4,875.47	2,237.80	2,033.81	2 grams
Phenol (ton)	23,358.02	13,477.00	13,975.00	14 grams
Cyanide (ton)	11,645.13	7,121.00	7,089.00	7 grams
Petroleum products (ton)	327,041.2	105,061.00	81,593.00	80 grams
Arsenic (ton)	1,716.85	1,208.70	1,386.82	1.4 grams
Mercury, cadmium (ton)	375.36	258.60	185.62	0.2 grams
Enterprise funds for pollution control (10,000 yuan)	196,966	218,579	204,340	1.99 yuan
% of national income	0.50	0.51	0.44	

■ Backward Technology and Pollution

As often emphasized here, a major cause of the severe environmental pollution in China is the low level of technology in the country and the serious lack of qualified personnel. The lack of education and technology which is at the root of the inefficiency and environmental degradation in agriculture also retards progress in industry. It seems that if a country is underdeveloped in terms of science and technology, then every other area is correspondingly handicapped.

In 1981, there were only 10,400 professional scientists and technicians working in China's environmental protection agencies, an average of one per 100,000 people. By 1983, the number had increased to 15,300, still an average of only about 1 per 70,000 people. In 1983, China only had 23,060 sets of instruments related to environmental protection, not even enough to supply one instrument to one in 17 of China's 40,000 mining enterprises.

China has also been slow to upgrade technology used in industry. The amount of waste generated per unit of product by industry is considerably higher than in developed countries, and almost 10 times greater in certain industries. Run-off, emissions, drips and leaks are common, and workers are at risk from toxic gases. The scale of China's industry is much smaller than Japan's, but the total quantity of gas, water and industrial residue emitted by China's factories is several times higher than in Japan—primarily because China has a low recycling rate and a high and inefficient consumption of raw materials and fuel.

For example, if China were able to lower coal consumption in steel production by 0.1 tons, 100 million cubic meters less contaminated air would be produced daily nationwide. If coal consumption in the steel industry could be reduced from 1.5 tons to 1.0 tons, the reduction in the amount of contaminated air produced would be nearly equivalent to reducing the air pollution from the top five steel factories in China. Furthermore, if we were able to recycle the 600,000 plus tons of sulfur dioxide discharged from nonferrous metal smelting each year, it would be equivalent to producing over 1 million tons more sulfuric acid each year *(see table 9.3)*.

Noise is a form of pollution that is often overlooked. China has one of the most serious noise pollution problems in the world, but many Chinese still do not really understand the hazards of noise pollution. According to measurements taken in Beijing, Shanghai, Tianjin, Hangzhou, Wuhan, Guangzhou, Chongqing, Harbin and other cities in China, the noise level is approximately 80 decibels or

TABLE 9.3 POLLUTION AND CONSUMPTION OF MATERIALS AND ENERGY RESOURCES BY INDUSTRY IN CHINA

	QUANTITY	WASTE & COMPARISON
Coal consumption for every ton of steel	1.5 tons	On average, higher by about 1/3 than average industrial countries
Waste water from paper production	1.7–2 billion tons/yr.	Containing 930,000 tons of oxygen-consuming organisms
Water consumed for manufacturing every ton of steel	over 100 tons	Higher than industrialized countries by several times
Rate of recycling for industrial water	about 20%	2/3 is discharged into the environment untreated. In more industrialized countries, 75% is recycled.
Annual waste from steel manufacturing— water gas solid waste	2.3 billion tons 484.3 cubic meters 28.65 million tons	
Solid industrial waste discharged annually	300 million tons	
Discharge of SO_2 from smelting nonferrous metals	600,000 tons/year	
Annual discharge of coal gases from coking 10 million tons of coal	3 billion cubic meters	

higher in municipal areas and in some cities it reaches 70 decibels in the evening, well above the levels of 65 decibels in the day and 45 decibels at night which are considered safe. Ventilators, gas turbines, water pumps, boiler exhausts, generators, transformers, stone crushers, electric saws, jackhammers, and lathes rumble and screech continuously day and night, and little or no attempt is made to control the noise. A number of regulations have finally been made, but for a variety of reasons it has been difficult to implement them thoroughly.

Recently the number of vehicles in Chinese cities has increased enormously (accounting for about 70% of urban noise), but there are not nearly as many as in advanced industrial countries. In China the noise level has increased faster than the number of vehicles. In 1985 there were about 150,000 motor vehicles in Beijing, not even 1/10 of the number in Tokyo, but average noise levels in Beijing were twice as high.

The same year, Hangzhou only had 4,000 vehicles, but the noise level exceeded that of New York City, where there are a million vehicles. In Nanjing the noise level along main transportation routes is 80 decibels, and in some places it reaches 85–90 decibels. In Guangzhou the noise level is 80 decibels along the main transportation routes. In 1985 the city government of Guangzhou received 616 letters of complaint, 255 (41%) of which were related to noise.

▮ The Top 3 Polluters: Bureaucratism, Ignorance, and Poverty

The Daxinganling forest fire discussed above provides a classic case of bureaucratism, ignorance, and poverty as the greatest polluters of the environment in China. When that forest erupted into a wild conflagration, it soon registered on satellite cloud charts, but no one noticed. When experts volunteered to put out the fire, some people did not understand, and even ridiculed them. The most incomprehensible thing is that it was not until 9 May that the *People's Daily* issued the first nationwide report on the fire, saying that it had "passed through the railroad tracks of four logging companies, and cut off roads and communications lines." In fact by 7 May, the county seat of Mohe had already become a flaming purgatory, as piles of dry timber blazed, but the report did not even mention it.

Throughout China the report met with two days of total silence and it was not until the third day, when a report of the destruction of Mohe was released, that everyone woke up. Even then, tens of thousands of soldiers were sent to extinguish the fire without proper fire-fighting equipment. Because this sudden and tragic event met with the slowest and most ignorant response conceivable, and it is not surprising that it turned into a disaster.

In the 1970s, the control of environmental pollution depended on the implementation of the administration's strategy, and the grace period allowed to carry out regulations generally meant that the job was assigned to lower-level offices. This improper practice does not encourage the internal offices of enterprises to take action. Recently several new measures have been implemented, but they are too late to create a sound system for controlling pollution. Some production work units include fines for excess pollution emissions in production costs, but the state has a policy of returning 80% of the pollution emission fines to enterprises without penalty.

Since the worldwide energy crisis of the 1970s, industrially developed nations have made enormous efforts to cut back the consumption of natural resources in the industrial sector. They have worked hard to reduce the consumption of raw materials in production, and to reduce the amount of waste in general. For example, within ten years of the oil crisis, Japan's energy consumption had fallen about 40% per unit of GNP, and oil consumption was reduced by 50%. China clearly needs to follow the same path and shift from the old emphasis of merely cleaning up pollution to eliminating its sources.

Even at this late date, environmental problems in China have still not received adequate attention from policy-makers. Environmental pollution, the scarcity of natural resources, and overpopulation present a fundamental threat to mankind, and in China they are deadly. Facing the problem of severe environmental pollution worldwide, China has unexpectedly emphasized "giving consideration to production, livelihood, and ecology." In fact, this really means that for the sake of production and livelihood, the ecological environment could be destroyed.

This approach to the environment enables us to understand why environmental protection regulations in China are not only vague but also lack the force of law. Even though the environmental protection laws were promulgated in 1979, they were not seriously implemented. People at environmental protection research institutes themselves believe that for many years they have merely been researching slogans. Even when an enlightened official creates a policy for the decisive management of environmental issues, conflicts of interest among the various bureaus often prevent the policy from being implemented.

The reason the Environmental Protection Law is ineffective is very simple: the biggest producers of pollution are factories, and because many factories are run by the state, punishing them would be equivalent to punishing the state itself. So environmental polluters only implement the regulations if they think it is to their immediate advantage. Therefore, even though pollution in many areas is outstripping efforts to control it, methods of pollution control are crude, outdated, and unreliable; funds and staff are scarce, and supervision often exists only in name.

There is nothing to indicate that things will improve in the near future. In China there is rarely an item on environmental protection in the policy agenda of officials at different levels. Most people are only concerned with immediate material benefits and very few look at long-term and far-ranging effects. They are more sensitive in their reactions to damages and losses than to social and health benefits, and because they are afraid of failure, they prefer to avoid attempts to change. And they have no concept of the notion of a crime against nature, even where the damage is most severe.

The central government has in fact announced some ambitious target goals for environmental protection to be reached by 1995. These include limiting sulphur dioxide emissions to 19 million tons; treating 70% of industrial waste water and gases, and converting half the urban residential use to gas or liquid fuel, which are far cleaner than coal. Official policy calls for using 15% of the total funds for planned industrial development to improve environmental quality by installing updated technology. But in China, actual results can fall quite short of policy goals and official proclamations. Consequently, there is no reason to assume that our environmental crisis will end soon or that we should relax our vigilance in protecting the ecosystem.

China must make an enormous effort to support enterprises that establish and promote clean technologies and recycling. Enterprises should be encouraged to reduce the consumption of natural resources, and motivated to reduce waste emissions. Environmental protection and production should be closely coordinated, and waste materials converted into resources.

How can we continue to be so ungrateful to nature, and how can we change our attitudes and actions? The most hopeful possibility was expressed by Professor Tanijima of Tokyo University in a speech in 1984 at China's Academy of Social Sciences: "Although China is one step behind advanced countries in starting to modernize, contrary to what one might expect, this may be fortunate. China can ... learn from the lesson of environmental damage in advanced countries. If the coexistence of China and nature during modernization were to succeed, it would be an unrivalled honor and a great, outstanding achievement."

Unfortunately, China is not highly industrialized, and damage to the environment and environmental pollution are already serious. Moreover, China is heedlessly spending the "original capital" of the environment by sacrificing it to the development of production. If this policy is not forcefully adjusted with more fundamental and effective measures, China's latent crisis may explode with increasingly severe deterioration of the environment, forcing her to pay an even higher price for economic development.

NOTES

▌ Chapter 1

1. "Zhongguo lixiang renkou mubiao de dinglian yanjiu he youhua fenxi" (Quantitative Research and Analysis for the Optimal Population Target of China), see *Renkou dili lunwen xuan* (Selected Essays on Population Geography), compiled by the Population Studies Group of Huadong Normal University.

2. Results of this study were reported in *Zhongguo qingnian bao* (China Youth Herald), 3 July 1989.

3. For English-language presentation of population data and other statistics see *China Statistical Yearbook 1990* (Beijing: International Center for the Advancement of Science and Technology, 1990) and *Beijing Review*, no. 46 (1990): 21–23. *Beijing Review* frequently reports official figures and policy statements on a variety of development-related and environmental topics.

4. Hu Guowen, "Lun qingdai de renkou pengchang" (On the Population Expansion during the Qing Dynasty), *Huadong shifan daxue xuebao* (Journal of Huadong Normal University), no. 2 (1984).

5. *Renkou fazhan guocheng de yuce he kongzhi* (The Process of Population Growth: Forecast and Control), see *Xitong gongcheng he kexue guanli* (Systems Analysis and Scientific Management), no. 2 (1980).

6. *Renkou yanjiu* (Population Studies), no. 4 (1984): 2.

7. Li Mengbai, *Woguo chengzhen fazhan de zhanwang* (Prospects for Township Development," see *Chengxiang jianshe* (Construction: Town and Country), December 1982.

8. *Renkou yanjiu* (Population Studies), no. 2 (1985): 50.

9. *Shehui kexue pinglun* (Commentary on Social Sciences), no. 6 (1985):

64.

10. After Bannister raised the question, Liu Zheng concluded that the current sex ratio of the total population had risen to 106.27% from 105.45% (higher than Bannister's original estimate), based on the newly disclosed figures that incorporated the number of soldiers currently in active service. See *Renkou yanjiu* (Population Studies), no. 6 (1985): 4–9.

11. *Renkou yanjiu* (Population Studies), no. 1 (1984): 39.

12. *Guangming ribao* (Guangming Daily), 25 August 1986.

13. See 1983 edition of *Lun zhongguo renkou de fengbu* (The Distribution of Chinese Population) and 1985 edition of *Renkou yanjiu lunwen ji* (Essays on Population Research), vol. 3, by *Huadong shifan daxue chuban she* (Hua Dong Normal University Press).

■ Chapter 2

1. For relevant data see *Baike zhishi* (Encyclopedic Knowledge), no. 11 (1985): 7; *Beijing wanbao* (Beijing Evening Journal), 3 March 1986; *Shijie jingji daobao* (World Economic Herald), 4 February 1986; and *Jingjin ribao* (Economic Daily), 5 May 1986.

2. Zhongguo shehui kexue (Social Science in China), no. 2 (1986): 69; and *Guang Ming Daily,* 2 January 1987.

3. *Kexue* (Science,) no. 4 (1990): 307.

4. *Zhongguo shehui kexue* (Social Science in China), no. 4 (1983): 207–217.

5. *Zhongguo keji bao* (Chinese Scientific Journal), 8 January (1985): 2. Also *Gongyuan erlinglingling nian de zhongguo* (China in 2000), by Keji wenxian chubanshe (Scientific and Technological Document Press, 1984) states that the forest cover in Xishuan Banna dropped from 69.4% in 1949 to 26% in 1980 (p. 82).

6. For figures on logging, see *Guangming ribao* (Guangming Daily), 25 May 1984; *Xuexi yu tansuo* "Study and Exploration," no. 1 (1982): 19; *Liaowang zhoukan* (Outlook Weekly), no. 11 (1986), article by Yang Jike; *Zhongguo kejibao* (Chinese Scientific Journal), 8 January 1986; *Fujian nongye* (Agriculture in Fujian), no. 4 (1983): 2; and *Mingzu tuanjie* (Fraternity between Nationalities), no. 3 (1985): 24.

7. See *Fazhan zhanlue yanjiu, huanjin ziyuan juan* (Researches on Development Strategy: Resources and Environment Volume), by Beijing keji chubanshe (Beijing Science and Technology Press, 1986): 56; and *Bengkui de huangtudi* (The Collapsing Yellow Earth), by Xueyuan chuban she (Scholar's Attic Press 1989): 19.

8. *Yuce* (Forecast), no. 5 (1989): 5.

9. *Kexue* (Science), no. 4 (1990): 307.

10. *Hebei xuekan* (Hebei Academic Journal), no. 2 (1986): 26–31.

11. *Weilai yu fazhan* (Future and Development), no. 1 (1982): 16; and *Guangming Daily,* 12 August 1986.

12. *Kaifang* (Opening), no. 7 (1985): 23.

13. *Caijing wenti yanjiu* (Researches in Financial Matters), by *Dongbei caijing wenti yanjiu* (Northeastern Institute of Finance), no. 6 (1985): 49.

14. *Fujian shida xuebao* (Fujian Normal University Journal), no. 2 (1983): 3.

15. *Hebei shelian tongxun* (Hebei Community Journal), no. 6 (1984): 45.

16. *Renwen zazhi* (Humanity Studies Journal), no. 6 (1983): 34; *Guangming ribao,* (Guangming Daily), 5 December 1986; and *Ziran ziyuan* (Natural Resources), no. 1 (1987): 1–6.

17. *Zhongguo shehui kexue* (Social Science in China), no. 3 (1985): 160; and *Hebei shifan daxue xuebao* (Hebei Normal University Journal), no. 1 (1981): 4.

18. *Tianjin jiaoyu* (Education in Tianjin), no. 2 (1986): 39.

19. *Ziranziyuan* (Natural Resources), no. 1 (1986): 1; Guangming Daily, 5 December 1986.

20. *Weilai yu fazhan* (Future and Development), no. 4 (1983): 9.

21. *Hong Kong Express,* 15 September 1986; *Dili zhishi* (Geographical Knowledge), no. 11 (1984): 4; and *Ziran zazhi* (Nature Magazine), no. 5 (1983): 345.

22. *Financial Times* of Hong Kong, 20 November 1987.

23. *Guangming ribao* (Guangming Daily), 17 May 1985.

24. *Shandong jingji* (Economy of Shandong), no. 5 (1985): 43.

25. *Qinghai shehui kexue* (Social Science in Qinghai), no. 11 (1984): 101.

26. *Weilai yu fazhan* (Future and Development), no. 4 (1984): 50.

27. *Guangming ribao* (Guangming Daily), 1 May 1985; *Chenshi wenti* (Urban Problems), no. 9 (1985): 54; *Dili zhishi* (Geographical Knowledge), no. 8 (1983): 3; and *Ziranziyuan* (Natural Resources), no. 1 (1986): 13.

∎ Chapter 3

1. Janos Kornai, *Economics of Shortage.* Amsterdam; New York: North-

Holland, 1980.

2. *Zhongzhou xuekan* (Central Journal), no. 2 (1981): 45.

3. *Minzu tuanjie* (Fraternity among Nationalities) Beijing, no. 8 (1985): 20.

4. See, for example, *Shehuixue yanjiu* (Researches in Sociology), no. 3 (1986).

5. *Wuhan Daxue Xuebao* (Wuhan University Journal), no. 6 (1982): 67. AUTHOR'S NOTE: The proportion of people with incomes below a certain level (W) is the horizontal axis, and the proportion of income (V) is the vertical axis. When W = V, giving the straight line OP, this indicates "absolute equality." The curve which is produced when W is greater than V, is called the Lorenz Curve (L), and the ratio of the area of OLP to the

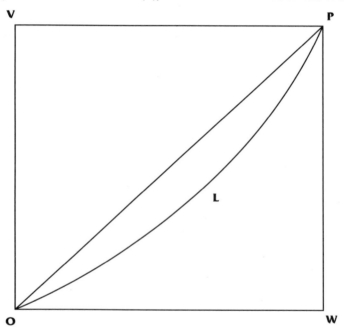

area of triangle OWP is the Gini Coefficient.

FIGURE 3.1A

6. National Income is the net output value of industry, agriculture, construction, transportation, and commerce after deducting material consumption. Gross National Product is a compound indicator used in some Western countries. Apart from the net output value of the five main production sectors listed above, it also includes revenue from services and

government, fixed asset depreciation, etc., but does not include transferred values like raw materials, fuels, power etc. China never used this indicator in the past.

7. Dwight Healt Perkins, with the assistance of Ye-chien Wang, Kuo-ying Wang Hsia, and Fung-ming Su. *Agricultural Development in China, 1368–1968*. Chicago: Alding, 1969.

8. Allen S. Whiting and Robert F. Dernberger. *China's Future: Foreign Policy and Economic Development in the Post-Mao Era*. Introduction by Bayless Manning. New York: McGraw Hill, 1977.

■ Chapter 4

1. Calculated on the basis of one kilogram of coal equal to 7,000 large calories. See *Jingji yanjiu* (Economic Research), no. 12 (1982): 4.

2. The energy flexibility index "P" equals the average annual increase in the rate of energy consumption divided by the average annual increase rate of economic development.

3. Data are quoted from *Weilai yu fazhan* (Future and Development), no. 2 (1985): 34; *Caijing wenti yanjiu* (Research in Finance), no. 6 (1985): 49; *Lilun yu xuexi* (Theory and Study), no. 5–6 (1984): 23; *Caijing yanjiu* (Research in Finance), no. 6 (1983): 53–54; *Jingji yu shehui fazhan* (Economy and Social Development), no. 3 (1985): 24; *Zhongguo tongji nianjian* (China Annual Statistics 1984): 230–231;*Guangming ribao* (Guangming Daily), 27 may 1987; 11 December 1986.
4. *Ibid.,* 29 May 1987.

5. *Gongyuan erlinglingling nian de zhongguo* (China in 2000) (Science and Technology Documents Publisher, 1984).

6. *Xueyuan xuebao jiangxi caijing* (Jiangxi College of Finance Journal), no. 2 (1985): 101; *Guizhou shehui kexue* (Guizhou Social Sciences), no. 6 (1981): 10; *Kexue, jingji, shehui* (Science, Economy, and Society), no. 2 (1983): 37; *Shentaixue zazhi* (Journal of Ecology), no. 4 (1985): 46.

7. *(Jingji wenti tantao)* (Economic Inquiry), no. 1 (1984): 9.

8. *Guangming ribao* (Guangming Daily), 12 January 1987.

9. *Ibid.,* 20 June 1986.

10. Calculation was based on data from Mao Hanying, *Shijie renwen dili shouce* (Handbook of World Human Geography) (Knowledge Press, 1984): 324.

11. *Caijing wenti yanjiu* (Research in Finance), no. 5 (Northeast College of Finance Press, 1985): 33; *Xuexi yu tansuo* (Study and Inquiry), no. 2 (1985), 77–78.

12. *Weilai yu fazhan* (Future and Development), no. 2 (1986): 6.

13. *Neimenggu shehui kexue* (Inner Mongolian Social Sciences), no. 2 (1984): 47; *Guizhou touzi yanjiu,* (Guizhou Investment Research), no. 6 (1985): 6.

14. *Shijie jingji daobao* (World Economic Herald), 10 June 1985.

15. *Caizheng Yanjiu* (Research in Finance) (Shanghai), no. 6 (1982): 11.

16. Zhang Xueli, "Current State and Prospect of China's Transportation," paper delivered to the Conference on China's Future, September 1984.

17. "Hot Currents," *Re Liu,* no. 2 (1986).

18. *Jingji wenti yantao* (Economic Inquiry) (Tianjin College of Finance), no. 2 (1984): 32–33.

19. *Weilai yu fazhan,* (Future and Development), no. 2 (1986): 10.

20. *Guizhou touziyan jou* (Guizhou Investment Research), no. 6 (1985): 15; *Wei shi* (Truth) (Jiangsu), no. 2 (1982): 14.

21. *Zhengming* (Contender) (Jiangxi), no. 1 (1985): 85; *Qinghai shehui kexue* (Qinghai Social Sciences), no. 3 (1985): 9; *Baike zhishi* (Encyclopedic Knowledge), no. 2 (1985): 7.

22. *Shanghai Haiyun xueyuan xuebao* (Shanghai College of Navigation Journal), no. 2 (1985): 12.

23. *Weilai yu fazhan* (Future and Development), no. 2 (1986): 6; *Wei shi* (Truth) (Jiangsu), no. 2 (1982): 14.

24. *Zhongguo shehui songji ziliao* (China Social Statistics): 112; *Weilai yu fazhan* (Future and Development), no. 2 (1986): 15–16.

25. Liu Fengchang, *Jingzi guanli* (Business Administration), no. 7 (1982).

▪ Chapter 5

1. See *Jining shizhuan xuebao* (Jining Teacher's College Journal), no. 2 (1982): 1–5; *Shanxi Jingji yu shehui fazhan* (Economic and Social Development in Shanxi), no. 3 (1985): 16–21, and *Renmin ribao* (People's Daily), 9 October 1981, 5l, and the 16 November editorial.

2. *Guangming ribao* (Guangming Daily), 17 and 30 April 1987. Estimates in the *American Business News* on 15 December 1987 put the value of unused eqipment in China at 20 billion yuan.

3. See *Fujian luntan* (Forum of Fujian), no. 7 (1985): 11; *Jingji yanjiu* (Economic Research), no. 4 (1985): 77–78; *Zhongzhou xuekan* (Zhongzhou Journal), no. 4 (1985): 22; *Weilai yu fazhan* (Future and Development), no. 2 (1984): 63–64; and *Xuexi yu tansuo* (Learning and Exploration), no. 6 (1984): 71.

4. Zhang Wenkui, *Guanyu xumuye xiandaihua de jige wenti* (Several Issues Relating to the Modernization of Animal Husbandry), by Nongye Chubanshe (Agricultural Publishing House, n.d., n.p.): 6; and *Xiandaihua* (Modernization), no. 7 (1983): 11.

5. *Lanzhou xuekan* (Lanzhou Journal), no. 4 (1985): 49.

6. *Quanguo xiangzhen qiye zhaiyao* (Exerpted Reports on the State of Agriculture), by the Ministry of Agriculture (1987); the article by Lei Guanghua in *Jingji wenti tansuo* (Exploration on Economic Questions), no. 11 (1987); and *Jingji ribao* (Economic Daily), 3 July 1987.

7. *Jingji wenti tansuo* (Exploration on Economic Questions), no. 5 (1987) and no. 7 (1987), articles by Zhou Fenglin and Duan Fulin.

8. *Jiangxi shehui kexue* (Social Science in Jiangxi), no. 3 (1986): 24.

9. *Nanfang ribao* (Southern Daily), 13 April 1987. A report in *Lilun xinxibao* (Information Journal on New Theories) on 12 January 1987 also said that between 1979 and 1985 45.772 million agricultural workers transferred to non-agricultural production, another million or so are working in the city, and 6 million workers are leaving the villlages each year as temporary workers. This means that about one-fifth of China's agricultural workers have changed their employment during this period.

10. *Jingbing luncong* (Capital City Soldier), no. 1 (1984): 49–50.

11. *Weilai yu fazhan* (Future and Development), no. 4 (1983): 9.

12. *Xuexi yu cankao* (Studies and References), by the Research Institute of the Chinese Academy of Social Science, no. 4 (1983): 22.

13. *Weilai yu fazhan* (Future and Development), no. 1 (1982): 19.

14. *Nongye xiandaihua tansuo* (Forum for Agricultural Modernization), nos. 30 and 31 (1981).

15. *Xueshujie dongtai* (Newest Trends in Academia), no. 18 (1985): 68.

16. *Weilai yu fazhan* (Future and Development), no. 4 (1983): 9.

17. *Guangming ribao* (Guangming Daily) 9 December 1986.

18. *Baike zhishi* (Encyclopedic Knowledge), no. 2 (1985): 68.

19. *Nanfang ribao* (Southern Daily), 12 January 1987.

20. *Jingji yanjiu* (Economic Research), no. 1 (1987).

■ Chapter 6

1. *Fujian luntan* (Forum for Fujian), no. 7 (1985): 13.

2. *Dandong jingji* (The Economy of Dandong), no. 3 (1985): 36; and *Fujian luntan* (Forum for Fujian), no. 7 (1985).

3. *Fujian luntan* (Forum for Fujian), no. 7 (1985).

4. *Fujian luntan* (Forum for Fujian), no. 9 (1985): 44–45.

5. *Jingji ribao* (Economic Daily), 22 February 5 February and 2 April (1985). Also *Xunxiabo* (Information Digest), 20 and 24 April 1985.

6. *Qiuji* (Earth Membership), by Baijia chubanshe (Hundred Schools Press, 1989): 127.

7. *Lunwenxuan* (Collected Papers), by Tianjin Jingji Xuehui (Tianjin Economic Association), from the 1986 annual conference: 124–128.

8. *Ibid.*

9. *Lilun xinxibao* (Information Journal on New Theories), 13 April 1987; *Frankfurter Zeitung* 29 March (1983); *Mingpao* (Hong Kong), 21 June 1987.

10. *Jinan xuebao* (Jinan Journal), no. 1 (1985): 19.

11. *Jingji yu shehui fazhan* (Economic and Social Development), no. 2 (1985): 7.

12. *Jinan xuebao* (Economic Journal): no. 1 (1985): 19.

13. *Shehui kexue xuebao* (Social Science Journal), by Xiang Shifan Xueyuan (Xiangtan Normal College), no. 1 (1985): 95.

14. *Weilai yu fazhan* (Future and Development), no. 4 (1986): 12–14; *Xuexi yu tansuo* (Studies and Explorations), no. 1 (1982): 18.

15. *Wenhuibao* (Hong Kong), 22 January 1986.

16. *Lilun xinxibao* (Information Journal on New Theories), 13 April 1987.

17. *Guangjiaojing* (Wide-Angle Lens), no. 161, February 1986.

18. *Guangzhou Daily*, 19 May 1984.

19. The figures quoted by Chen were properly researched but differed somewhat from the Liangxiang report. The original figures are used here.

20. *Guangjiaojing* (Wide-Angle Lens), no. 152 (May 1985): 58.

21. *Wenhuibao* (Hong Kong), of 9 November 1984, reported that investment in Shenzhen by central ministries and committees had already reached 1.6 billion yuan, not including investment by provinces. Yet gross investment in capital construction for the whole city was only 1.96 billion yuan.

22. *Touzi yu jianshe* (Investment and Construction), no. 5 (1985).

23. *Xiandai jingji yicong* (Modern Economics in Translation), no. 3 (1985): 3.

24. *Kaituozhe* (Pioneers), no. 11 (1985): 2.

25. *Liaowang* (Outlook), 11 June 1984.

26. *Shenzhen tequ bao* (SEZ Daily News), 22 November 1982.

27. *Wenhuibao* (Hong Kong), 29 March 1985: 2.

28. *Guangjiaojing* (Wide-Angle Lens), no. 152 (May 1985): 55, 63.

29. *Guangzhou yanjiu* (Guangzhou Research), no. 3 (1988); *Shijie jingji daobao* (World Economic Herald), 26 May 1988; *Guangjiaojing* (Wide-Angle Lens), no. 5 (1987): 76.

■ Chapter 7

1. *Mao Zedong xuanji* (Selected Works of Mao Zedong), vol. 4, 1323–1324.

2. *Jingji yu shehui fazhan* (Economic and Social Development), no. 2 (1985): 33.

3. *Jingji kaifa* (Economic Opening), no. 2 (1985): 15. The article claims that up until June the increase was 23.1%.

4. *Xuexi yu tansuo* (Studies and Explorations), no. 5 (1985): 94; and *Caizheng yanjiu ziliao* (Financial Research Journal), nos. 6 and 7 (1983).

5. *Nihon keizai shimbun* (Japan Economic News), 31 July 1983.

6. *Kaifa yanjiu* (Researches on Economic Opening), no. 1 (1985): 7.

7. *Xibei faxue xuebao* (Northwestern Legal Journal) no. 1 (1984): 35–37.

8. *Xinjiang shehui kexue* (Social Sciences in Xinjiang), no. 4 (1984): 2.

9. *Jingji dili* (Economic Geography), no. 1 (1986): 22.

10. *Guizhou shehui kexue* (Social Sciences in Guizhou), no. 6 (1985): 10.

11. *Guizhou touzi yanjiu* (Guizhou Investment Studies), no. 6 (1985): 3–11. The West is referred to here as 10 provinces and regions, including Inner Mongolia, Sichuan, Shaanxi, and Guangxi.

12. *Jingji ribao* (Economic Daily), 19 June 1985, gives same definition of West as above.

13. *Zhongzhou xuekan* (Zhongzhou Journal), no. 2 (1981): 42.

14. *Shehui kexue biankan* (Collected Journals in Social Sciences), no. 4 (1983): 49.

■ Chapter 8

1. *Hanshan shizhuan xuebao* (Hanshan Teachers College Journal), no. 1 (1986): 35.

2. *Bai ke zhishi* (Encyclopedic Knowledge), no. 3 (1983): 15.

3. *Shijie jingji daobao* (World Economic Herald), 30 March 1981.

4. *Xueshu luntan* (Academic Forum), no. 4 (1983): 43.

5. *Hongqi* (Red Flag), no. 8 (1983): 2.

6. *Meiguo de keji qianli* (The Technological Potential of the USA): 1.

7. *Gaodeng jiaoyu xuebao* (Journal of Higher Education), no. 1 (1985): 64.

8. *Xueshu luntan* (Academic Forum), no. 4 (1983): 43.

9. *Waiguo jiaoyu qingkuang* (Reports from the Education Sectors Abroad), nos. 3 and 9 (1982); *Shijie jingji daobao* (World Economic Herald), 30 March 1981.

10. *Zhongguo jiaoyu bao* (Chinese Education), 18 September 1984.

11. *Xibei renkou* (Population in the Northwest), no. 3 (1983): 19.

12. *Shehui kexue* (Social Science), no. 5 (1983). At the time annual expenditures for education were only 10-billion-plus yuan.

13. *Guangming ribao,* (Guangming Daily), 10 June 1985.

14. *Jiangsu gaojiao* (Higher Education in Jiangsu), nos. 3 and 6 (1985).

15. Shen Zhenghua, *Rencai yuce gongzuo de chubu shijian* (Initial Experiments in Forecasts in Professional Demands), from *Shanghai gaojiao yanjiu* (Researches in Shanghai Higher Education), series no. 8.

16. *Guanli rencai yu guanli jiaoyu* (Management Talents and Management Education). Collection put out by the editorial department of *Kexue guanli yanjiu* (Researches in Scientific Mangement): 116.

17. Jilin University *Yuce fangfa yu rencai yuce* (Professional Demand: Forecasting and Its Methodology) Collection: 132; *Xinhua News* 8 November 1982.

18. *Guangming ribao* (Guangming Daily), 1 and 21 September (1984); *Zhongguo jiaoyu bao* (Chinese Education Daily), 5 May and 31 December (1983); and *Zhongguo tongji nianjian yijiubasi* (China Statistical Yearbook 1984).

19. *Zhongguo jiaoyu bao* (Chinese Education Daily), 31 December (1985).

20. *Xibei renkou* (Population of the Northwest), no. 3 (1983): 18.

21. *Gaodeng jiaoyu ziliao* (Information Journal on Higher Education), no. 1 (1981): 13.

22. *Gaodeng jiaoyu (*Higher Education), no. 3 (1984).

23. *Gaodeng jiaoyu ziliao* (Information Journal on Higher Education), no. 1 (1981): 13.

24. *Liaoning shida xuebao* (Journal of Liaoning Normal University), no. 3 (1984): 26.

25. *Liaoning Jiaoyu* (Education in Liaoning), no. 3 (1984).

26. *Shijie jingji daobao* (World Economic Herald), 30 March 1981.

27. *Zhongguo tongji nianjian 1981* (China Statistical Yearbook 1981).

28. *Bijiao jiaoyu* (Comparative Education), by Jiaoyu Kexue Chubanshe (Education Science Press), n.p., n.d.

29. *Jiaoyu yanjiu ziliao* (Research Journal for Education), 1980.

30. *Zhongguo jiaoyu bao* (Chinese Education Daily), 15 September 1984.

31. According to 1984 statistics, the percentage of boys and girls entering school nationwide was 97% and 93% respectively. In the Southwest, Northwest, Inner Mongolia, Guangxi and other provinces alone there were 3 million girls who did not enter school. See *Xinmin wanbao* (New Citizen's Evening News) report on 29 September 1985.

32. *Zhongguo jiaoyu bao* (Chinese Education Daily), 26 April and 5 May 1988; *Xueshu yanjiu* (Academic Research), no. 2 (1988).

33. *Renkou yanjiu lunwenji* (Collected Essays on Population Research), by Zhongshan University Press, no. 49 (1984). For other figures see *Zhongguo jiaoyu bao* (Chinese Education Daily), 1, 8, 15, 18 September 1984.

34. *Tongji* (Statistics), no. 6 (1984).

35. *Zhongguo jiaoyu bao* (Chinese Education Daily), 31 December 1985.

36. *Gaodeng jiaoyu weilai yu fazhan* (Future Development of Higher Education), no. 2 (1985): 57.

37. *Luelun gaodeng jiaoyu de fazhan sudu he danchun zhuiqiu shengxue de wenti* (A Brief Discussion of the Speed of Development in Higher Education and the Problems of Excessive Focus on College Entrance), from *Renmin jiaoyu* (People's Education), no. 1 (1982).

38. In 1985 the total number of students accepted into institutions of higher education was 619,200, including students sponsored by their work units who don't have to pass the regular entrance examination and students in continuing education courses for cadres. The National Education Committee has already declared that "development is too fast."

39. *Hongqi* (Red Flag), no. 14 (1983): 33.

■ Chapter 9

1. For figures on damage and relevant photographs, see Su Ya's on-site investigation in the special issue of the magazine *Humen* (Tigergate), June 1987.

2. *Shandong jingji* (Economy of Shandong), nos. 5 and 43 (1985) and *Guangming ribao* (Guangming Daily), 10 October 1986 and 23 December 1986.

3. *Nanjing daxue xuebao* (Nanjing University Journal), no. 3 (1985): 509; *Weilai wushinian* (The Next Fifty Years), (Joint Publishing Co., 1985): 75; and *Xinhua wenzhai* (New China Exerpts), February (1983): 228.

4. *Ziran zazhi* (Nature), no. 12 (1987): 920–924.

5. *Gongyuan erlinglinglingnian de zhongguo* (China in the Year 2000), by Keji Wenxian Chubanshe (Science and Technology Literature Press, 1984): 190; and *Huanjing yu ziyuan* (Environment and Resources), no. 1 (1984): 18.

6. *Guangming ribao* (Guangming Daily), 8 April 1987.

7. *Wuhan daxue xuebao* (Wuhan University Journal), no. 3 (1984): 43.

8. *Jingji ribao* (Economic Daily), 23 February (1986).

9. *Weilai yu fazhan* (Future and Development), no. 2 (1985): 29; *Zhengming* (Contention), no. 2 (1985): 21.

10. *Jingji yu shehui fazhan* (Economic and Social Development), no. 3 (1985): 25; *Guangming ribao* (Guangming Daily), 10 October 1986.

NOTES TO FIGURES AND TABLES

(NOTE: figures and tables have been updated, where appropriate, using data from the 1990 Chinese census, *China Statistical Yearbook 1990*, and official government publications.)

Figure 1.1 *Renkou yanjiu* (Population Studies), no. 6 (1984): 50.

Figure 1.2 Tian Xueyuan, *Zhonguo renkou kongshi he fazhan qushi yanjiu* (Research on Control and Development Trends of the Chinese Population), (Jinji Kexue Chubanshe, 1984): 385.

Figure 1.3 See footnote 6, chapter 1.

Figure 1.4 Tian, 171.

Figure 1.5 *Zhonguo shehui kexue* (Social Sciences in China), no. 6 (1983): 184.

Figure 1.6 *Ibid.*

Figure 2.1 (Derived from table 2.2.)

Figure 2.2 *Shanghai jiaotong daxue xuebao* (Journal of Shanghai Jiaotong University), no. 4 (1983): 65.

Table 1.1 Cheng Yuqin, *Woguo renkou de jintian he mingtian* (Population of China: Today and Tomorrow) Keji Wengzian Chuban [Scientific Document Press], 1984): 6.

Table 1.2 *Statistical Yearbook of China 1990*.

Table 1.3 *Renkou yanjiu* (Population Studies), no. 1 (1984): 39.

Table 1.4 *Renkou yanjiu* (Population Studies), no. 6 (1984): 50.

Table 2.1 *Welai yu fazhan* (Future and Development), no. 1 (1982): 18; *Atlas of the People's Republic of China* (Atlas Press, 1987) figure 20.

Table 2.2 *Sichuan daxue xuebao congkan* (Sichuan University Journal), no. 3 (1979)10: 104–111; *Renkou yuanjiu* (Population Studies), No. 2 (1980): 58 , and no. 5 (1985): 21; *Zhonguo shehui kexue* (Social Sciences of China) no.3 (1985): 152–160; *Fujian shida xuebao* (Fujian Normal University Journal, no. 2 (1984): 12; *Gonyuan erlinglingling nian de zhongguo* (China in the Year 2000) (Kexue jishu chubanshe [Science and Technology Press, 1984]): 56, 60; *China Statistical Yearbook 1990*.

Table 3.1 *Fuyang shifan xuebao* (Academic Journal of Fuyang Teachers College), no. 2 (1984): 57.

Table 4.1 *United Nations Statistics Monthly* (June 1981); *Caijing wenti yanjiu* (Research in Finance), no. 6 (1982): 16–20; *People's Daily*, 18 July 1985; *Weilai yu fazhan* (Future and Development), no. 4 (1983): 37–38; *Shijie renwen dili shouce* (Handbook of Human Geography), (Knowledge Press, 1984: 213–219; *Xinjiang nengyuan* (Xinjiang Energy), (Xinjiang People's Press, 1982): 6–49.

Table 4.2 *Fuyang shifan xuebao* (Academic Journal of Fuyang Teachers College), no.2 (1984): 57.

Table 4.3 *Gongyuan erlinglingling nian de zhonguo* (China in 2000) (Science and Technology documents Press: 1984); *Zhonguo tongji nianjian* (China Statistical Yearbook) (1984, 1990); *Baiki zishi* (Encyclopedic Knowledge) (1983): 5; *Shijie jingji daobao* (World Economic Herald), 10 June 1985; *Zhonguo shehui tongji ziliao* (China Social Statistics) (China Statistics Press, 1985): 110–111; *Weilai yu fazhan* (Future and Development), no. 2 (1986): 15; *Zhejiang xuekan* (Zhejiang Journal), no. 5 (1984): 9.

Table 4.4 *Nanpang renkou* (Population of the South), no. 3 (1986): 14–16.

Table 5.1 *Welai yu fazhan* (Future and Development), no. 1 (1982): 16; *Ibid.*, no. 4 (1984): 32; *Fujian shida xuebao* (Journal of Fujian Normal University), no. 2 (1984): 10; *Dili zhishi* (Geographical Digest), no. 7 (1985): 4; *China Statistical Yearbook 1990*.

Table 5.2 *Jiaoyu lunfenji* (Education Department of Nanjing Normal University, 1984): 22.

Table 6.1 *Guang jiaojin* (Wide-Angle Lens), no. 149 (1985): 49.

Table 8.1 *Kyiku to joho* (Japan) (December 1979); *Waiguo jiaoyou dongtai* (February 1986): 6; UNESCO statistics.

Table 8.2 *Zhonguo jiaoyubao* (Chinese Education Daily), 5 May 1983; 4 September 1984; 31 December 1985.

Table 9.1 Yu Yufu, et al., *Huanjing wuran yu renti baojian*, (Fudan University Press, 1985), vol. 56.

Table 9.2 *Zhongguo shenbui tongji ziliao* (China Statistical Press, 1985, vols. 239–249).

Table 9.3 You Qingchuan, *Huanjing wuran he fangzhi*, 1983, 18; Ziran zazhi, 1984.

About the Author

He Bochuan sent a shock wave through Chinese political and intellectual circles in the late 1980s with the publication of this outspoken book on ecological and development problems. A lecturer in the Department of Philosophy at Sun Yat-sen University in Guangdong, in 1983 he was asked to write a section on education in the series *China in the Year 2000,* a publication sponsored by the Foundation for Chinese Futurology. Research for this piece became a catalyst for a number of articles on the related issues of population, ecology, energy, and economics.

China on the Edge sold over 400,000 copies before a halt in printing was ordered in the aftermath of June 4, 1989. However, He Bochuan continues to teach at the university, remaining critical and outspoken, a testimony to the persistence and resilience of dissent in China.

Born in the early 1940s during the Sino-Japanese war and raised in an orphanage, He is unsure of his exact birth date. Nor does he know his original given name. In 1961, when a junior majoring in mathematics at the Normal College of Guangdong, he was selected by his professors to participate in research for creating the first generation of computers in China. He joined the army in hopes of being able to continue this research, but was assigned to propaganda work instead. After finishing his army service he worked as a secondary school teacher until accepting his present position.

GOOD DEEDS & GUNBOATS
Two Centuries of American-Chinese Encounters
by Hugh Deane

A collection of Chinese encounters by famous American missionaries, businessmen, opium merchants, poets, singers, soldiers and journalists, reveals the formation of American perceptions toward China over the last 200 years.

#2378-2	cloth	$29.95

LIVING IN CHINA:
A Guide to Teaching, Studying, and Living in the People's Republic and Taiwan
By Rebecca Weiner, Margaret Murphy and Albert Li

An essential handbook for anyone planning on going to China to study or teach; includes a comprehensive directory of Chinese schools, as well as U.S. sending organizations.

#2480-0	paper	$16.95

CHINESE FOR TODAY
by The Beijing languages Institute

An excellent text for beginning Chinese language study, incorporating the better elements of earlier texts from China.

#1840-1	Chinese for Today, Book 1	$24.95
#1841-X	Exercise Book 1	$10.95
#1842-8	Six Audio Cassettes, Book 1	$70.00
#2425-8	Chinese for Today, Book 2	$24.95
#2426-6	Reader Book 2	$10.95
#2427-4	Six Audio Cassettes, Book 2	$70.00

CRISIS AT TIANANMEN
REFORM AND REALITY IN MODERN CHINA
compiled by Yi Mu and Mark V. Thompson

The only book about China's pro-democracy movement written from the viewpoint of an independent mainland Chinese journalist.

#2290-5	paper	$14.95

ALL THE TEA IN CHINA
by Kit Chow and Ione Kramer
An entertaining, informative, and beautifully illustrated guide to the world's most popular beverage.

#2194-1   paper $14.95

CHINESE ARTISTIC KITES
by Ha Kuiming and Ha Yiqi
These world renowned kite-makers from Beijing provide an in-depth guide to the art and craft of Chinese kite-making. Lavish color photos showcase the beauty of their award-winning creations.

#2279-4   paper $16.95

LÓNG IS A DRAGON
Chinese Writing for Children
by Peggy Goldstein
A beautifully illustrated introduction to Chinese writing with explanations about how the language developed and clear instructions on how to draw the characters. For children, parents, tourists and anyone interested in the art of Chinese writing.

#2375-8   cloth $14.95

MOONCAKES AND HUNGRY GHOSTS
Festivals of China
by Carol Stepanchuk and Charles Wong
The perfect introduction to the many celebrations of the Chinese calendar year, including information on the food, costumes, religious significance, song-and-dance performances, and symbolism. Richly illustrated with color photos.

#2481-9   paper $14.95

QUOTATIONS OF CHAIRMAN MAO TSETUNG
Mao's "Little Red Book" has been out of print in China for some time, but we have arranged a new printing, in the original red plastic cover. Widely used as a text in courses on modern China, it is easily one of the most important and influential books of the twentieth century.

#2388-X   original red plastic cover $7.95

Would you like our catalog?

Just write us and we'll send you our latest catalog featuring books on China and Chinese culture, as well as periodicals, handicrafts, software, films on video, Chinese music on CD, and books for children. You'll find books on travel, art, history, contemporary affairs, culture, and for professional reference and learning Chinese. CHINA BOOKS, an employee-owned and managed cooperative, distributes books in the U.S. and Canada to your local bookstore or through our mail order service.

Write to:

CHINA BOOKS

Box E

2929 Twenty-fourth Street

San Francisco, CA 94110

(415) 282-2994